A Financial Revolution
in the Habsburg Netherlands

County of Holland, 1570

Medemblik

Enkhuizen

Horn

Alkmaar

De Schermer

De Beemster

Edam

Monnikendam

Haarlem

Amsterdam

Muiden

Weesp *Ij*

Naarden

Haarlemmermeer

Brasemeer

Leiden

Utrecht

The Hague

Rijn

Oudewater

Delft

Gouda

Ijsel

Ijselstein

Schoonhoven

Lek

Maas

Schiedam

Rotterdam

Leerdam

Asperen

Vlardingen

Heukelom

Brill

Gorcum

Maas

Dordrecht

Geertrudenberg

Zevenbergen

A Financial Revolution

in the

Habsburg Netherlands

Renten and *Renteniers* in the
County of Holland, 1515–1565

James D. Tracy

UNIVERSITY OF CALIFORNIA PRESS

Berkeley / Los Angeles / London

University of California Press
Berkeley and Los Angeles, California

University of California Press, Ltd.
London, England

Library of Congress Cataloging in Publication Data

Tracy, James D.
   A financial revolution in the Habsburg Netherlands.

   Bibliography
   Includes index.
   1. Debts, Public—Netherlands—History—16th
century.   2. Annuities—Netherlands—History—16th
century.   3. Finance, Public—Netherlands—History—
16th century.   I. Title.
HJ8707.T73   1985   336.3′4′09492   84–24426
ISBN 0–520–05425–3

Printed in the United States of America

1 2 3 4 5 6 7 8 9

For
Lee and Loretta Tracy

For
Lee and Loretta Tracy

Contents

Tables

Acknowledgments

The research on which this book is based was done at Belgian and Dutch archives between September 1979 and August 1980, thanks to a sabbatical leave from the University of Minnesota, Fulbright research grants from the Belgian American Commission for Educational Exchange (Brussels) and the Netherlands America Commission for Educational Exchange (Amsterdam), as well as smaller grants from the American Council of Learned Societies, and the University of Minnesota Office of International Programs. I began, and worked most extensively, at the Algemeen Rijksarchief/Archives Generaux du Royaume in Brussels, where Dr. Carlos Wyffels and his staff were most kind in helping a relative neophyte become oriented to archival research. For what progress I have made in coming to understand the fascinating but little studied world of the Habsburg Netherlands, I am most indebted to two colleagues in the Netherlands who have been generous with their time, criticism, and encouragement, Hugo de Schepper, now of the Catholic University of Nijmegen, and Jeremy Bangs, of the Leiden Stadsarchief. Finally, two colleagues at Minnesota, Russell Menard and Kathryn Reyerson, were kind enough to give portions of the manuscript a good critical reading.

Abbreviations

AJ   Andries Jacobszoon, "Prothocolle van alle die reysen . . . bij mij Andries Jacops gedaen . . ." 2 vols., Gemeente Archief, Amsterdam.

ASR   "Stadsrekeningen," extant from 1531, Gemeente Archief, Amsterdam.

Aud.   "Papiers d'Etat et de l'Audience," Algemeen Rijksarchief, Brussels.

Baelde   Michel Baelde, *De Collaterale Raden onder Karel V en Filips II, 1531–1578* = *Verhandelingen van de Koninklijke Vlaamse Akademie voor Wetenschappen, Letteren, en Schone Kunsten van België, Klasse der Letteren*, XXVII (Brussels: 1965).

Balen   M. Balen, *Beschryving van der Stadt Dordrecht* (Dordrecht: 1677).

Blécourt   A. S. de Blécourt, E. M. Meijers, *Memorialen van het Hof van Holland, Zeeland, en West-Friesland van de Secretaris Jan Roosa*, 3 vols. (Haarlem: 1929).

Boitet   R. Boitet, *Beschryving der Stad Delft* (Delft: 1729).

Brouwer-Ancher   A. J. M. Brouwer-Ancher, J. C. Breen, "De Doleantie van een Deel der Burgerij van Amsterdam in 1564 en 1565," *Bijdragen en Mededelingen van het Historisch Genootschap te Utrecht* XXIV (1903): 59–200.

CC   "Chambre des Comptes," Algemeen Rijksarchief, Brussels.

De la Torre   Aud. 1441; 4, no. 2 (see chap. 5, n. 106).

Elias   Johan E. Elias, *De Vroedschap van Amsterdam, 1578–1795* (2 vols., reprint Amsterdam: 1963).

GRK   "Grafelijkheids Rekenkamer," Rijksarchief van Zuid-Holland, The Hague.

GRM   J. Th. De Smidt, E. I. Strubbe, J. van Rompaey, H. de Schepper, eds. *Chronologische Lijsten van de geëxtendeerde sententiën en procesbundels berustende in het archief van de Grote Raad van Mechelen*, 3 vols. (Brussels: 1966–1978).

GSR   "Stadsrekeningen," Stadsarchief, Gouda.

GVR   *Goudsche Vroedschapsresolutiën betreffende Dagvaarten der Staten van Holland en de Staten Generaal (1501–1572)*, ed. L. M. Rollin Couquerque, A. Meerkamp van Emben, *Bijdragen en Mededelingen van het Historisch Genootschap te Utrecht*, 37 (1916): 61–81, 38 (1917): 98–357; 39 (1918): 306–407.

Holleman   F. A. Holleman, *Dirk van Assendelft, Schout van Breda, en de zijnen* (Zutfen: 1953).

Houtzager	Dirk Houtzager, *Hollands Lijf- en Losrenten voor 1672* (Schiedam: 1950).
HTR	"Tresoriers Rekeningen," Stadsarchief, Haarlem.
Lille B	"Comptes des Receveurs Generaux de toutes les finances," in "Chambres des Comptes, Série B," Archives du Département du Nord, Lille (available on microfilm, Algemeen Rijksarchief, Brussels).
LTR	"Tresoriers Rekeningen," Stadsarchief, Leiden.
Maddens	N. Maddens, *De Beden in het Graafschap Vlaanderen tijdens de Regering van Keizer Karel (1515–1550)* = *Standen en Landen/Anciens Pays et Assemblées d'Etats* LXXII (Houle: 1978).
Meilink	P. A. Meilink, *Archieven van de Staten van Holland voor 1572* (The Hague: 1929).
Nübel	Otto Nübel, *Pompeius Occo* (Tübingen: 1972).
RSH	*Resolutiën van de Staten van Holland*, 289 vols. (Amsterdam: 1789–1814).
Sandelijn	Adriaan Sandelijn, "Memoriaelboek," 4 vols., Gemeente Archief, Amsterdam.
SH	"Staten van Holland voor 1572," IIIe Afdeling, Rijksarchief van Zuid-Holland, The Hague.
Ter Gouw	J. ter Gouw, *Geschiedenis van Amsterdam*, 8 vols. (Amsterdam: 1879–1893).
Verhofstad	Karel Jan Willem Verhofstad, *De Regering der Nederlanden in de Jaren 1555–1559* (Nijmegen: 1937).
Walvis	J. Walvis, *Beschrijving der Stad Gouda* (Gouda: 1714).

Provinces of North and South Holland, 1976

Introduction

To students of English history, the term "financial revolution" connotes a dramatic rise in public borrowing during the 1690s, coupled with a shift from short-term to long-term debt. Financiers' loans at high rates gave way to low-rate securities such as life or perpetual annuities, each of which was guaranteed by Parliament and funded by specific revenues. To enhance the popularity of these instruments, Parliament made the income free of tax. In 1694, holders of this new debt pooled their credits to form the Bank of England, which in turn began issuing its own interest-bearing shares. To prevent indebtedness from accumulating to unmanageable proportions, Parliament decreed in 1717 that redeemable annuities would either be reduced to a lower rate of interest or, if the holder preferred, redeemed from a sinking fund that was established at the same time. P. J. Dickson, a recent student of these developments, believes it was this system of public borrowing, enabling England to spend on war out of all proportion to its tax revenue, which best explains why Britain prevailed against a larger and wealthier France during the long series of wars from 1689 to 1815.[1] Though state annuities were new to England in the 1690s, proponents of the new system drew consciously on long-established precedent in the Dutch Republic, just as critics were quick to observe that "stock-jobbing" of this particular kind had never been heard of before England acquired a Dutch sovereign in 1688.[2] Unfortunately, however, the Netherlands' financial revolution, a precursor of England's, is shrouded in obscurity. Dutch historians have, curiously, neglected the topic of public debt,[3] perhaps because the essential features of Netherlands public borrowing are not properly Dutch[4] at all, since their origin traces back to the time when most of the provinces making up the present Benelux Countries were grouped together under a single Habsburg

[1]P. J. Dickson, *The Financial Revolution in England: A Study in the Development of Public Credit, 1688–1756* (London and New York: 1967); the quote, 8–9.

[2]Dickson, *The Financial Revolution*, 17, 51.

[3]H. De Buck, *Bibliographie der Geschiedenis van Nederland* (Leiden: 1968): the small section (440) on public finance has no entry on public debt. A. C. J. de Vrankrijker, *Geschiedenis van de Belastingen* (Bussum: 1969), does not deal either with the Habsburg period or the annuities at issue here. The two studies of Holland's finances prior to independence are: P. J. Blok, "De Financiën van het Graafschap Holland," *Bijdragen en Mededelingen voor Vaderlandsche Geschiedenis*, 3e Reeks, III (1886): 36–130; and H. Terdenge, "Zur Geschichte der holländischen Steuern im 15en und 16en Jahrhundert," *Vierteljahrschrift für Sozial- und Wirtschaftsgeschichte* XVIII (1925): 95–167; neither makes use of the accounts on which this study is based (GRK and SH). Recent Belgian scholars have shown more interest in fiscal history: see especially M. Baelde, "Financiële Politiek en Domaniale Evolutie in de Nederlanden onder Karel V en Filips II, 1530–1560," *Tijdschrift voor Geschiedenis* LXXVI (1963): 14–33; *Récherches sur les Finances Publiques en Belgique—Acta Historica Bruxellensia*, III (2 vols., Brussels: 1967–1970); of particular interest for the sixteenth century are the articles by M. A. Arnould and J. Craeybeckx; and Maddens.

[4]"Dutch" is a somewhat confusing appellation, since it commonly refers only to the Netherlands and its people, whereas the term of which it is properly a translation (*nederlands;* an older form, *diets,* is now archaic) also refers to the literary language shared among Netherlanders and the Flemings (Dutch-speakers) who make up a majority of Belgium's population. In Charles V's time, the people of Holland, Flanders, and (save for a francophone strip in the south) Brabant all spoke related west-netherlandish dialects.

sovereign. The Bank of Amsterdam, it is true, does not appear until 1605, when rebel provinces of the north had already thrown off Spanish rule. But life-term and perpetual or heritable annuities, the heart and soul of public debt in the seventeenth-century Netherlands, had been in constant use since the early decades of the sixteenth century, and have seldom been the subject of historical inquiry, except as a preface to the study of the modern life insurance industry.[5]

This study is an investigation of the "financial revolution" that took place in the Low Countries during the reign of Charles V, focusing on Holland in particular. Holland was far from being the most important of the seventeen provinces whose hereditary ruler was Charles V—Flanders and Brabant, most of which are now located in Belgium,[6] were notably larger and more populous—but for present purposes there are two good reasons for making Holland the center of discussion. It is one of the provinces for whose fiscal history during this period a wealth of documentation is preserved,[7] and it

[5]The best study of life annuities or lijfrenten, though it deals only with eighteenth-century variants not relevant to the sixteenth century, is J. C. Riley, "Life-Annuity Based Loans in the Amsterdam Capital Market toward the End of the 18th Century," Economisch- en Social-Historisch Jaarboek XXXVI (1973): 102–130. See also Houtzager, and Bouwstoffen voor de Geschiedenis van de Levensverzekeringen en Lijfrenten in Nederland, edited by the Directors of the Algemene Maatschappij voor Levensverzekering en Lijfrenten (Amsterdam: 1897).

[6]The northern quarter of Brabant, centered on 's Hertogenbosch, and a coastal strip of northern Flanders have been part of the Netherlands since the early seventeenth century. In the beden, or subsidies, to which each province consented, Brabant paid five-sixths of Flanders' total, and Holland paid either one-third as much as Brabant (according to the Hollanders), or one-half (according to the central government): see the correspondence between Assendelft, for the Council of Holland, and Mary of Hungary, 23, 30 January, 7 February 1552 (Aud. 1646:2 and 1646:3).

[7]GRK contains the accounts of the Ontvanger van de beden in Holland, an official appointed by the Council of Finance and responsible for the collection of all ordinary and extraordinary subsidies. SH contains the accounts of the Ontvanger van 't gemeen land, an official answerable only to the provincial States, who collected only the (usually) small levies or omslagen needed by the States for their own purposes, but who, after 1542, began assuming responsibility for collecting extraordinary subsidies, including those raised by sales of annuities. These records may be checked against the annual accounts of the Receveur General de toutes les Finances (Lille B) at a higher level

played such a prominent role in the history of the later Dutch Republic that its name has become (to foreigners, if not to natives of the Netherlands) synonymous with that of the country as a whole.[8]

Chapter 1 contains a brief survey of the various types of public debt to be found on the European continent at the close of the Middle Ages. Chapter 2 gives a description of the fiscal system of the Habsburg Netherlands and Holland in particular, with emphasis on annuities issued by the provincial parliaments but funded by the annual *bede*, or subsidy. Chapter 3 contains a description of innovations tracing to a brief period during the 1540s when the government was strong enough to induce the States,[9] or parliaments, of various provinces, including Holland, to introduce a second series of annuities funded by new taxes of their own devising. Chapter 4 shows how these changes, together with advantageous terms of sale made necessary by a temporary contraction of credit, permitted the development of a voluntary market for state annuities, in a province where previous issues of such instruments had met their quotas only because certain groups were compelled to subscribe. Chapter 5 contains an examination of occupational and other characteristics of the Hollanders who, in the 1550s, set a pattern for the future when they freely came forward with unprecedented

---

of the fiscal hierarchy, and against city treasury records (ASR, GSR, HTR, LTR) at a lower level. Tax records for Flanders are equally well preserved (see Maddens), but those for Brabant were devastated in a late seventeenth-century fire which gutted the old archducal palace in Brussels.

[8]The sixteenth-century County of Holland has since been divided into the two provinces of North and South Holland.

[9]"States" is the common English rendering for this meaning of the Dutch *staten* and the French *états,* all three being plural forms. At the root of Europe's parliamentary history lies the conception that society is made up of three different orders (in Latin, *status*, usually "estates" in English), the clergy, the nobles, and the burghers. By the fourteenth century, most of the provinces that would later make up the Habsburg Netherlands had developed parliaments reflecting this tripartite division, although in some cases (as in Holland) the clergy was not deemed important enough to merit formal representation. English usage favors "estates" for parliamentary bodies in France and Germany, but "states" for the largely Dutch-speaking Netherlands.

sums of cash to invest in these state annuities. Finally, in chapter 6, the subsequent history of long-term public debt in the seventeenth-century Dutch Republic will be briefly traced, up to the time when England was ready for its financial revolution.

I

Forms of Public Debt in
Renaissance Europe

Though the distinction between long- and short-
term public debt was (according to Dickson) unknown in
England prior to about 1690, it had long been familiar on the
Continent. The reason for England's insularity in this respect
is perhaps to be found in the sphere of private credit; for
although land was not commonly used in England as security
for private credit until the middle of the seventeenth century,[1]
Continental landholders had, since the twelfth century or
earlier, been possessed of a technique for converting their
property to credit. In France, at least, the practice of borrowing by "constituting" a *rente* on one's land, or of extending

[1]Dickson, *The Financial Revolution in England,* 4–5.

credit on this basis, was pioneered by monastic institutions. As the agrarian economy improved, twelfth-century lords found they could obtain credit from the local monastery by pledging the usage fees (*cens*) paid by their peasants instead of having to mortgage the land itself. From this practice there derived the idea of creating an artificial income on one's property by constituting a rente (= annual income) on it. In default of annual interest payments at the stipulated rate, creditors had the right to seize the property against whose "income" the contract had been secured. Such rentes could either be for the life of the creditor or his assignee, or, at an appreciably lower rate, perpetual. By the late Middle Ages, however, all perpetual or "heritable" rentes in France were generally considered redeemable in principle, in deference to canon law prohibitions against usury.[2] It was this form of private credit, widely diffused in Spain, Germany, northern France, and the Low Countries, which subsequently became the basis for long-term public credit in the same regions.

At this point it will be useful to clarify terms. *Short-term debt* refers to loans at high rates of interest by financiers who expect repayment in full (or renegotiation of the loan) within a few years or less. *Long-term debt* refers to obligations at lower rates but over a more extended period, with vaguer expectations about recovery of the initial capital. Long-term debt will usually be *funded* in the sense that interest payments (and sometimes redemption of the capital as well) are assigned to one or more regular sources of governmental income, often with the stipulation that collectors of these revenues are legally bound to meet interest payments to debtholders before employing their receipts for other purposes. Bankers to whom a government was indebted could thus sometimes be induced (or constrained) to accept conversion of their short-term loans into appropriately funded long-term

---

[2]The best general overview is Winfried Trusen, "Zum Rentenkauf im Späten Mittelalter," *Festschrift für Hermann Heimpel* (3 vols. Göttingen: 1972), II, 140–158; on the origins of private rentes in northern France, Robert Genestal, *Les Monastères comme établissements du credit en Normandie aux XIIe et XIIIe siècles* (Paris: 1901), 87–119. For the sixteenth century, the best study is B. Schnapper, *Les Rentes au XVIe siècle* (Paris: 1957), 1–133. On Castilian *censos*, Bartolomé Bennassar, *Valladolid au siècle d'or* (Paris: 1967), 258–259.

obligations. Continental historians use the terms *floating* and *consolidated* to describe this distinction between short-term and long-term debt.

From the thirteenth through the sixteenth century, long-term debt usually consisted either of rentes backed by the revenues of a prince or a town government, or of interest-bearing forced loans levied on wealthy subjects or citizens. The distinction between these two forms of public credit can be merely a theoretical one—for instance, when a government compels wealthy subjects to buy its rentes.[3] Also, both forms of credit could be sold or transferred to third parties, though usually at a discount, unless the government in question had been scrupulous about meeting its annual interest payments.[4] There is, however, an important difference between the two in terms of their political implications. On one hand, forced loans are more equitable because the wealthy are not given a choice of whether or not to support the state in its hour of need; on the other hand, there are limits as to how much can be raised in this way, since forced loans depend on a government's knowledge of who its wealthy citizens are, and on their willingness to have portions of their private wealth appropriated by the state. Conversely, the voluntary sale of rentes, though it may permit wealthy subjects to escape the burden altogether, has at least the potential for harnessing to public ends the full strength of capital markets both domestic and foreign, since rentes may attract capital from people of middling wealth, or from those whose prosperity has gone undetected by the government, as well as from beyond the frontiers. Broadly speaking, Italian city-states preferred the more equitable practice of forced loans, whereas northern cities opted for the potentially more lucrative technique of selling rentes on the open market.

In the Middle Ages, long-term public debt makes its earliest appearance in the city-states of north and central Italy. The

---

[3]For example, when Henri II raised 3,100,000 *livres tournois* from the sale of rentes in the late 1550s, "most of these issues . . . appear to have been forced on the Parisians" (Martin Wolfe, *The Fiscal System of Renaissance France* [New Haven: 1972], 111).

[4]See below, notes 7 and 10.

Genoese *compera* traces to the thirteenth century, if not earlier. When the commune needed capital, investors, each holding one share per 100 lire, formed a syndicate (compera), which was then vested with ownership of a tax specially created to pay interest and retire the loan. For example, when the city wished to construct a war fleet of twelve galleys in 1432, a *compera securitatis* was formed and given control of a new excise of 0.5 percent on maritime insurance contracts; each share was to receive 7 percent annual interest, and was declared redeemable at 90 percent of par. In fact, it was quite rare for a debt thus contracted ever to be liquidated. In 1407, shareholders of the larger *compere* had pooled their assets to form the famed Banco di San Giorgio. Though it had to suspend banking operations after a few decades, the San Giorgio continued to function as a supersyndicate for debt-holders, absorbing more and more compere, and issuing shares of its own, backed by the revenues vested in them. By this time, the capital value of Genoa's long-term debt, estimated at 600,000 lire, vastly exceeded the annual revenues (some 80,000 lire) not already in the hands of compere.[5] While the intricacies of the San Giorgio are peculiar to Genoa, the compera was used in other north Italian towns under one name or another. Milan, for example, was still raising capital in this way during Charles V's rule in Lombardy.[6]

Venice experimented with the practice of alienating revenues to creditors, but its preference for forced loans appeared as early as 1172, when Venetian citizens were required to contribute a fixed percentage of their moveable wealth as recorded in an *estimo* of moveable property drawn up by officials of the commune. Such loans, or *prestiti*, were at first interest-free, yet lenders had little cause for complaint, since the rapid growth of Venice's population and economy permitted loans to be repaid in full from excise tax revenues within a few years. By 1262, however, public debt was beginning to accumulate, and new measures were deemed necessary. Although lenders were henceforth promised an annual return

[5]Jacques Heers, *Gênes au XVIe siècle* (Paris: 1961), 97–146.
[6]Federico Chabod, *Lo stato e la vita religiosa a Milano nell'epoca di Carlo V* (Turin: 1971), 112–120.

of 5 percent, a *ligatio pecuniae* solemnly decreed by the Venetian senate and the Grand Council obligated the collectors of eight specified excises to make these interest payments before meeting any other "extraordinary" expenses, and also to set aside funds for redeeming a portion of the capital each year. Gino Luzzato, the historian of medieval Venetian finance, comments that one can properly speak of a "public debt" only at this point. Even so, prestiti credits were not employed for private purposes—that is, there was no secondary market—until the fourteenth century, when scheduled repayments of capital had been postponed so regularly that the loans came to be regarded as bearing interest in perpetuity. Such credits now became attractive as investments in certain circumstances; for example, one could save money by purchasing someone else's loan credits at a discount, while counting them at face value for purposes of a dowry. Market value of the credits fluctuated widely, and was deeply depressed during Venice's hour of danger in the Chioggia War (1378–1381), when interest payments had to be suspended for two years. By the 1450s, citizen resistance to further levies forced the government to abandon prestiti, at least temporarily. Forced loans were resumed in 1482, on the basis of a new estimo of real property; credits derived from these loans—known as the *monte nuovo*, as distinct from the old debt (*monte vecchio*) based on the estimo of moveable property—traded at values closer to par. The monte nuovo was fully retired by 1552, but in the meantime a *monte novissimo* had been created in 1509, and a *monte di sussidio* in 1526.[7]

Beginning in the fourteenth century, Florence and Siena also relied on forced loans, here called *prestanze*, to raise capital in time of war or other emergency. The relative novelty of such public borrowing in these Tuscan republics is indicated by the unusual measures that were taken to assure lenders that revenues allocated to the payment of interest on their loans would actually be used for that purpose. Florence,

[7]Gino Luzzato, *Il debito pubblico della Repubblica di Venezia, 1200–1500* (Milan: 1963); for the ligatio pecuniae and the proper beginning of public debt, 29. Frederic C. Lane, "Public Debt and Private Wealth, particularly in 16th Century Venice," *Melanges en honneur de Fernand Braudel* (2 vols., Toulouse: 1973), I: 317–325.

with its Guelph traditions, regularly had its obligations to prestanze creditors guaranteed "by the lord Pope." Ghibelline Siena, not having the same access to Rome, threatened its officials with heavy fines if they even suggested diversion of the allotted revenues.[8] As in Venice, interest payments were assigned to excise taxes of various kinds, but these revenues were not sufficient to retire the debt, which therefore mounted steadily over the years. Interest rates in both Florence and Siena were as high as 15 percent during the first half of the century, but were fixed at 5 percent in Florence after 1381.[9] In both cities, loan credits could be sold to third parties, a process facilitated in Florence by the creation in 1347 of a Monte Commune, which pooled outstanding public debt; as subsequent prestanze were levied, lenders were credited with an equivalent amount of Monte Commune stock. The value of the credits fluctuated in keeping with expectations about the commune's ability to pay. In 1427, efforts were made to provide the city with a broader base of assessment by requiring a detailed declaration of all one's patrimony (the *catasto*) in place of an estimate made by officials of the commune. But a disastrous war with Lucca forced a temporary suspension of interest payments—monte stock traded at only 15 percent of par in 1433—and under Cosimo de' Medici, who came to power in 1434, Florence relied less on prestanze than on voluntary investments in the "bank of dowries." This pre-Medicean institution permitted fathers to make, in the names of their infant daughters, investments that yielded a handsome sum for a dowry after a term of fifteen years, provided that the girl was still living; if she was not, the money became the property of the commune.[10]

[8]William Bowsky, *The Finances of the Commune of Siena, 1287–1355* (Oxford: 1970), 177–180; Richard Trexler, "Florence by Grace of the Lord Pope . . ." *Studies in Medieval and Renaissance History* IX (1972): 115–212. For public debt based on forced loans in other Tuscan cities, see C. E. Meek, "Il debito pubblico nella storia finanziaria di Lucca," *Actum Luce* (III) 1974: 7–46, and Cinzio Violante, "Imposte dirette e debito pubblico a Pisa nel Medioevo," *L'Impôt dans le cadre de la ville et d'Etat* (Brussels: 1966), 45–94.

[9]Bowsky, 180–181; Anthony Molho, *Florentine Public Finance in the Early Renaissance* (Cambridge, Mass.: 1971), 66–67.

[10]Molho, 79–87, 162; Professor Julius Kirshner at the University of Chicago is currently engaged on a study of the Florentine bank of dowries.

The Florentine bank of dowries bore some resemblance to the life annuities of the day in that both could be used to provide for the security of one's children, and were thus attractive to investors. Insofar as the bank of dowries was a product of market considerations, one would think that the same considerations might have prompted Italian statesmen to introduce the transalpine *rente viagère* in some form or another. In fact, however, *lijfrenten* seem not to have played any role in Italian public finance until the Venetian mint (*zecca*) began offering life annuities at 14 percent between 1536 and 1540. During the great naval war against the Turks in the early 1570s, the mint also issued what northern Europeans would call heritable annuities, offering 8 percent per annum until such time as the mint would redeem them. But annuities were not to be a permanent feature of Venetian fiscal policy. In a great project for freeing the zecca, Venice expended some 10,000,000 ducats between 1577 and 1600 to redeem all outstanding annuities as well as outstanding shares of the various *monti* which had not been retired already.[11]

North of the Alps, urban excise taxes were widely used to fund annuities rather than forced loans. As early as 1260 or thereabouts, northern French cities like Douai and Calais were issuing the two kinds of rentes already common in the realm of private credit, that is, rentes viagères and *rentes heritables*. From northern France the idea spread to the County of Flanders and the Duchy of Brabant in the Low Countries, while ecclesiastical centers like Cologne were focal points for diffusion of the same practice among German towns.[12] In

[11]Lane, "Public Debt and Private Wealth . . . in 16th Century Venice;" Brian Pullan, "The Occupations and Investments of the Venetian Nobility in the middle and late Sixteenth Century," in *Renaissance Venice*, ed. J. R. Hale (Totowa, N.J.: 1973), 388.

[12]Hans van Werveke, *De Gentsche Stadsfinanciën in de Middeleeuwen* = *Academie Royale de Belgique, Classe des Lettres, Sciences Morales et Politiques, Memoires in 8o,* 2e Serie, XXXIV (Brussels: 1934), 282–290; Georges Espinas, *Les Finances de la Commune de Douai des Origines au XVe Siècle* (Paris: 1902), 314–346 (p. 315, note 2, the author gives references for heritable or perpetual rentes in fifteen cities in France, Germany, and the Low Countries during the fifteenth century). For the origins of life and heritable rentes and their

Flanders, the great city of Ghent issued its first series of lijfrenten between 1275 and 1290; purchasers were found among the financiers of nearby Arras, who had previously been extending short-term credit to the city, and now accepted a conversion of what was owed them into these new, long-term obligations.

Both the lijfrenten and a subsequent issue of *erfrenten* (heritable or redeemable rentes) were guaranteed by the Count of Flanders; as in the case of the pope's role in Florentine public debt, the count did not assume any responsibility for Ghent's liabilities, but rather undertook to see to it that the city lived up to its promises. Despite good intentions, Ghent could not keep up with interest payments, and these early lijfrenten were practically worthless by the 1330s. A further series of lijfrenten was issued between 1346 and 1356, but buyers were now sought in Brabant (Brussels and Leuven) rather than in Arras. Except for one sale of erfrenten, buyers for Ghent's issues were found outside the city.[13] In contrast, Florence had but a limited interest in peddling prestanze credits to foreigners. Like investment in Italian forced loans, investment in the rentes of northern cities seems to have provoked some scruples relating to the Church's prohibitions against usury, though the canonical issues involved appear to have been effectively thrashed out during the course of the fifteenth century.[14]

North of Flanders and Brabant, towns in the smaller and less developed County of Holland began issuing *renten* only during the fourteenth century. In Leiden, the city archives boast continuous records of renten sales and interest pay-

---

use by towns in Germany, Bruno Kuske, *Das Schuldenwesen der deutschen Städten im Mittelalter* (Tübingen: 1904) = *Zeitschrift für die Gesamte Staatswissenschaft, Ergänzungsheft* XII, 12–38.

[13]Van Werveke, 285, 289.

[14]Molho, *Florentine Public Finance*, 142. On canon law issues, see Julius Kirshner, "The Moral Problem of Discounting Genoese *Paghe*, 1450–1550," *Archivum Fratrum Praedicatorum* (1977): 109–167; Fabiano Veraja, *Le origini della controversia sul contratto di censo nel XIII secolo* (Rome: 1960); the section from Genestal, cited in note 2; and Jeremy D. Bangs, "Holland's Civic *Lijfrente* Loans (XVth Century): Some Recurrent Problems," *Publication du Centre Européen d'Etudes Burgundo-Medianes* 23 (1983): 75–82. I am indebted to Professor Kirshner and Dr. Bangs for copies of their articles.

ments stretching into the eighteenth century, offering a rich but hitherto untapped source of social as well as economic history.[15] As with Venice's ligatio pecuniae, a city's most important revenues were legally pledged to interest payments on the debt. In Amsterdam, for example, tax farmers who contracted each year to collect the *groote accijns* (excise taxes on beer, wine, and grain), assumed the obligation of meeting interest payments from their excise receipts.[16] Lijf- or erfrenten were sold by the cities in time of war, to build fortified walls (many of which were still standing in the sixteenth century) or even to meet their quotas in the annual *beden*, or subsidies, which became somewhat more burdensome after the Dukes of Burgundy were recognized as Counts of Holland (1428).[17] Like cities elsewhere, those of Holland had difficulty servicing a mounting debt, and in 1494 Archduke Philip the Handsome—grandson of the last Burgundian Duke and father of Charles V—authorized them to suspend interest payments for a year or more.[18] Some towns were slow to recover from the financial crisis of the late fifteenth century, but others prospered during the following decades. Table 1 shows the relative solvency of Holland's towns during a decade (1531–1540) for which at least some records are extant for five of the six "great cities" with voting rights in the

[15]Dr. Bangs, of the Leiden Stadsarchief, is currently engaged on a study of that city's lijfrenten from the fourteenth to the eighteenth century.

[16]Ter Gouw, III, 407–415. ASR lists each year the names of contractors for this and lesser *accijnsen*, with sums they contracted to pay the treasury each quarter. Payments to holders of city lijfrenten or *losrenten* are not recorded in ASR, since they were made by farmers of the groote accijns, whose accounts have not survived.

[17]Ter Gouw, III, 135, 169, 187–189. A city issued renten to meet a bede payment because of insufficient income (see GSR xli, 21 May 1516; lxxviii, 19 June 1543), or merely because of a cash flow problem: ASR, 1552, 1553, 1554, Amsterdam sells renten for the stated purpose of meeting bede installments, even though in each of these years the city treasurers eventually passed on to their colleagues for the next year a surplus well in excess of what the city paid in ordinary and extraordinary subsidies.

[18]I. Prins, *Het Faillissement der Hollandsche Steden: Amsterdam, Dordrecht, Leiden en Haarlem in het jaar 1494* (Amsterdam: 1922). The most recent treatment is an unpublished typescript to be found in the Leiden Stadsarchief: W. Downer, "De Financiële Toestand van de Stad Leiden omstreeks 1500" (1951), of which Dr. Jeremy Bangs was kind enough to furnish me a copy.

TABLE 1

INDEBTEDNESS OF THE GREAT CITIES OF HOLLAND
(Figures in Holland pounds = 20 silver *stuivers* or 40 groats)

	Annual income (% of income) spent on renten interest				
Source	Amsterdam ASR	Dordrecht DSR	Gouda GSR	Haarlem HTR	Leiden LTR
1531	56,310 (60)			19,481 (55)	
1532	51,024 (63)			18,085 ( )*	35,871 (42)
1533	50,196 (64)		19,572 (65)	18,377 (58)	30,140 (50)
1534	45,768 (69)		21,450 (66)	18,855 (55)	23,405 (71)
1535	53,130 (60)	28,536 (42)	21,666 (58)	18,765 (55)	
1536			18,990 (56)	19,190 (52)	23,057 (63)
1537	58,632 (67)		22,452 (61)	8,662 (68)**	24,926 (58)
1538	56,502 (72)		19,470 (62)	19,237 (51)	24,566 (55)
1539	64,920 (74)		18,732 (67)		31,972 (45)
1540	64,926 (67)		18,360 (71)		24,739 (59)

*Suspension of payments authorized by the central government.
**Totals for six months only, due to change of accounting period.

provincial parliament, or States, of Holland (Amsterdam, Dordrecht, Gouda, Haarlem, and Leiden; accounts for Delft, the sixth great city, perished in a fire in 1536) (see table 1).

The figures given in table 1 show a clear contrast between Amsterdam, whose revenue base was two or three times that of the others and rising, and Gouda, Haarlem, and Leiden, whose revenues were stationary or even declining. In fact, Amsterdam could increase its debt almost at will.[19]

[19]Though roughly equal in population to Haarlem and Leiden at the tme of a 1514 assessment of provincial wealth—see *Informatie op den Staet van Holland in 1514*, R. Fruin, ed. (Leiden: 1866)—Amsterdam had clearly outdistanced them by 1550, rising from about 14,000 to 30,000 or 35,000 while the others remained virtually stationary. Available information is summarized by Jan De Vries, *The Dutch Rural Economy in the Golden Age* (New Haven: 1974), 89–90. In addition, there is a document of ca. 1535 (Aud. 1526, folios 8–9) which gives a contemporary estimate of the relative populations of

Income levels for Leiden[20] as well as Gouda and Haarlem[21] reflect difficulties with the traditional industries of these towns. Taken singly, Amsterdam (with its Baltic trade) and Dordrecht (with its control of river traffic from Germany) were the only cities whose credit was strong enough to be exploited directly by the central government.[22] Taken collectively, however, the six great cities, together with the nobles of Holland,[23] spoke for a province that included eighteen smaller towns[24] and a thriving rural economy.[25] It was the great merit of Charles V's officials that they envisioned and carried out plans for inducing bodies like the States of Holland to pledge their corporate or collective credit to the service of the Habsburg state.

Holland's towns and villages: in case of war, twenty-two cities in Holland were expected to provide 429 able-bodied men, led by Amsterdam with 60, while Haarlem, Delft, and Leiden were assessed a quota of 50 each. The increase in Amsterdam's revenues during the 1530s is largely explained by an increase in the proceeds of the *bieraccijns*, the most important component of the groote accijns, as this thriving commercial center was thronged by thirsty sailors and merchants. That there was a ready market for lijfrenten is suggested by a comment in ASR 1552 (when purchases totaling 11,040 pounds were made) to the effect that sales were limited to six pounds of annual income per beneficiary, "so that everyone may be satisfied" (cf. a similar comment in ASR 1560, when purchases were held to a limit of twelve pounds per beneficiary).

[20]Leiden's major industry, the manufacture of heavy woolen cloth, experienced grave and continuous difficulties during the Habsburg period: N. W. Posthumus, *Geschiedenis van de Leidsche Lakenindustrie*, vol. 1 (The Hague: 1908).

[21]Brewing, the major industry in Haarlem and especially Gouda, suffered from a decline of traditional markets in Flanders and in other parts of Holland: J. C. van Loenen, *De Haarlemse Brouwindustrie voor 1600* (Amsterdam: 1950); GVR xiv, cxl, clxiv.

[22]In 1522, four cities in Holland were asked individually to sell renten secured by various parcels of the emperor's domain income: Amsterdam (total capital of 8,000 pounds), Dordrecht (4,800), Hoorn (1,600), and Edam (1,600): see GRK 3424, 3427. In 1555, Amsterdam and Dordrecht were each requested to sign "obligations" of 60,000, as surety for some of the emperor's major creditors: Mary of Hungary to Cornelis Suys, 18 August 1555 (Aud. 1656:2).

[23]See chapter 6, note 23.

[24]E. C. G. Brünner, *De orden op de buitennering van 1531* (Utrecht: 1918): in 1531 the "walled cities" given the privilege of banning the practice of certain industries (brewing, cloth manufacturing, etc.) within a given distance of their walls included, besides the six "great cities," St. Geertruidenberg,

Like their English cousins, French monarchs were slow to develop a short-term debt. Jacques Coeur of Bourges gained fame as banker and financial broker for Charles VII (1420–1460), but he had neither predecessors nor successors.[26] Instead, kings usually preferred the traditional method of "squeezing" their officials through forced loans at no interest. Even the huge expenditures of Francis I's (1515–1547) campaigns against Charles V did not require recourse to the German and Italian banking houses represented in Lyons, and it was not until the *Grand Parti* of 1555–1559 that these foreign firms were brought to invest in the king's debt, with results sufficiently discouraging to both sides to send subsequent rulers back to squeezing the *officiers*.[27]

Long-term royal debt in France has a more continuous history. Princes could sell rentes by mortgaging their more secure or desirable sources of income. During the fourteenth century, when taxes granted by parliamentary bodies were still something of a novelty, creditors preferred the older domain revenues, the king's "ordinary" income. By the late fourteenth century if not earlier, rentes were being sold on the income from various parcels of the royal domain. Buyers were often royal officials who purchased their rentes at discounts that seemed scandalous to reform-minded contemporaries.[28]

Alkmaar, Hoorn, Medemblik, Enkhuizen, Edam, Monnikendam, Naarden, Weesp, Muiden, Woerden, Oudewater, Schoonhoven, Gorcum (Gorinchem), Rotterdam, and Schiedam. In addition, The Hague and Vlaardingen, though not walled, were counted as "cities" for purposes of the provincial excise tax, which began in 1542 (see chapter 3). Finally, six other towns lay within the jurisdiction of private lords, and thus were not subject either to the Court of Holland in The Hague, or to the assessment by which Holland's ordinary subsidy was paid. But they too would be included in the provincial excise tax: Zevenbergen, Asperen, Heukelom, Leerdam, Woudrichem, and Ijsselstein (see SH 2278). Jan De Vries has estimated that as of the 1514 *Informatie* cited in note 19, 140,180 of Holland's 274,810 people, or roughly 51 percent, lived in cities: *The Dutch Rural Economy*, 81.

[25]De Vries, *Dutch Rural Economy.*

[26]H. De Man, *Jacques Coeur, königliche Kaufmann* (Bern: 1950).

[27]Wolfe, *Fiscal System of Renaissance France*, 63–65.

[28]Maurice Rey, *Le Domaine du Roy et les Finances Extraordinaires sous Charles V* (2 vols., Paris: 1965), I, 49.

Martin Wolfe and Alvaro Castillo Pintado believe that obligations of this kind ought to be regarded as the personal debt of the monarch rather than as "public" debt in a modern sense, since, to quote Wolfe, "it was only in the advanced city-states of Italy that loans could be made on the full faith and credit of the government."[29] Though Wolfe is wrong to suggest that it was only in Italy that government borrowing came to rest on something more than the promise of a prince, he and Castillo are correct in saying that the promise of a prince was of itself not sufficient to obligate the full resources of the commonwealth.

That creditors viewed things in this light, at least in the sixteenth century, is evident in the numerous lay principalities in Germany where parliamentary bodies were induced, by appropriate concessions, to take over debts charged against the prince's domain, or *Kammergut*. In Württemberg, Duke Ulrich's debts mounted to 950,000 Rhine *gulden* (roughly 1,360,000 Holland pounds at conversion rates prevailing in 1500)[30] at the time of the treaty of Tübingen (1514), in which his Estates took over administration of the debts and also of the revenues intended to pay them off. There followed a period of intermittent disorder, when Ulrich's high-handed rule led to his expulsion by the Swabian League, which then sold its rights over Württemberg to the Habsburgs, who in turn were evicted by the Schmalkaldic League when it returned a suitably Protestant Duke Ulrich to power in 1534. By the time Ulrich's son Christoph succeeded in 1550, there was an accumulation of new debt totaling 1,700,000 gulden, at an annual interest charge of 86,000, or roughly 5 percent. Christoph persuaded his Estates to assume responsibility for this sum, but only by surrendering full control over territorial revenues and expenditures into the hands of a permanent

[29]Wolfe, *Fiscal System of Renaissance France,* 92–93; Alvaro Castillo Pintado, "Los Juros de Castilla: Apogeo y Fin de un Instrumento de Credito," *Hispania* (Madrid) 23 (1963): 43–70, here p. 44, believes Castile's juro debt was not "modern" because the crown was only obligated so long as the specific revenues by which juros were funded remained adequate.

[30]See Appendix A (by John Munro), values of gold coinage ca. 1500, in *The Correspondence of Erasmus,* vol. 1, trans. R. A. B. Mynors and D. F. S. Thomson, annotated by Wallace Ferguson (Toronto: 1974), 336–338.

committee of the Estates (dating from the Habsburg period, and consisting of six burghers and two prelates), which subsequently continued to function in this capacity until 1808.[31] Bavaria had a well-articulated financial administration by about 1300, earlier than most German territories, but in the fourteenth century the initiative in fiscal matters passed to the Estates. Beginning in 1356, all taxes were collected as disbursed by agents responsible to the Estates rather than to the prince. In succeeding centuries the dukes raised money outside this framework by mortgaging their Kammergut, but by the 1540s William IV was so heavily in debt he was forced to yield control of domain revenues to the Estates, which now approved (1543) a new, provincewide excise tax on common articles of consumption for the specific purpose of freeing the Bavarian Kammergut from debt.[32]

Bradenburg's Hohenzollern margraves of the late fifteenth century were able to persuade their Estates to introduce a provincial beer excise without having to accede to their demands for control of the debt. But under Margraves Joachim I (1499–1535) and Joachim II (1535–1571) the debt mounted as high as 1,145,000 Rhine gulden, and the Estates demanded and got (1540) collection chests controlled by their own agents as the price for an agreement to assume responsibility for most of this total.[33]

Later in the sixteenth century, between 1570 and 1600, the Estates of the Habsburg County of Tyrol,[34] the Duchy of Braunschweig-Wolfenbüttel, and the Rhineland Palatinate[35] assumed similar responsibilities for managing the prince's debts and collecting his revenues. Where the Estates had

[31]F. L. Carsten, *Princes and Parliaments in Germany* (Oxford: 1959), 6–52.

[32]Heinz Dollinger, *Studien zur Finanzreform Maximilians I von Bayern in der Jahren 1598–1618* (Göttingen: 1968), 475–479, a sketch of the development of Bavaria's public debt (for so it may be called at this point) from 1545 to 1598.

[33]Herbert Helbig, *Gesellschaft und Wirtschaft der Markgrafschaft Brandenburg im Mittelalter* (Berlin: 1973), 59–69; Johannes Schulter, *Die Markgrafschaft Brandenburg* (5 vols., Berlin: 1961–1969), IV, 58–76.

[34]See the discussion of Tyrol in Peter Blickle, *Landschaften im alten Reich* (Munich: 1973), especially 246–254 (on taxation).

[35]*Braunschweigische Landesgeschichte im Überblick*, Richard Moderhack, ed. (Braunschweig: 1977), 76; Volker Press, *Calvinismus und Territorialstaat: Regierung und Zentralbehörden der Kurpfalz, 1559–1619* (Stuttgart: 1968), 166–167.

gained leadership in fiscal affairs they did not necessarily retain it; for example, Maximilian II reasserted ducal control over the administration of taxes in Bavaria in the early seventeenth century.[36] But the fiscal development of these six important territories shows how commonplace it was for parliamentary bodies to intervene to shore up a prince's credit, and make his debts "public."

By the sixteenth century, French monarchs had a similar need to expand the credit that was available to them on a long-term basis, secured by future revenues, but France's political institutions did not permit application of what might be called the German model. Here, the Estates General had briefly assumed control of collecting and disbursing royal tax revenues amid the confusion of the 1350s, when the hapless Jean II had been captured by the English and a huge ransom was demanded. After about 1440, however, the Estates General had no further role even in consenting to taxation, while provincial Estates, where they existed, were limited to apportioning taxes whose amount had already been determined by the king and his officials.[37] Since parliamentary bodies were thus in no position to act as guarantors of the royal debt, it was necessary to look elsewhere for persons whom lenders would regard as more creditworthy than the king himself. Beginning in 1522, certain particularly lucrative royal revenues in the Paris region were placed in the hands of the city's government, or *bureau de ville*, which then sold heritable rentes on the income at the customary rate of 1:12 or 8.33 percent. Buyers apparently found these new instruments more attractive than the older domain rentes, since the revenues on which they were based were controlled by sober merchants and *rentiers* in the *hôtel de ville*, not by the king or his officials. Amid the jumble of royal finance, it was notorious that payment orders, even if signed by the king himself, were not automatically honored by the revenue collectors to whom they were addressed.[38]

---

[36]Dollinger, *Studien zur Finanzreform Maximilians I.*

[37]Pierre Chaunu, "L'Etat de Finance," in *Histoire Economique et Sociale de France*, ed. Fernand Braudel, vol. 1 (Paris: 1977), 129–148; Wolfe, *Fiscal System of Renaissance France*, 1–66.

[38]The best account is Schnapper, *Les Rentes au XVIe Siècle*, 151–173.

Francis I, who introduced the new *rentes sur l'hôtel de ville*, used them sparingly, raising only 725,000 *livres tournois* by this means in all the years of his reign. But Henri II collected some 6,800,000 from rente sales during a much shorter reign (1547–1559). Great nobles and royal officials had a strong interest in these securities, but wealthy townsmen apparently did not. For example, it seems that much of the 3,100,000 in rentes purchased by the burghers of Paris under Henri II was due to forced buying, a practice reminiscent of the forced loans in Italian city-states.[39] During the 1560s, successive alienations of Church land to the crown provided security for a new series of rente issues, but not enough for the huge total of rentes the crown cajoled or compelled its subjects to buy during the early years of France's religious wars (25,900,000 livres between 1559 and 1574). Already in the 1570s interest payments were becoming irregular, and sporadic sales under Henri III (1574–1589) met with little enthusiasm. During the seventeenth century new rentes continued to be sold—mostly to royal financial officials at great discounts—until the whole burden of a now ancient rente debt was largely eliminated by Colbert.[40]

The Spanish monarchy managed its long-term debt a good deal more carefully, even though it rested on the faith and credit of the king alone, without the intervention of his subjects in any corporate capacity. In the conventions of Castilian finance, the crown's "ordinary income" (*rentas ordinarias*) included certain tax revenues, such as the traditional sales tax,

[39]Schnapper, *Les Rentes*, 159–161, notes a dispute between scholars as to whether the rapid subscription of early rentes sur l'hôtel de ville represented strong interest among the bourgeoisie, or a policy of forced buying. Schnapper himself finds, from a study of rente contracts recorded in several notarial registers during the 1550s, that these rentes "sont souscrites avant tout par deux categories des personnages: les officiers royaux . . . et aussi la plus haute noblesse d'epée," with huge purchases by Court figures like the Constable Anne de Montmorency. See also Wolfe, *The Fiscal System of Renaissance France*, 91–93, 109–115.

[40]Wolfe, 121–129, 154; Schnapper, 155–156, notes that after 1572, almost all rentes sur l'hôtel de ville were sold to *partisans*, or banker syndicates, like the Rucellai and the Gondi, who put up only half the purchase price, and a fair portion even of that in the form of royal debt recognizances; Julian Dent, *Crisis in Finance: Crown, Financiers and Society in 17th Century France* (Newton Abbot: 1973), 46–54.

or *alcabala,* as well as other rights that might elsewhere have
been considered part of the king's domain, such as customs
duties. The crown's "extraordinary income" consisted of subsidies granted by the Cortes and, in later times, the revenues
of the three grand-masterships of the Spanish military orders,
which would be annexed to the crown under Ferdinand and
Isabella, and shipments of treasure from the Indies. Since
the twelfth or thirteenth century, the kings of Castile had also
been issuing instruments of long-term debt, known as *juros,*
secured by the crown's ordinary income. Much of this old
debt was extinguished in financial reforms of the 1480s,
but a new and much larger series of issues began under
Charles V.[41] The juros had interest rates ranging from 3 to 7
percent. Like the private rentes, which in Castile were known
as *censos,* they could either be for life only, or heritable and
redeemable. Already by 1522, only five years into Charles's
reign in Castile, 37 percent of the crown's rentas ordinarias
was expended on interest payments to juro holders, a figure
which swelled to nearly 60 percent by the time of Charles's
abdication in 1555.[42] In addition, a new type of security, the
so-called *juros de resguardia,* had been created in 1542 for the
benefit of those among the emperor's Italian and German
bankers who voluntarily agreed to accept these annuities,
secured by choice revenues, in exchange for cancellation of
some of Charles's short-term debt. But even the notable increase in the influx of Peruvian silver was not enough to keep
pace with the crown's expenses between 1552 and 1559, the
longest and far the costliest of the Habsburg-Valois wars. The
"bankruptcies," which Philip II was compelled to declare in
1557, and again in 1575 and 1594, really amounted to a non-
voluntary conversion of short-term loans into juros. By 1560,

[41]The standard accounts of Spanish royal finance in this era are: Ramon
Carande, *Carlos V y sus Banqueros* (3 vols., Madrid: 1943–1957); Modesto
Ulloa, *La Hacienda Real de Castilla en el reinado de Felipe II* (Madrid: 1977); and
Miguel Artola, *La Hacienda Real del Antiguo Regimen* (Madrid: 1982). For these
and other pertinent reference I am indebted to my colleague at Minnesota,
Professor Carla R. Philips.

[42]On juros, Artola, *La Hacienda Real del Antiguo Regimen,* 62–72; Antonio
Dominguez Ortiz, *Politica y Hacienda de Felipe II* (Madrid: 1960), 315–332; and
Felipe Ruiz Martin, "Un expediente financiero entre 1560 y 1575," *Moneda y
Credito* 92 (1965):1–58.

the amount of the rentas ordinarias pledged to juro holders reached 98 to 100 percent, and the *rentas extraordinarias* were becoming increasingly burdened. Over the whole century, the capital value of outstanding juros rose from 5,000,000 ducats in 1515 to 83,000,000 by 1600, a growth that is impressive but still moderate in comparison with the twenty-fivefold increase in royal rentes in France between 1547 and 1574. Contrary to what happened in France, there were no suspensions of payment on juro interest during the reigns of Charles V or Philip II. As Castillo Pintado remarks, however, the temptation to default on debt secured only by the king's word was too attractive to resist forever, and juro holders found their incomes frequently taxed, reduced, or suspended in the following century, under Philip III and Philip IV.[43] Why such practices were not resorted to by earlier monarchs is not clear. Perhaps one may hazard a guess that sixteenth-century royal officials were shrewd enough to see the juros as a kind of strategic reserve in the competition for precious credit resources; firms like the Fuggers might just acquiesce in the conversion of their loans into juros, but only if the latter were instruments of unimpeachable reliability.[44]

During the sixteenth century, when interest was paid faithfully, the juros were quite popular among investors in Spain. In Valladolid, the favored residence of Castilian monarchs prior to Philip II, Bennassar finds that ecclesiastical corporations were the most prominent buyers of juros, followed by members of great noble families domiciled in the city, and royal officials. Castillo Pintado suggests that most juros were held by members of the clergy prior to about 1560, with laymen becoming the most prominent investors after the second great royal bankruptcy, or forced conversion, in 1575.[45]

[43]Carande, *Carlos V y sus Banqueros*, I, 71–120; Alvaro Castillo Pintado, "Los Juros de Castilla," 47–52, as well as "Dette flottante et dette consolidée en Espagne de 1557 à 1600," *Annales* XVIII (1963): 745–759, and "Decretos y medios generales dans le system financière de Castille: la crise de 1596," *Melanges en l'honneur de Fernand Braudel* (2 vols., Toulouse: 1973), I, 137–144.

[44]Castillo Pintado, "Los Juros de Castilla," 47: so close was the connection with bankers' loans (*asientos*) that juros came to be sold by Genoese *asiento* contractors instead of by royal officials.

[45]Bennassar, *Valladolid au Siècle d'Or*, 252–259; Castillo Pintado, "Dette flottante et dette consolidée," 759.

It is a matter for discussion among students of Spanish history whether the Castilian bourgeoisie turned to juros in order to enjoy the social prestige of "living nobly," that is, as a rentier, or because state securities were a sensible investment alternative in an already declining economy. Either way, it seems clear that the juros, while providing a nearly inexhaustible source of the revenue that was needed for the wars of Philip II, siphoned off a great deal of capital that might otherwise have been available for productive investment.[46]

If Spanish juros became somewhat less attractive to investors during the seventeenth century, investment in papal debt, created principally after 1550, continued to flourish. The first papal monte was established in 1526 by the Medici pope, Clement VII. Florence and Genoa provided models for long-term debt in the Papal States, but the system as practiced after 1550 soon took on some distinctive features of its own. When capital was needed, a monte was "erected" and offered to the highest bidder among Roman banks or syndicates of financiers, with the winner then offering interest-bearing shares (*luoghi*) to the general public. Shares were either extinguishable at the death of the original proprietor or, at a lower rate of interest, indefinitely transmissible to heirs or assigns; shares of the latter kind came to be thought of as perpetual, since, although some monti were created with the intention of amortizing the principal over a period of years, principal was in fact seldom if ever retired. There was no question of parliamentary involvement in papal debts, for the popes were in the process of becoming absolute monarchs in their temporal dominions during the second half of the sixteenth century. In the absence of parliamentary guarantees, however, successive popes won the confidence of investors by means of privileges and rights that have no parallel in other territories discussed in this chapter. Shareholders were solemnly promised that their title to these investments could not be confiscated for any reason, not even the gravest crimes

---

[46]Bennassar, 558–565, emphasizes the importance of the social ideal of living nobly; for a different view, see Carla Philips, *Ciudad Real, 1500–1700* (Cambridge, Mass.: 1979), 110–112. Castillo Pintado, "Los Juros de Castilla," 48–49, contends that capital invested in juros was lost to the building of Spain's economy.

against God or man. Investors in each individual monte were authorized to form a college among themselves (rather like the Genoese compere, it seems) vested with direct control of the papal revenue by which the monte was funded. Whether or not they availed themselves of this right, they had a Cardinal-Protector to look after their interests at the Curia. As a result, confidence in papal monti was such that shares of favored issues sold for as much as 120 percent of par on the secondary market. No less than forty monti were erected between 1526 and 1603 and, by Delumeau's reckoning, brought in a total monetary equivalent of one and a half years of Spanish silver imports during the period when shipments from Latin America were at their peak. In these circumstances, the Camera Apostolica had no difficulty reducing its burden of annual interest payments by converting lifetime-only shares to perpetual shares, or by lowering the rate for a perpetual monte, always with the proviso that shareholders who did not wish to accept the reduction could reclaim their original capital instead.[47]

One may conclude that there was a certain convergence in the mechanisms of Continental public debt during the sixteenth century. No government could do without the services of great financiers who were often agents of firms domiciled beyond its frontiers. Indeed, it was not unknown for financial brokers of this period surreptitiously to boost profits by lending to two hostile rulers at the same time.[48] The only alternative to high rates charged by the bankers was long-term debt of one form or another. State-backed annuities, already in use north of the Alps, made some headway in Italy, as in Venice. Further, in most places (Spain and the Papal States excepted) princely promises no longer sufficed to provide creditors the assurance they required. The prince's subjects had to intervene in some corporate capacity, whether like the city government of Paris assuming control of the royal revenues by which

[47]Jean Delumeau, *Vie Economique et Sociale de Rome dans la Seconde Moitié du XVIe Siècle* (2 vols., Paris: 1957–1959), II, 783–824.

[48]J. A. Goris, *Etude sur les Colonies Marchandes Meridionales à Anvers de 1478 à 1567* (Leuven: 1925), 375–381, on Gasparo Ducci's financial role in France and the Habsburg Netherlands during the 1540s.

the rentes sur l'hotel de ville were funded, or like the Estates of German territories such as Bavaria or Württemberg taking over the duke's debts. The rest of this book will be devoted to showing how, in the Habsburg Netherlands, these common elements were blended together in a distinctive combination: as the government's borrowing needs on the Antwerp exchange expanded at an incredible rate, as much as seventyfold over the last thirty years of Charles V's reign,[49] debt service costs were held to manageable limits only by paying off the bankers with funds raised through the sale of annuities—which in turn became more attractive to investors in proportion as the provincial parliaments, or States, assumed full responsibility for them.

[49]See chapter 2, notes 5, 43, and 49: a Council of Finance summary for the years 1521–1530 indicates total borrowing for the decade of 538,870 (405,889 on obligation, plus another 133,961 in loans from officials), while other figures suggest outstanding loans of 3,801,992 for 1554 alone, which would be slightly more than seventy times the annual average of indebtedness for 1521–1530.

II

Netherlands Finance and the Origins of Provincial Renten

The Burgundian-Habsburg monarchy of Charles V was Spanish by adoption, but French by language and tradition. Between 1506 and 1567, Charles and his son Philip II were represented in Brussels (or Mechelen) by three ladies of their family who governed as regents: Charles's aunt, Margaret of Austria (1506–1514, and 1519–1530); his sister, the widowed Queen Mary of Hungary (1531–1555); and his illegitimate daughter, Margaret of Parma (1559–1567).[1] The

[1]Jane de Iongh, *Margaretha van Oostenrijk* (Amsterdam: 3d printing, 1947), and *De Koningin: Maria van Hongarije, Landvoogdes der Nederlanden, 1505–1558* (Amsterdam: 4th printing, 1966); F. Rachfahl, *Margaretha von Parma, Statthalterin der Niederlanden* (Munich: 1898). On Emmanuel-Philibert of Savoy,

regents governed through a network of advisory councils, which Charles reorganized in 1530: a Council of State, chiefly consisting of great nobles, for military and foreign affairs; a Privy Council, made up of jurists, for domestic matters; and a Council of Finance, staffed by "long robes" but always including a few great nobles with fiscal experience.[2] At the provincial level, the authority of the regent (and ultimately of Charles V, who was recognized under separate titles in each of his territories as Duke of Brabant, Count of Flanders, Count of Holland . . .) was vested in a governor, or stadtholder, usually chosen from among the "great lords" who sat in the Council of State. In Holland, the man who served longest as stadtholder during the Habsburg period was Antoine de Lalaing, lord of Montigny and Count of Hoogstraten, who was also head of the Council of Finance and a leading member of the Council of State.[3] Since Hoogstraten was in Brussels or Mechelen most of the time, tending to other affairs, governing authority in Holland was in practice exercised by a judicial and financial bureaucracy known collectively as the *Hof van Holland,* or Court of Holland, in The Hague; its chief components were a Chamber of Accounts (*Rekenkamer*) and a Council of Holland (*Raad van Holland*) whose members combined judicial and administrative responsibilities.[4] At the higher levels, servants of the Habsburg crown were familiar with fiscal expedients of many different kinds, and, in the great city of Antwerp, they had access to the leading Italian, Iberian, and South German banking houses. Accordingly, the fiscal system that evolved under their direction was eclectic and in many ways creative, even if it never achieved the

---

who functioned as regent between 1555 and 1559, see Verhofstad, and Carlo Evasio Petrucco, *Lo Stato Sabaudo al Tempo di Emmanuele Filiberto* (3 vols., Turin: 1928).

[2]See Baelde.

[3]M. L. J. C. Noordam-Croes, "Antoon van Lalaing, Graf van Hoogstraten," *Jaarboek Koninklijke Hoogstratens Oudheidkundig Kring* 36 (1968): 1–174.

[4]For a description of the Hof van Holland in the fifteenth century, see the introduction to Blécourt; Tracy, "Heresy Law and Centralization in the Habsburg Netherlands: Conflicts between the Council of Holland and the Central Government over Enforcement of the Placards," *Archiv für Reformationsgeschichte* 73 (1982): 284–307.

blessed state of solvency. In what follows, it will be appropriate to consider first the government's chief annual revenues (I), and then the means by which it could convert future revenues into cash (II). On this basis, it will be possible to explain how the tax system worked in the province of Holland (III), and to examine the practice of having provincial parliaments, like the States of Holland, sell annuities backed by tax revenues (IV).

I. The regent and her advisers disposed of an annual income based, as in other princely states, on domain receipts and on subsidies granted by representative bodies. Domain income was much the smaller of the two. For example, a ten-year summary of the income and expenses drawn up for Charles V (1521–1530) has the following totals.[5] (All figures in this book are given in Holland pounds equal to 20 silver stuivers or 40 silver groats).[6]

Domain receipts	2,509,044
Subsidies	10,110,757
Parties extraordinaires	1,051,717
Rentes on future subsidies	1,016,051
Loans raised on *obligations*	405,889

[5]Aud. 867:71–91.

[6]The Holland pound of 20 stuivers or 40 groats was a unit of account, used in requests for subsidies. There was also a coin of the same official value, the *Karolus gulden,* first minted in gold (1521), and later in silver (1541): see H. A. Enno van Gelder, Marcel Hoc, *Les Monnayes des Pays-Bas Bourguignons et Espagnols, 1434–1713* (Amsterdam: 1960), and Jelle Riemersma, *Religious Factors in Early Dutch Capitalism* (The Hague: 1967), 37–43. In fact, the Karolus gulden circulated at a value somewhat in excess of 20 stuivers (AJ, 3 November 1530; Council of Holland to Mary of Hungary, 29 July 1537, Aud. 1540) and hence is not referred to here. The purchasing power of the Holland pound changed slightly over the years, since there were slight variations in the silver content of the stuiver and the groat in 1521, 1553, and 1559: H. van der Wee, *Growth of the Antwerp Market* (3 vols., Antwerp: 1963), III, graph 7. Also, the purchasing power of a constant amount of silver declined somewhat as the sixteenth-century price revolution began to take effect in the Netherlands during the 1550s: De Vries, *The Dutch Rural Economy in the Golden Age,* 180–185. But no attempt is made here to take these changes into account.

(*Parties extraordinaires* included a variety of small items like confiscations and the alum toll; rentes on future subsidies and loans raised on *obligations* will be explained in the course of this chapter.) Though it is not inconsiderable, the sum for domain receipts is also somewhat misleading, since many of the choicest parcels of domain rights, such as the Antwerp toll and the Zeeland toll, had already been pledged well into the future by the time Charles was elected emperor in 1519, to provide handsome pensions for the electors who voted for him, and for other important imperial princes.[7] Still other income-producing princely rights had been mortgaged through sales of rentes—either heritable rentes at the customary 1 : 16 (6.25%) or life rentes at a higher rate—as had been customary in the Burgundian realm at least since the reign of Duke Philip the Good (1419–1467).[8] According to a 1535 census of domain receipts, only about 20 percent of the income from forty-six different collecting districts was allocated to interest payments on rentes. It is notable, though, that the larger rente-free incomes are found in northern provinces like Holland and Friesland, where domain rentes were just beginning to be sold in the 1530s.[9] Still other documents make it clear that if one counted all the pensions and salaries that had been assigned to domain receipts, together with overhead expenses paid by local receivers, the result was a net annual deficit.[10] One can understand the government's reluctance to sell parcels of domain outright, instead of pledging their income either through the sale of rentes or as surety for loans,[11]

[7]Aud. 867: 116–123 (summary of domain income and expenditures on this income for 1527).

[8]Aud. 868: 62–64, among charges on the domain receipts for Leuven (Brabant) is a rente at 1 : 18 "at the cost of the late Philip, Duke of Burgundy."

[9]Aud. 868: 62–90; the estimated annual income is 438,671, and the annual rente interest is 86,501.

[10]Aud. 867: 116–123, total domain receipts for 1527 were 194,214, but expenditures on these receipts amounted to 204,250.

[11]Aud. 867: 132–136, financial report brought to the emperor in Spain by Rosimbois and Banes, to which his reply is dated Saragossa, 8 April 1529. Margaret of Austria informed her nephew she had ordered one revenue official to give obligations on his receipts five years ahead of time rather than sell a parcel of domain, because "domaine vendue" was the same as "extraordinaire vendu," that is, domain once sold could no longer be used as security for loans. See Charles V to Mary of Hungary, 2 March 1536, in M. Baelde,

but disposable receipts from the domain played only a small part in the calculations of those who ruled the Netherlands on Charles V's behalf. Far more important were the two kinds of subsidy revenue. Ordinary subsidies were voted by the provincial States more or less as a matter of course, only the amounts of such grants and the number of years they would run being subject to negotiation. Extraordinary subsidies were sought by the government in time of emergency, but not always obtained (subsidies were called *aides* in the Walloon provinces, and *beden* in the Dutch-speaking lands). Within each province, the *aide ordinaire* or *ordinaris bede* was levied according to a system of repartition determined by the States and revised periodically, at least until the sixteenth century.[12] The *aide extraordinaire* or *extraordinaris bede* was usually collected the same way. Both were collected by Receivers of Subsidies who often (as in Holland) had responsibility for an entire province, whereas the collectors of domain receipts had much smaller circumscriptions.[13] Like these other officials, the Receivers of Subsidies were appointed by the Council of Finance, and made payments by authorization of the Receiver-General for All Finances,[14] who was, *ex officio*, a member of the Council

---

"Onuitgegeven Dokumenten, betreffende de Zestiende-eeuwse Collaterale Raden," *Bulletin de la Commission Royale d'Histoire* CXXXI (Brussels: 1965), 141–152.

[12]In Holland this assessment was known as the *schiltal*, and was last carried out in 1514: (*Informatie op het Stat . . . van Holland van 1514*, R. J. Fruin, ed. [Leiden: 1866]). The transport of Flanders is discussed in Maddens, 13–72.

[13]See the *Inventaris* (no. 61) for GRK at the Rijksarchief voor Zuid-Holland in The Hague: there were separate collection districts and collectors for domain revenue in North Holland, Kenemerland and Westfriesland, Amstelland, Rijnland, South Holland, and Gouda (with Schoonhoven and *het land van Stein*) plus several smaller jurisdictions. The earliest "Ontvanger Generaal" for beden for the whole province seems to have been Meester Jacob Goudt, 1507–1510, who was perhaps the father of Willem Goudt, Receiver-(General) for the beden in Holland from 1511 until his death in 1543.

[14]Disputes between the States of Holland and Willem Goudt (see note 13) sometimes turned on the fact that Goudt was answerable for how he disposed of bede receipts not to the States, but to his superiors in the Council of Finance: for example, Gerrit van Assendelft, First Councilor of the Council of Holland, to Hoogstraten, 21 October, 21 November, 17 December 1531, 7 August 1532 (Aud. 1525). Not even the Stadtholder could countermand instructions Goudt had received from the Council of Finance: Assendelft to Hoogstraten, 4 July 1536 (Aud. 1530), 28 January 1537 (Aud. 1532).

of Finance. If towns or villages were slow in meeting one of the semiannual payment dates, the Receiver of Subsidies had power to grant extensions,[15] and if they were altogether too slow he could place their leading men under detention in the provincial capital until some agreement was made.[16]

Not everyone was subject to the provincial assessment on which the subsidy was based. Certain categories of privileged persons—nobles, clerics, and government officials—enjoyed personal exemptions.[17] More importantly, whole villages and towns were exempt because they lay within enclaves of noble jurisdiction, subject to Charles V in person, but not to the provincial States, nor to the province's fiscal and judicial bureaucracy.[18] From the standpoint of those who did pay, it is worth noting that not all taxes were subsidies voted by the provincial States. First, a regent sometimes boldy dispensed with the formalities of parliamentary consent, as when Mary of Hungary imposed an unpopular export duty "by virtue of the Emperor's absolute power" in 1543.[19] Second, the States of each province regularly voted smaller levies, collected on the same basis as the subsidies, to cover their own administrative expenses. The *omslagen*, as these taxes were called in Holland, were rarely of any consequence compared with the beden, at least not prior to the 1550s.[20]

Even in times of peace, the ordinary subsidies were probably not sufficient to meet the government's recurring needs.

---

[15]Such delays, or *atterminatiën*, are discussed for Flanders by Maddens, and for Leiden in Holland by W. Downer, "De Financiële Toestand van Leiden omstreeks 1500" (chapter 1, note 18).

[16]Detention (gijzeling) in The Hague was not an uncommon experience for magistrates from Gouda: GVR 4 July 1524, 6 November 1529, 8 January 1530.

[17]Beginning in the 1540s, the regent promised to override certain of these exemptions as part of bede agreements with the States, but it was easier said than done: see chapter 3, note 40. In the States of Holland, the nobles, who usually supported the government on other fiscal issues, defended the exemptions of these privileged enclaves as well as their own: Assendelft to Mary of Hungary, 23 February 1544 (Aud. 1646:3).

[18]A 1553 10th penny tax levied on income from real property "outside" as well as "inside" the schiltal lists, as exempt from the assessment and hence from "most subsidies, thirty-seven villages or parts of villages, and six towns (Leerdam, Zevenbergen, Asperen, Heukelom, Woudrichem, and Ijsselstein).

[19]RSH 25 February, 7 March, 1543.

[20]Accounts for these omslagen levied by schiltal are listed in Meilink, 1762–1798, but have not been consulted for this study.

But the dominant fact of Low Countries history during this period was the long series of wars with France and her allies, including the Duchy of Guelders and, sometimes, the King of Denmark. While the rolling hills of Artois and Hainaut offered no barrier to the advance of French troops from the south, Guelders lay astride the several branches of the Rhine and could thus interdict river traffic through the northern Netherlands. Holland in particular could be threatened in two ways, either by invasion from Guelders, through the intervening ecclesiastical principality of Utrecht, or when Denmark pinched off its vital Baltic trade by closing the Danish Sound to Netherlands shipping.[21] In the period covered by this study, there were major Habsburg-Valois wars from 1515 to 1517, 1521 to 1525, and 1526 to 1528; after occasional skirmishes during the 1530s, there was full-scale war again between 1542 and 1544, followed by the long and brutal conflict that dragged out from 1552 to 1559.

These wars made the government totally dependent on the goodwill of the States, which were already in a position to be rather demanding because of the decentralization of power in the Low Countries, which coincided with the beginning of Habsburg rule. Under Charles the Bold, last of the Burgundian Dukes (1467–1477), the States General functioned as a national parliament, capable of agreeing to taxation after prior consultation with the component provincial States, and it granted the ambitious and somewhat terrifying Duke Charles sums of money undreamed of by his predecessors.[22] But in a reaction, which followed Charles's death on the field of battle, his daughter and heiress, Mary of Burgundy, had to restore the freedom of each provincial parliament not to be bound by the decisions of the others, so that the States General was

[21]For the general history of the Habsburg-Valois wars as they affected the Low Countries, Alexandre Henne, *Histoire du Règne de Charles V en Belgique* (10 vols., Brussels: 1858–1860); for conflicts with Guelders and Denmark, J. E. A. L. Struik, *Gelre en Habsburg, 1492–1528* (Arnhem: 1960); and Rudolf Häpke, *Die Regierung Karls V und der europäische Norden* (Lübeck: 1914).

[22]Richard Vaughan, *Duke Charles the Bold* (London: 1973), especially p. 189; Michel Mollat, "Récherches sur les finances des ducs Valois de Bourgogne," *Revue Historique* CCXIX (1958): 285–321; Peter Spufford, "Coinage, Taxation, and the Estates General of the Burgundian Netherlands," *Standen en Landen— Anciens pays et Assemblées d'Etat* XL (1966): 61–88.

no longer a decision-making body. In some cases Mary was constrained to carry the process of devolution one step further, acknowledging that no one city with voting rights in the States of a particular province could be bound by the decisions of other "members" of the States. This latter concession, at least as it applied to Holland, was abrogated in 1494 by Archduke Philip the Handsome, son of Mary of Burgundy and Maximilian of Habsburg and father of Charles V, but sixteenth-century Habsburg regents still had to contend with the principle of provincial autonomy.[23]

When a bede was needed under Habsburg rule, the States General was convoked solely to hear a "general proposition" in which the president of the Council of State or some other high official set forth the reasons why funds were needed, as well as the total amount required. Deputies from each provincial States were then convened separately to hear a "particular proposition" explaining how much was being asked of them. Within the bosom of the Council of Finance there were, of course, set quotas for each province, but it was a settled policy during Charles V's reign that officials would never discuss these quotas in a plenary session of the States General, lest the meeting be wholly disrupted by interprovincial quarrels.[24] Having heard their "particular proposition," deputies returned home and reported to the full States of their own province, which then referred the request for a subsidy to the individual towns or other "members" which made up the States. Special commissioners appointed by the regent negotiated with each provincial assembly, and often with their component members, since the consent of a province could be held up by the recalcitrance of a single town (the others making their consent conditional on the willingness of all to pay), while provinces that had already signaled their agreement might retract it for similar reasons. In an extreme

[23]Henri Pirenne, *Histoire de Belgique* (7 vols., Brussels: 1902–1932), III, 10–15; P. J. Blok, *Geschiedenis eener Hollandsche Stad* (4 vols., The Hague: 1910–1918), II, 57–69.

[24]N. Maddens, "De Invoering van de 'Nieuwe Middelen' in het Graafschap Vlaanderen tijdens de Regering van Keizer Karel," *Belgische Tijdschrift voor Filologie en Geschiedenis = Revue Belge de Philologie et d'Histoire* 57 (1979): 342–363, here 348–354.

case, one of the component "members" of one town government in one province could hold up the entire process for several months.[25] If all went smoothly, and it usually did not, the States General would be convoked again so that deputies from all the provinces could present their formal assent to the original request, or at least something resembling it.

Meanwhile, the business of war did not await the outcome of such negotiations. But deputies to the provincial States had a tendency to be unimpressed by military dangers remote from their own districts.[26] They had other fish to fry in their discussions with the regent's commissioners and, consciously or not, exploited the government's need to extract concessions in a number of areas, notably in the matter of tax rebates. These *graces*, or (in Dutch) *gratiën*, trace back to the fifteenth century or earlier.[27] To judge from the accounts of the receiver for the beden in Holland, each full or partial remission of the bede quota for a particular town or village had to be justified by a statement of need and endorsed by the Council of Finance upon recommendation of the provincial Chamber of Accounts.[28] According to a summary for the year 1531 drawn up by the Council of Finance, the real value of the three most important provincial ordinary subsidies for that year was reduced by about one-third because of gratiën:[29]

[25]Lodewijk van Schore, president of the Council of State, to Mary of Hungary, 14 November 1543, and 1 January 1546, Aud. 1642:3a. In the first instance, the magistrates and the former magistrates of Antwerp give their consent to a bede, but the other two "members" of the city government, the burghers and the guilds, do not; in the second, the upper two members of the Brussels city government are agreeable to a new bede, but the "nations," or groupings of guilds, are not. For similar problems the central government had with Brabant towns in the 1550s, see Verhofstad, 74, 98–104. Except for Dordrecht, Holland's cities, smaller and of more recent vintage, were ruled in the old-fashioned way by self-perpetuating patrician oligarchies, and did not have governments divided into "members."

[26]Tracy, *The Politics of Erasmus: A Pacifist Intellectual and His Political Milieu* (Toronto: 1978), 78–81.

[27]Blok, "De Financiën van het Graafschap Holland," Bijlage.

[28]Capsule summaries of these *brieven van gratie* are found under the entries for gratie in GRK; contrary to what one might think, rebates were usually treated in the accounts as expenditures rather than as deductions from income.

[29]Aud. 875:4–10. These three provinces accounted for 78.79 percent of the gross ordinaris bede income expected for the year. Ordinaris beden or aides

	Nominal sum	Gratiën	Gratiën as percentage
Brabant	200,000	64,659	32.33
Flanders	200,000	65,807	32.90
Holland	80,000	28,193	35.24

Gratiën were often higher in *extraordinaris beden*, at least for cities that had voting rights in the States, since consent to an extraordinaris bede could not be taken for granted.[30] Though rebates were granted to towns and villages not represented in the States, it was above all the "great cities," those with voting rights, which could profit from the government's wartime needs by bringing their rebates to unprecedented levels. At least in regard to Holland, this point will be documented a bit farther on.

The selfishness of the great cities was not, however, the only reason for the government's inability to raise the money it needed in a timely manner. For reasons that have never been fully understood, Habsburg rulers did not employ Dutch-speaking troops to defend their Dutch-speaking provinces. The few *compagnies d'ordonnance* that were maintained on a year-round basis were recruited from the francophone

---

ordinaires for other provinces and districts were: Zeeland, 30,000 (canceled because of flooding); Hainaut, 29,000, counting 5,000 from the prelates; Lille, Douai, and Orchies, 16,000; Mechelen (a separate enclave lying within the Duchy of Brabant), 4,000; Voorne, 2,650; Putte and Stryen, 1,000 (Voorne, Putte, and Stryen were located in Holland, but were not "under the schiltal"; through separate receivers, they paid, respectively, 1/27 and 1/80 of the beden approved by the States of Holland); Luxembourg, Overmaas and Limburg, O. For Artois no aide ordinaire is listed, but there are four aides extraordinaires totaling 47,600.

[30]Between 1524 and 1545, the six great cities (Dordrecht, Delft, Gouda, Haarlem, Leiden, and Amsterdam) received between 66 and 80 percent of the total gratiën alloted to Holland for ordinary subsidies (GRK 3427, 3429, 3430, 3433, 3436, 3437, 3440). For extraordinary subsidies between 1523 and 1552, they received between 77 and 100 percent of the total rebates (GRK 3425, 3426, 3428, 3431, 3432, 3436, 3438, 3439, 3441, 3443, 3445, 3451). Since it was harder for small cities and villages to obtain rebates for extraordinary subsidies, the total gratie remained about the same for both kinds of beden; that is, about 27,000 or 28,000 on a bede of 80,000 during the 1530s.

provinces, while mercenary companies were hired as needed by military contractors from north or south Germany.[31] Charles V's Dutch-speaking subjects were thus defended by foreigners, men who may have come cheaper, or whose very distance from home may have made them more reliable as soldiers,[32] but who, in the absence of timely payment, readily extracted what was due them, and a bit more into the bargain, from those they were intended to protect. Nothing was more likely to make the States flatly refuse a subsidy request than the government's inability to control its own troops.[33] It was, then, a vicious circle. Because the States would not consent without wrangling, the regent could not pay her troops, who then behaved in such a way as to make the States absolutely unwilling to consent. As Margaret of Austria once complained to her imperial nephew, "In the long run, I do not see how it is feasible to conduct a war in these countries."[34]

II. Such a government could only survive by converting future revenues into ready cash. One way of doing so was to persuade towns or even whole provinces to "anticipate" one or more "terms" of a subsidy (ordinary subsidies fell due on St. John's day and Christmas, extraordinary subsidies at various times, but usually twice a year). Anticipations of both subsidy and domain receipts were especially common in time of war, as may be seen from the following table of average annual receipts over five-year intervals:[35]

---

[31]Tracy, *The Politics of Erasmus*, 74–77.

[32]Geoffrey Parker, *The Spanish Road and the Army of the Netherlands* (Cambridge: 1972), 30, reports the common view that men were better soldiers the farther they were from home.

[33]Tracy, *The Politics of Erasmus*, 77.

[34]Alexandre Henne, *Histoire de Belgique sous le règne du Charles V* (2 vols., Brussels: 1865), I, 396, quoting Margaret to Charles V, 22 April 1523, "à la longue, je ne vois conduisable le fait de la guerre en ces pays."

[35]Annual totals for the gross receipts of Jean Micault as Receiver-General for All Finances between 1508 and 1533 are given in Aud. 867:35–38; figures for subsequent years are from the annual accounts, Lille B 2386, 2392, 2398, 2404, 2410, 2418, 2424, 2430, 2436, 2442, 2448, 2454, 2460, 2476, 2482. Note that the accounts for 1534, 1539, and 1549 are not extant.

1508–1510	688,651
1511–1515	658,984
1516–1520	950,430
1521–1525	1,229,955
1526–1530	919,951
1531–1533, 1535	1,342,490
1536–1538, 1540	896,328
1541–1545	2,202,439
1546–1548, 1550	756,870

Income bulges in the early 1520s and 1540s represent periods of heavy fighting, whereas that of the early 1530s betokens an effort by Charles V to cleanse his ledgers of debts stemming from wars of the 1520s.[36] In each case there followed a period of diminished receipts, since a portion of the income for these years had already been collected ahead of time. This method of borrowing against the future had obvious limits, since for the provinces it was neither desirable to raise so much money at once, nor safe to have the local fisc stripped of resources normally brought in by the ordinary subsidy. For example, by the fall of 1523, Holland's ordinaris bede through the St. John's term of 1526 had already been collected, which meant that the receiver for the beden might not have any cash

[36]In the Receiver-General's account for 1531 (Lille B, 2363), payments from certain domain receipts in Flanders were pledged up to twenty years in advance in order to retire a total debt of 448,825 owed to merchants of Antwerp. In March 1531 the regent submitted to the emperor a plan drafted by the Council of Finance for avoiding "past and future" interest charges on the Antwerp exchange: Mary of Hungary to Charles V, 23 March 1532 (Aud. 52). The next year the emperor sent a special instruction specifying which pensions and other expenses assigned to domain income were actually to be paid: to Mary of Hungary, 5 April 1533 (Aud. 52). Still later, however, it was necessary for the Council of Finance to explain to the emperor how certain expenses not included in the budget ("non couchées") for the years 1531–1534 had disrupted plans to reduce the deficit: Aud. 868:1–2v.

on hand for hiring soldiers or sailors in an emergency.[37] Borrowing on the Antwerp exchange—the other method of realizing future assets—was acknowledged to be a "cancer" on the body politic, since, during Margaret of Austria's regency, rates for loans to the central government could go as high as 22 percent and were never lower than 12 percent.[38] Nonetheless, it was only in Antwerp that the regent could find men like Gasparo Ducci of Lucca, who could raise as much as 60,000 pounds in cash on twenty-four hours' notice.[39] (To give some idea of the magnitude of such a sum, be it noted that 60,000 pounds would buy as many as thirty homes along Amsterdam's most fashionable street,[40] or 90,000 bushels of wheat on the local grain exchange.)[41] Even at the

[37]The States of Holland agreed in 1522 to "anticipate" ordinaris bede payments over the next two years (GVR 17 August, 10 September, 1522). By October 1523, the three-year ordinaris bede whose last payment date was St. John's day 1526 had already been collected in full (AJ 3 October 1523, GRK 3423, 3427, 3429). For the argument that such anticipations left the province without means to defend itself, AJ 18 July 1528.

[38]For loan rates of 22 percent or higher, see the interest payments listed under "Betalingen aan officiers" (payments to officials) in GRK 3432. A list of state loans on the Antwerp exchange during the reign of Charles V has been prepared by Mme. G. Bellart, currently director of the Archives du Départment du Nord in Lille, who had the great kindness to allow me to examine her notes. Though it is regrettable that this valuable material has not been published, there is a summary by Fernand Braudel, "Les Emprunts du Charles V sur le Place d'Anvers," *Charles-Quint et son Temps* (Paris: 1959), 190–201.

[39]? to the Marquis of Arschot, 20 June 1541, Aud. 129: Gasparo Ducci of Lucca has offered to deliver 60,000 Karolus gulden (see above, note 6) within twenty-four hours if certain conditions are met. On Ducci and his role as financial broker for Mary of Hungary during the 1540s, see J. A. Goris, *Etudes sur les Colonies Marchandes Meridionales à Anvers, 1488–1577* (Leuven: 1925), 363, 375–381.

[40]I. J. G. Kam, *Waar Was Dat Huis in de Warmoesstraat* (Amsterdam: 1968): in 1543, when property-owners paid a 10th penny on actual or hypothetical rental income (estimated at 1/16 the market value of the property), the typical house along fashionable Warmoesstraat paid a tax of between ten and twenty pounds; a fifteen-pound tax would mean (15 × 160) a market value of 2,400. The owner of a house then called "Reval," but currently known by its prosaic modern street address, No. 96, paid a tax of 16.5 pounds, equivalent to a sale value of 2,640; in 1561 the same house was valued at 4,300.

[41]Grain prices per *last*, a measure of volume equivalent to about 85 bushels, are discussed in Tracy, "Habsburg Grain Policy and Amsterdam Politics: The Career of Sheriff Willem Dirkszoon Baerdes," *Sixteenth Century Journal* XVIII (1983): 293–319.

high rates just mentioned, lenders had no confidence in the personal bond of Charles V or in any of his princely kin. Already by the 1520s they were demanding, as reliable surety for their loans, the personal bond, or obligation, of one or more of the great lords in the Council of State.[42] In these circumstances neither Margaret nor her advisers resorted willingly to the Antwerp exchange. Though the figure probably does not represent the full extent of Habsburg borrowing in Antwerp, the 1531 memo prepared for Charles V, which was quoted above, gives only 405,889 as having been raised during the previous ten years by loans on obligation, plus (under Parties extraordinaires) 133,961 by loans from officials. Of this total, 126,000 was a loan from the Augsburg firm of Hochstetter obtained during the campaigns of 1528, which officials in Brussels were at pains to justify to the emperor, as well they might be, since the Hochstetter had demanded 200,000 in principal and interest payments over the next five years.[43]

Matters got worse instead of better in succeeding decades, especially with the outbreak of another major war with France in 1542. By now the personal credit of the great lords was perhaps diminished,[44] and it was in any case not sufficient for the emperor's expanded borrowing needs. Gasparo Ducci, who was then serving as the crown's factor, or loan-broker,

[42]Charles V to Margaret of Austria, 30 October 1522 (Lanz, I, 72): Charles is informed by his brother Ferdinand that Duke George of Saxony will not accept the emperor's personal obligation (transmitted to him via Ferdinand) as adequate surety for a debt of 200,000 florins (= Karolus gulden, see note 6) in connection with the purchase some years earlier of Saxon claims to the province of Friesland.

[43]Aud. 873:53v–57v (405,889 "anticipations of future *aides*, loans from officials," and 133,961 "obligations in regard to Overijssel"); Aud. 867:132–136. In the letter quoted below, note 44, Mary of Hungary apologizes to Charles V because she had been forced to borrow 300,000 in Antwerp, contrary to his instructions in 1533.

[44]On the indebtedness of the great families from whose ranks most provincial governors were chosen, see Gordon Griffiths, *William of Hornes, Lord of Hèze, and the Revolt of the Netherlands* (Berkeley: 1954), 10–14. A chance comment by Mary of Hungary suggests that Charles V sought to attach these families to the dynasty by making them its creditors: the regent has collected obligations from the great lords, "bien sachant que voudriez que pour le service de votre majesté ilz fussent interessé": Mary to Charles, 14 July 1533, *in* Baelde, "Onuitgegeven Dokumenten betreffende de Zestiende-eeuwse Collaterale Raden," 134–140.

in Antwerp, now devised the so-called *rentmeesterbrieven* (tax-collectors' letters), by which the officials who collected the emperor's beden and domain revenue pledged money to lenders or lender syndicates on the surety of their future receipts.[45] These officials were in any case already involved directly in the government's credit operations in Antwerp. Most of the money collected by (for example) Holland's receiver for the beden never found its way to his superior, the Receiver-General for All Finances. Instead, the bulk of his receipts was expended on what were called *décharges*. These were quittances signed by the Receiver-General and two or three other members of the Council of Finance, "discharging," or acquitting, the local receiver of liability for certain of his receipts, with the amount and (usually) the bede in question specified. The décharges are no longer extant, but capsule summaries of them in the accounts of Holland's receivers for the beden (GRK) show that the receiver obtained a décharge from his superiors after presenting certain named bankers in Antwerp with a promissory note against his future receipts. In other words, the décharges were counterparts of the obligations of tax collectors, of the type which were, it seems, formalized in Ducci's "invention" of the *rentmeester-brief*.[46] As for what happened to the "ringing coin" (*espèces sonnantes;* one Flemish coin was called the *klinkaert*) in which Holland's beden were paid, one must look to the small entries under "travel expenses" for details about carts loaded with silver—naturally accompanied by armed guards—rolling off from The Hague in the direction of Maassluis, and thence across the great river to Antwerp, where the emperor's creditors awaited payment.[47]

But all the resources of Charles V's well-managed fiscal bureaucracy could not keep pace with the rising cost of war

---

[45]Richard Ehrenberg, *Capital and Finance in the Age of the Renaissance* (New York: 1928), 223; see above, note 39.

[46]"Betalingen aan officiers," the rubric which makes up the bulk of expenditures in bede accounts (SH as well as GRK), consists mainly of décharges and of smaller entries for payment of loan interest owing in Antwerp, though some payments are made directly to the Receiver General for All Finances or to the Treasurer of War.

[47]See, for instance, the entries under "Reisen" (journeys) in GRK 3427, 3441.

and the imperious need for credit. For the first eight months of 1543, wartime military expenses in the Netherlands were reckoned at 2,765,658 pounds; for the six-month campaigning season of 1558, the last full year of the longest Habsburg-Valois war, the figure was 5,377,421.[48] Even in 1538, a year of relative peace, the Council of Finance reported a net deficit of 1,421,836, which translated into an equivalent amount of borrowing. By 1554, the total owing to lenders in Antwerp had risen to 3,801,992, roughly seven times what had been borrowed on "obligation" during the entire decade of the 1520s.[49] In effect, the sum by which the government's liabilities exceeded its income was parceled out among the various collectors. Holland's receiver for the beden thus reported in the same year (1554) that he had outstanding *obligatiën* totaling 596,404 for which he had no corresponding receipts in the offing.[50] Antwerp's merchant bankers were not slow to discern that rentmeesterbrieven were no longer to be trusted. Already in 1553 the States of Holland were asked, as surety for loans in Antwerp, to give their corporate *obligatie* for a loan to be repaid out of future beden. With the proviso that interest charges be paid by the central government and not by the States, this practice became common during the 1550s.[51] Credit operations on the Antwerp exchange thus evolved in such a way that the precious quality of credit-

---

[48]Aud. 650:293–294, 159–162.

[49]Aud. 1407:1, list of bankers' loans arranged according to the traditional quarterly payment dates: *koudemarkt* (Candlemas), Easter, Pentecost, and *bamis* (St. Bavo's day). The list runs from Pentecost 1554 through Candlemas 1556. It seems most loans were extended for two quarters, from Pentecost to Candlemas, then again to Pentecost, or from Easter to St. Remy, then again to Easter. Hence to arrive at a figure for total indebtedness I have added the sums owed for Pentecost (1,506,630) and St. Bavo's day (2,295,332) 1554. Using a different source, Baelde, "Financiële Politiek en Domaniale Evolutie," 26–27, reports loans of 3,071,000 for 1554; he also notes that some state loans on the Antwerp exchange were for the use of Habsburg governments elsewhere than in the Netherlands. See chapter 1, note 49, and chapter 3, note 76.

[50]GRK 3454.

[51]See the "Regestenlijst" in Meilink, nos. 443, 448, 449; RSH 8, 23, 31 August 1553. Maddens, "Invoering van de 'Nieuwe Middelen' in Vlaanderen," 867, mentions that some of the four "members" of the States of Flanders (the rural Franc of Bruges, plus the cities of Bruges, Ghent, and Ieper) were already providing obligations against future bede payments in 1544.

worthiness passed from the emperor to his great nobles, thence to his revenue agents, and finally to the States, which had to give their consent to taxation. In the ensuing discussion, it will be seen that this evolution was but one part of a larger process by which the States came to exercise direct control over tax receipts and expenditures.

Long-term debt was the obvious and indeed the only alternative to ruinous interest rates demanded in Antwerp. As noted above, rentes on the prince's domain had been known in the Low Countries since the later fifteenth century at least, and there were still handsome and relatively unburdened incomes in the northern provinces on which rentes were being sold in the 1530s and 1540s.[52] But beden were the mainstay of Habsburg revenue, and it was to this source that the government had to turn in any real quest for low-interest

[52]Aud. 868:62–90, a 1535 inventory of domain receipts shows the following for collection districts whose expected annual income exceeded 10,000 pounds:

Collection district	Income	Rente interest
Brussels	24,358	4,143
Antwerp	24,300	10,172
Flanders	86,000	32,107
Cassel (Flanders)	21,300	1,019
South Holland	22,800	275
Kenemerland (Holland)	20,000	2,000
North Holland	17,000	2,803
Voorne (Holland)	13,500	523
Zeeland Bewesterscheldt	32,700	6,940
Friesland	56,000	0

In the sales of rentes on domain revenue, which are reported almost every year in Lille B, under "Vendicions," buyers from Holland are relatively prominent in the 1530s and 1540s, and the revenues in which they took an interest were almost always located in their own province or (after 1538) in Friesland: Lille B 2380, 2386, 2392, 2398, 2404, 2410, 2418, 2436, 2442, 2448, 2454, 2482.

credit. Just as a particular district or town might agree to "anticipate" its bede quota, it might also be induced to stand surety for an issue of renten, with principal and interest to be paid from money coming in from subsequent terms of an ongoing bede. The town or village treasurer would then remit interest payments (and sometimes installments of the principal) to renten-holders in his area, before handing over the balance of his receipts to the provincial receiver for beden. Renten sales on this basis are found in the early years of the sixteenth century among some castleries in the County of Flanders, and likewise in the great city of Antwerp.[53] In Holland, four cities—Amsterdam and Dordrecht, plus Rotterdam and Hoorn—agreed in 1522 to raise a total of 16,000 pounds by selling erfrenten, or heritable annuities, at the usual rate of 1 : 16, each on the surety of its own ordinaris bede quota.[54]

To take full advantage of this method of raising capital, it was necessary to persuade the "members" of a given provincial parliament to obligate themselves in their collective capacity, pledging the full subsidy receipts for the whole province. Given the rivalries that always pitted one town or district against another, it was not easy to bring the members of a provincial States to accept the novel principle of collective responsibility for debt. For example, throughout the early decades of Charles V's rule, the States of Flanders steadfastly refused to sell renten against the ordinaris bede income for the whole province, though individual castleries continued to be willing to do so for their respective quotas.[55] Nonetheless, in or about 1515 the ministers of a boy prince—Charles was then fifteen, and not yet emperor—somehow induced the States of Artois, Brabant, Hainaut, Holland, and Lille to make a first issue of renten against their provincial ordinaris bede.[56] This is the point at which the story of this book prop-

[53]Maddens, 349–364; for rentes sold during the 1520s by the States of Brabant, and by cities or corporations within Brabant, Aud. 873:126–129.

[54]Aud. 873:130v; see GRK 3424, 3427 (Amsterdam's entire quota of 8,000 was purchased by Jean Micaut, Receiver-General for All Finances).

[55]Maddens, 349–364; see chapter 3, notes 16 and 17.

[56]Charles V to Margaret of Austria, 31 October 1522 (Lanz, I, 70): the States of Brabant have agreed to sell annual rentes of 15,000 on their ordinaris bede,

erly begins. Before going further, it would be well to take a brief look at the character and institutions of the one province that will be the center of attention.

III. The present provinces of North and South Holland comprise an area slightly larger than 2,000 square miles, roughly the size of the state of Delaware. As may be seen by comparison of the two accompanying maps of Holland, the sixteenth-century County of Holland, though roughly coterminous with the two modern provinces, was smaller in land area because much of its surface was then covered by inland lakes.[57] North and South Holland are densely populated now, and sixteenth-century Holland was already one of Europe's most urbanized regions. On the basis of the 1514 *Informatie*, Jan De Vries calculates that 140,180 of an estimated 274,810 people, or about 51 percent, lived in cities.[58] Apart from the six "great cities" already mentioned, there were eighteen small cities that did not have voting rights in the States of Holland, but were still assessed regular quotas in the ordinaris bede. Some of the small cities, like Rotterdam and The Hague, were thriving economic centers. Six other cities lay within enclaves of noble jurisdiction, where the writ of the provincial States normally did not run, so that they were not included in the assessment.[59] Unlike the larger cities of Flanders and Brabant, towns in Holland had for the most part never passed through the guild revolutions of the fourteenth

---

which at the usual 1 : 16 rate would mean a capital of 240,000. See above, note 53. The earliest issues of rentes by the States of Namur were for capital sums of 9,600 in 1523 and 6,000 in 1531, the latter secured by an *obligacion* signed by Jan Stercke, the Receiver-General: P. Brouwers, *Les Aides et Subsides dans le Conté de Namur au XVIe Siècle* (Namur: 1934), xlix–lviii. According to Aud. 868:19–46, the beden of various provinces were burdened as follows with annual interest in 1534: Brabant, 42,011; Holland, 20,775; several castleries in Flanders, 8,100 (see Maddens, 363–364; the States of Flanders, prior to 1544, refused to issue rentes in its corporate name); Hainaut, 1,900; Lille, Douai, and Orchies, 1,500; and Artois, 600.

[57]According to the *Encyclopedia Brittannica*, 1965 edition, XVI, 277, the combined area of the present provinces of North and South Holland is 2,375 square miles.

[58]De Vries, *The Dutch Rural Economy in the Golden Age*, 81–85.

[59]Chapter 1, note 24.

century. Thus while the city governments of places like Ghent and Antwerp were composed of different "members," representing in various ways the craft guilds, the merchants, and the old patrician families, Amsterdam, Haarlem, and most other Holland towns were still ruled in the old-fashioned way, by a town council whose members were chosen for life by co-option.[60] This council was generally called the *vroedschap*, a term signifying "men of ease." Magistrates who conducted the city's daily business—a college of burgomasters and a college of judges, or *schepenen*—were usually chosen by or from the vroedschap.[61] Unlike the provincial assemblies of Brabant or Hainaut,[62] the States of Holland had no ecclesiastical member to dilute the voting strength of the great cities and their urban oligarchies.[63] There was a college of nobles, which had one vote in the States, as did each of the cities, so that a bede proposition obtained the necessary majority as soon as it was approved by three cities and the nobles, who almost always supported the central government.[64] With their extensive landed wealth, the nobles,

[60]Ferdinand H. M. Grapperhaus, *Alva en de Tiende Penning* (Zutphen: 1982), 18; for interpretations of the guild revolutions in the Netherlands, Henri Pirenne, *Early Democracies in the Low Countries* (New York: 1914), and R. van Uytven, "Plutokratie in de 'Oude Demokratiën' der Nederlanden," *Handelingen van de Koninklijke Zuid-Nederlandse Maatschappij van Taal en Letterkunde en Geschiedenis* XVI (1962): 373–409. The best history of a Holland city is Ter Gouw on Amsterdam.

[61]Amsterdam's constitution is described in Ter Gouw, III, 360–415; on Leiden, P. J. Blok, *Geschiedenis eener Hollandsche Stad*, vol. 2; and on Dordrecht, J. S. van Dalen, *Geschiedenis van Dordrecht* (2 vols., Dordrecht: 1931–1936), vol. 1.

[62]The most recent study of the States of Brabant, albeit at a somewhat later period, is G. Janssens, "Een Onderzoek naar het Bronnenmateriaal voor het Bestuderen van de Politieke Aktiviteiten van de Staten van Brabant, 1567–1577," *Standen en Landen—Anciens Pays et Assemblées d'Etat* LXX (1977): 339–353. On the twelve abbots who together constituted a separate "member" of the States of Brabant, see P. Gorissen, "De Prelaten van Brabant onder Karel V: hun Confederatie, 1534–1544," *Standen en Landen* VI (1953): 1–127.

[63]Meilink, 1–3, says there was no clerical estate in the States of Holland, although when the important Peace of Cambrai was to be approved by the provincial States, two heads of religious houses in Holland were summoned to affix their seals along with those of the nobles and the great cities (AJ 8 February 1530: Abbot William of Egmond, Abbot Conrad of Bernhem near Heusden; cf. RSH 3 January 1530).

[64]See chapter 1, note 23.

though exempt themselves from most forms of taxation, were expected to represent the interests of the rural population, and commissioners sent by the regent could indeed count on the nobles to oppose what were perceived as selfish attempts by town oligarchies to load off the burden of taxation on the peasantry.[65]

The great question, which is not any easier to answer now than it was in the sixteenth century, is how seriously the great cities' complaints of poverty and economic decline should be taken. Amsterdam, whose population at the time of the 1514 *Informatie* has been estimated at about 14,000, was then about the same size as Haarlem and Leiden; its quota in the *schiltal*, or assessment, on which the ordinaris bede was based was slightly lower than those for Delft and Leiden. Dordrecht and especially Gouda were smaller and had lower assessments.[66] Amsterdam's prosperity rested on the flow of Baltic rye through the Danish Sound, a traffic largely controlled by ships from Holland, and increasingly profitable in a century of rising population and hence rising demand for grain.[67] On the negative side, the Sound trade was sharply curtailed from

[65]For the nobles' defense of rural interests, RSH 10 July 1528, 12 October 1538; Assendelft to Hoogstraten, 12 October 1528 (Aud. 1527); Council of Holland to Mary of Hungary, 26 May 1544 (Aud. 1646:1). For the government's reliance on the nobles in its negotiations with the great cities, Mary of Hungary to the lords of Assendelft, Cruningen, Schagen, and Wassenaar, plus Gerrit van Poelgeest, Gerrit van Lokhorst, Adriaan van Matenesse, *baljuw* of Schiedam, and Willem van Alkmade, *ruwaard* of Rijnsburg, 18 May 1539 (Aud. 1531); to Assendelft, 11 January 1543 (Aud. 1646:1); and to Assendelft again, 14 March 1544 (Aud. 1646:3). Needless to say, the nobles also had interests, and tax exemptions, of their own to protect, as is indicated by the exasperated comment of Andries Jacobszoon, Amsterdam's perceptive town secretary, when the nobles refused to contribute to a new kind of bede "tis genouch (god betert) dat zy altyt de eerste zyn omme consent te dragen tot laste vanden anderen" (AJ 11 July 1524: "'tis enough, God help us, that they are always the first to give consent to burdens borne by the rest of us").

[66]For population estimates, see chapter 1, note 19. For a bede of 100,000 (e.g., GRK 3441), the quotas of the great cities were as follows: Delft, 8,516; Leiden, 8,067; Amsterdam, 8,017; Haarlem, 6,334; Dordrecht, 5,583; and Gouda, 5,449.

[67]J. A. van Houtte, *An Economic History of the Low Countries* (New York: 1977), 182–187; Aksel E. Christensen, *Dutch Trade to the Baltic around 1600* (Copenhagen: 1941), corrected at some points by N. W. Posthumus in his *De Uitvoer van Amsterdam* (Leiden: 1971), 174–187.

time to time by war in the Baltic, and Amsterdam's middle-man role was threatened by the development of direct trading connections between Antwerp and North Sea ports like Hamburg.[68] Moreover, the city's woolen cloth industry, briefly flourishing during the 1530s, was hurt by disruptions in the overland routes to Germany during the 1540s and 1550s.[69] But despite the tales of woe told by Amsterdam's deputies, nothing could be too amiss in a city whose population swelled to around 30,000 by 1550, and whose treasurers regularly passed on a hefty cash surplus to their successors for the following year.[70] Similarly, Dordrecht prospered as the "staple" or obligatory transfer point for the lucrative trade in Rhine wine, despite the resentment which its unique privileges caused among other Holland towns.[71] But the important North Sea herring fishery, centered in small cities like Rotterdam and Enkhuizen, had many unprofitable years owing to attacks on herring busses by French and Scottish privateers.[72] Towns that specialized in the production of

[68]Christensen, *Dutch Trade to the Baltic*, 39–47: though the volume of Holland shipping through the Sound continued to grow in absolute numbers ca. 1500–1560, it declined somewhat as a proportion of the whole, owing to a more rapid increase in volume for north German ports; see also Alfred Schmidtmayer, "Zur Geschichte der bremischen Akzise," *Bremisches Jahrbuch* 37 (1937): 64–69. Rudolf Häpke, *Niederländische Akten und Urkunden zur Geschichte der Hanse* (2 vols., Leipzig: 1913–1923, I, nos. 504, 509), contains documents concerning a secret commercial treaty of 1546 to further direct exchange between Antwerp and the Hanseatic cities; for Amsterdam's fearful reaction, ASR 1546, under "Reysen," 58–73v, trip by Meester Floris van Hougaerden, 15 March–17 April.

[69]Export of Amsterdam cloths (via Antwerp) to central and south Germany is discussed in Tracy, "Shipments to Germany by Erasmus Schetz and other Antwerp Merchants during the Period of the 100th Penny Tax, 1543–1545," forthcoming in the *Journal of European Economic History*.

[70]Chapter 1, note 19; ASR 1544–1564 (at times, the surplus exceeded 50,000).

[71]B. van Rijswijk, *Geschiedenis van het Dordtsche Stapelrecht* (The Hague: 1900).

[72]Nelly Gottschalk, *Fischereigewerbe und Fischhandel der niederländischen Gebieten im Mittelalter* (Bad Worishofen: 1927); A. Beaujon, *Overzicht der Geschiedenis der Nederlandsche Zeevischerijen* (Leiden: 1885), 1–31; and Rogier De Gryse, "De Gemeenschappelijke Groote Visscherij van de Nederlanden in de XVIe Eeuw," *Bijdragen voor de Geschiedenis van de Nederlanden* 7 (1952): 32–54, and "De Konvooieering van de Vlaamse Vissersvloot in de 15e en 16e

heavy green woolen cloth were facing hard times, as lighter, combination fabrics (English kerseys, Flemish says) gained a larger share of the market.[73] Drapers in Leiden, Holland's major cloth center, were having difficulty buying wool on credit,[74] while Haarlem's effort to subsidize the export of its woolens to Spain was abandoned as unproductive.[75] Finally, cities that brewed beer for export—Haarlem, and especially Gouda and Delft—faced keen competition from Hamburg beer imported to Antwerp, while towns in Flanders, the traditional market for brewers in Gouda and Delft, were placing new taxes on "foreign" beer.[76]

Meanwhile, Holland's agriculture prospered. Its fields lay within a zone of innovative specialized farming in the Low Countries,[77] and wealthy investors were beginning to put their capital into reclamation projects along the Maas delta in south Holland, and along the North Sea.[78] According to the accounts for a provincial land tax that began in the 1540s, Holland had only about 300,000 *morgen*, or 1,055 square miles,

---

Eeuwen," *Bijdragen voor de Geschiedenis van de Nederlanden* 2 (1948): 1–24. Holland's herring busses, which made up the bulk of the Netherlands fleet, have not been the subject of any special study, though there is a voluminous correspondence between Brussels and The Hague on how they should best be defended from privateers; see, for example, Assendelft to Mary of Hungary, 10, 14 August, 12 September 1552 (Aud. 1646:3).

[73]N. W. Posthumus, *Geschiedenis van de Leidsche Lakenindustrie in de Middeleeuwen* (3 vols., The Hague: 1908–1933), vol. 1; Sandelijn, 3 October 1550, mentions that all Holland cloths are green.

[74]AJ 10 September, 29 December 1523, 28 January 1524.

[75]HTR 1520–1532, under "miscellaneous expenditures;" subsidies eventually rose to 2.5 pounds for a whole cloth, which usually sold at less than 15 pounds. The two men involved were Frans de Witte, frequently a burgomaster during the 1520s, and his son-in-law, Gregorio de Ayala. See chapter 4, note 34.

[76]GVR 20 February 1509, 13 April 1537, and an undated petition from Gouda to Hoogstraten (Aud. 1524:18–19); Sandelijn, 12 February 1552; E. M. A. Timmer, "Grepen uit de Geschiedenis der Delftsche Brouwenering," *De Economist* LXX (1920): 358–373, 415–430; and, the fullest study to date, J. van Loenen, *De Haarlemse Brouwindustrie voor 1600*. Professor Richard Unger of the University of British Columbia is presently engaged on a study of Holland's brewing industry in the early modern era.

[77]De Vries, *The Dutch Rural Economy in the Golden Age*, 127–164.

[78]S. J. Fockema Andreae, *Het Hoogheemraadschap van Leiden* (Leiden: 1934), 227–231.

of land lying outside town and village limits,[79] but this total was gradually being increased due to reclamation.[80] Barring an economic history of Holland—a worthy though unlikely project, since provinces are not usually considered meaningful units of economic history—it is not possible to bring all of these strands of development together into a judgment of the relative prosperity of town and countryside. One can only say that the rural population probably could have borne a greater portion of the tax burden than was allotted to it in the 1514 schiltal, if not the dramatic realignment in favor of the cities, which will be described in chapter 3.

The 1514 schiltal was a perpetual source of disputes within the States of Holland. Delft's deputies never accepted the fact that their city had been assessed for 8.58 percent of the ordinaris bede, slightly more than the quotas for Leiden and Amsterdam.[81] By the 1540s, central government officials were

[79]Sandelijn (14 March 1549) reports a total of 274,000 morgen "under the schiltal." In land tax records dating from the 1540s, the number of morgen in Holland varies slightly from one account to another:

Account	"Under the schiltal"	Outside the schiltal	Total
SH 2210	271,191		
SH 1792	266,661		
SH 2280			296,757
SH 2281		37,001	
SH 2282			296,198
SH 2283		36,360	

Hence Assendelft's estimate of 300,000 morgen, in contrast to a larger figure current in government fiscal circles, seems reliable: to Mary of Hungary, 23 February 1544 (Aud. 1646:3).

[80]The progress of reclamation in certain districts may be measured by the number of morgen listed as "buiten dijks," or outside the dikes, in successive land tax accounts like those mentioned in note 79, especially for selected villages in southern Holland (e.g., Ablasserdam, het land van Arkel), and Grootebrouck in the north. See chapter 5, note 108.

[81]See above, note 66. Delft's complaints: GVR 10 October 1523; AJ 10 October 1523, 25 January, 30 April, 1524, 19 March, 24 June, 1528; Assendelft to Hoogstraten, 22 March 1531, and to Mary of Hungary, 28 December 1543 (Aud. 1646:3).

inclined to agree that the schiltal needed revising to reflect new economic realities, as had often been done in the past. Except for Delft, however, deputies to the States were not interested in providing the emperor's tax-collecting officials with up-to-date information on the wealth of his subjects, and the project was allowed to die a quiet death.[82] In fact, the schiltal had been altered in practice by granting gratiën, or rebates. Letters of *gratie* from the Council of Finance always specified the reason why a portion of the town or village bede quota had been remitted—for example, for flooding or fire, or to deepen a harbor or repair fortifications.[83] But letters of gratie for the great cities contain vague statements about economic decline, and were probably viewed on all sides as a matter of form, since the real point was that these cities and they alone had voting rights in the provincial States. As was noted earlier, four votes were needed for approval of a bede. As Holland's oldest city, Dordrecht had the right of speaking first and, like the nobles, it usually supported the government's position. Haarlem and (with some exceptions) Amsterdam could usually be brought round when the commissioners made a few concessions, but the other three cities almost always withheld their consent.[84] Technically, three recalcitrant cities could be "outvoted" (*overstemt*) or "substi-

---

[82]Meester Vincent Corneliszoon van Mierop to Hoogstraten, 9 September 1530 (Aud. 1525). The matter was pressed upon the States by government representatives twenty years later, but to no avail: RSH 15 April–4 July 1550, and letters to and from the Council of Holland of 7, 12 April, 13 May, 4, 5, 7 July, 1550 (Aud. 1646:2); and E. C. G. Brünner, "De Adviezen van de 'Conseil et Chambre des Comptes de Hollande' en van den Conseil Privé in zake der Voorgenomen Nieuwe Verponding van 1550," *Bijdragen en Mededelingen van het Historisch Genootschap te Utrecht* XLIII (1922): 129–160.

[83]Brief summaries of these letters of gratie are given in the bede accounts (GRK) as justification for the rebates granted.

[84]Amsterdam spoke last in sessions, or *dagvaarten*, of the States and hence enjoyed a certain tactical advantage. With slight variations, the pattern described held true for the States' consent to raise 48,000 by sales of renten in 1523 (AJ 13 February 1523; GVR 9 July 1523), 80,000 in 1523 (AJ 9 October 1523; GVR 23 October 1523), and another 80,000 in 1528 (AJ 19 February 1528; RSH 16 February, 13 March 1528), and likewise for their agreement to raise in each case 80,000 extraordinaris beden by the more usual method of a schiltal levy in 1524 (AJ 18 April 1524; GVR 27 April 1524), 1525 (AJ 25 June 1525; GVR 21 August 1525), and 1527 (AJ 20 December 1527).

tuted for" (*vervangen*) by a majority consisting of three other cities plus the college of nobles, though the Council of Holland seemed to believe that the consent of four cities was required, at least for an extraordinaris bede.[85] But commissioners knew from experience that however a majority was defined it could easily evaporate if one or more cities flatly refused to pay its share; hence they were at pains to obtain the consent of all cities, and Delft, Gouda, and Leiden could use this opportunity to increase their levels of gratie.

Table 2 shows how the great cities were able to increase their rebates on the ordinary subsidy over a period of twelve years.[86]

TABLE 2
GRATIËN ON THE ORDINARIS BEDE, SIX GREAT CITIES

	gratie 1524 (%)	gratie 1536 (%)
Dordrecht	64	64
Haarlem	64	64
Leiden	17	66
Delft	15	50
Gouda	8	50
Amsterdam	5	25

Why Dordrecht and Haarlem should have been so highly favored in the early 1520s is not immediately clear, but very likely it had something to do with the process by which the great cities consented to subsidies. As was just mentioned,

[85]Instances when three cities were declared to have been "outvoted" or "substituted for": AJ 15 September 1525; RSH 24 March 1542, 9 April 1552. For the presumption that the consent of four cities was required, Assendelft to Hoogstraten, 25 September 1531 (Aud. 1525), 13 August 1536 (Aud. 1526), 14 October 1538 (Aud. 1527). Sandelijn, 4 December 1551, records a belief that money could only be voted in the presence of noble deputies.

[86]GRK 3419, 3420, 3422, 3423, 3427, 3429, 3430, 3433, 3436, 3437, 3440–3442, and 3446–3451.

Dordrecht had the right of speaking first in the States, and, if it did not always accept the government's "proposition," it was more receptive than other cities. Dordrecht had at least two important privileges that were the envy of other cities— relating to the "staple" for goods moving along the Rhine, and to the manner in which its schiltal quota was assessed— both of which were upheld by organs of the central government during Charles V's reign.[87] In light of this background, Dordrecht's cooperative attitude with regard to subsidy requests and its high level of gratie have the earmarks of a quid pro quo arrangement. For Haarlem the case is clearer. Its *vroedschapsresolutiën*, or city council resolutions, contain a notation for 1518, the first year for which this record is extant, that Count Hendrik van Nassau, then Stadtholder of Holland, assured Haarlem's deputies he would promote their wishes in regard to gratie, if they in turn were mindful of "the judgment or contract of Duke [Albert] of Saxony [Stadtholder of Friesland, 1495–1505], that if two of the great cities consent to a bede request, we should be the third."[88] In fact, it often did happen that agreement to a subsidy came about when Dordrecht and the nobles accepted the government's request rather quickly, Amsterdam gave its consent in return for concessions, usually relating to trade policy, and Haarlem added the necessary third urban vote.[89]

What happened during the 1520s and 1530s, then, was that other cities gained for themselves something equivalent to the special treatment which Dordrecht and Haarlem already enjoyed. Leiden and Gouda would eventually have rebates in excess of 70 percent, and Delft was acquitted of all tax liabilities for twenty years after a disastrous fire in 1536.[90] Amsterdam's situation is perhaps the most interesting. Its

---

[87]On the staple, above, note 71; on Dordrecht's favorable assessment in the 1514 schiltal, Van Dalen, *Geschiedenis van Dordrecht*, I, 1093–1095.

[88]Stadsarchief Haarlem, "Vroedschapsresolutiën," 1518, p. 13. Albert of Saxony (d. 1500), presumably the duke referred to, had been Stadtholder of Friesland: O. Sperling, "Herzog Albrecht der Beherzte als Gubernator von Friesland," *Abhandlungen zu den Jahresberichten des königlichen Gymnasiums zu Leipzig*, 1891–1892.

[89]See above, note 84.

[90]GRK 3437 (full remittance of the last term of the ordinaris bede expiring Christmas 1536).

deputies sometimes branded the whole principle of granting rebates, in which small cities and the countryside had no chance of sharing proportionally, as "unreasonable," even "ungodly." Occasionally the city would put its principles into practice, renouncing gratie and paying its full quota for a particular bede. But self-abnegation of this kind proved somewhat tiresome as gratiën for the other cities steadily climbed; from 1531 on, Amsterdam insisted on a 25 percent rebate.[91]
· The combined schiltal quotas for the six great cities totaled 41.96 percent, but their share of gratiën for the province was seldom less than two-thirds for ordinary subsidies, and higher still for extraordinary subsidies, in which cities with voting rights in the States had greater negotiating leverage[92] (see table 3).

TABLE 3
GRATIËN FOR THE GREAT CITIES AS A
PERCENTAGE OF ALL GRATIËN

Year	Type of bede	Nominal sum	Gratie as % of nominal sum	Cities' % of gratie
1524	Ordinary	80,000	21.29	64.14
1536	Ordinary	80,000	34.24	73.76
1524	Extraordinary	80,000	34.16	81.04
1528/1529	Extraordinary	80,000	18.44	85.58
1536/1537	Extraordinary	80,000	39.85	81.34

Government officials knew perfectly well what was happening. In September 1530, Meester Vincent Corneliszoon van Mierop, an influential member of the Chamber of Accounts in The Hague, reported to the stadtholder on his discussions with leading magistrates in several of the great cities regarding the need for a new bede assessment, or schil-

[91] AJ 25 January 1524, 2 October 1526, 31 March 1528, 27 March 1531.
[92] For the ordinaris beden, GRK 3423, 3427, 3437; for the extraordinaris beden, GRK 3426, 3432, 3439.

tal. These gentlemen refused to see the point, said Meester Vincent, despite the complaints which small cities and especially villages had addressed to the Gracious Lady (Mary of Hungary) concerning tax inequities, and her expressed wish that "burdens be borne equally."[93] Similar criticisms of the selfishness of the great cities could be heard from Lord Gerrit, lord of Assendelft, First Councilor of the Council of Holland; from nobles in the States of Holland, who protested "as a matter of conscience" against higher levels of gratie for the cities; and from the highest levels of the government in Brussels.[94] The greatest inequity was that mercantile and industrial wealth in the more prosperous large towns was virtually untouched by taxation in any form. Some among the great cities in Holland had truly fallen on hard times, so that in Gouda, for instance, it was not uncommon for magistrates to compel wealthy burghers to buy town renten so the city could use the capital to pay its portion of a bede.[95] Elsewhere, as in Amsterdam, bede payments were made out of the excise taxes, which were every city's chief source of revenue, and which struck most heavily at items of common consumption like beer and grain.[96] Townsmen who owned land in the

[93]Letter cited above, note 82.

[94]Assendelft to Mary of Hungary, 23 February 1544 (Aud. 1646:3) and 23 January 1552 (Aud. 1646:2); Council of Holland to Mary of Hungary, 24 May 1544 (Aud. 1646:1) and 17 August 1549 (Aud. 1646:2); RSH 12 October 1538, Assendelft to Hoogstraten, 4 October 1538 (Aud. 1527); cf. comments about the gratiën enjoyed by Ghent and Bruges in Flanders by Lodewijk van Vlaanderen, lord of Praet (who was then Stadtholder of Holland) to Mary of Hungary, 8 October 1545 (Aud. 1661:3d).

[95]To raise money for its share of certain beden, Gouda used forced loans as well as forced purchases of town renten: GVR 21 May 1516, 4 June 1519, 30 July 1528, 18 December 1528, 19 June, 17 August, 1543. Leiden was encouraged to do the same: Assendelft to Hoogstraten, 22 February 1540.

[96]ASR. Those who contracted each year to farm the groote accijns (excises on beer, wine, and grain milling), Amsterdam's most lucrative revenue by far, had to pay interest on city renten out of their receipts (chapter 1, note 16), but always had something left over. By the time other excise income was added in, there was more than enough for the city to meet its bede obligations. The social inequity of such *accijnsen* was a matter for common discussion: see Erasmus, *Institutio Principis Christiani*, Otto Herding, ed., *Des. Erasmi Opera Omnia*, IV:1 (Amsterdam: 1974), 190–191: ". . . Quarum igitur rerum vsus infimae quoque plebis communis est, has quam minimum gravabit bonus princeps veluti frumenti panis cervisiae vini pannorum ac

countryside shared in at least some of the tax burdens of the rural population,[97] but fellow burghers who invested in cloth production or in the grain trade went unmolested. In particular, and for reasons too complicated to explain here, efforts by Margaret of Austria and Mary of Hungary to impose an export duty on the huge quantities of Baltic rye shipped into and out of Amsterdam were a total failure.[98] What the government lacked was not the will to achieve greater equity, but the capacity to do without the cooperation of urban elites who controlled the purse strings. Important as it was to have equality, it was more important to satisfy the Antwerp bankers whose ready cash was the only thing that kept invading French armies at bay—and this meant placating town oligarchies represented in the States rather than launching a frontal assault on their privileges. Whatever strategy the government might devise for creating a low-interest, long-term debt would have to take into account this fundamental political reality.

IV. In Holland there was already a precedent for pledging the credit of the province as a whole. In 1482, during a war with the neighboring ecclesiastical principality of Utrecht, the States agreed to sell renten secured by parcels of the prince's domain income which were entrusted for this purpose to their administration (this procedure resembled the later rentes sur l'hôtel de ville in France, save that princely revenues were entrusted to a provincial parliament rather than to the city government of Paris). These "renten of the common land" had a corporate character even though Amsterdam insisted

---

caeterarum item rerum, sine quibus humana vita non potest transigi. Atqui haec nunc potissimum onerantur idque non vno modo: primum gravissimis exactionibus, quas redemptores extorquunt, vulgus asisias vocat." The "redemptores" here are urban excise farmers.

[97]Hence the complaint of double taxation by burghers of Amsterdam, Schoonhoven, and Oudewater when the province of Utrecht, newly incorporated into the Habsburg dominions, imposed a land tax in which the burden was to be shared among working farmers and urban investors (AJ 12 May, 2 October, 1530, 6 January 1531; RSH 4 October 1530, 8 January 1531).

[98]P. A. Meilink, "Rapporten en Betoogen nopens het Congiegeld op Granen, 1530–1541," *Bijdragen en Mededelingern van het Historisch Genootschap te Utrecht* XLIV (1923): 1–124; see also the article cited above, note 41.

on standing apart, so as to sell one-sixth of the total under its own name rather than joining with the other five cities to issue renten in the name of the States. Amsterdam's reasons for this proud isolation may readily be inferred, though the other cities presumably did not welcome it.[99] In the legal practice of the Low Countries, when a city failed to keep up with interest payments on renten issued over its seal, renten-holders could recover damages by seizing the goods of any burgher of that city who chanced within their grasp. Hollanders knew from experience that *renteniers* outside the province were not shy about resorting to this procedure, especially in Flanders, which was a principal market for the issues of nearby Delft and Gouda.[100] By acting alone, then, Amsterdam was shielding its merchants from the possibility of reprisals occasioned by nonpayment of interest by one of the other cities—for if renten were issued by the States as a body, merchants from all the cities that guaranteed the issue were equally subject to reprisals. In fact, the payment schedule set for the 1482 renten could not be met from the domain receipts in question, and had to be renegotiated in 1503, and again in 1518, whereupon payments were made regularly until the debt was retired in 1526.[101]

In 1515 the States were asked to do as they had done in 1482, save that the renten would be secured against Holland's ordinaris bede, with the principal to be retired within a few years from the same source. As before, these renten were to be issued in the name of "the common body of the territory"

---

[99]Meilink, 53. "Tweede Memoriaalboek van Adriaan Sandelijn" (Rijksarchief van Zuid-Holland, The Hague), 1–30, records that the total debt, including interest arrears of about 7,000, was 207,356, at the rate of 1:13 or 7.69 percent. In 1522, Gouda sought to claim the privilege of "selling apart" for itself, but in vain: GVR 11 November 1522, 10 April 1523.

[100]Reprisals against Delft and Gouda by Flemish renteniers were frequently alluded to as the States discussed selling provincial renten: GVR 9 November 1522, AJ 9 October 1523, 1–4 October 1527. There was at least one case when Holland ships were seized at Sluys in Flanders for nonpayment of interest on the new provincial renten (AJ 31 December 1530), and fear of further such incidents lingered on: Assendelft to Mary of Hungary, 28 December 1543 (Aud. 1646:3).

[101]Meilink, 53; HTR 1521/1522–1526/1527.

(*'t gemeen corpus van 't land*).[102] When a city issued its own renten, buyers were furnished with individual certificates (*rentebrieven*) to which a wax effigy of the city's great seal was affixed. In the same way, the corporate character of the new provincial renten required affixing seals of all the cities that made up "the common body of the territory," that is, those with voting rights in the States. Rentebrieven were first engrossed by clerks of the Council of Finance and sent to the receiver for the beden in The Hague. Meanwhile, local jurisdictions supplied the receiver with lists of potential buyers in Holland (the important question of who these buyers were will be taken up in chapter 4). The receiver or his clerk would then make a circuit of "foreign" markets (that is, towns in other Habsburg Netherlands provinces, like Bruges in Flanders, or Brussels in Brabant) to find buyers for the remaining amount. Armed with a full list of subscribers, the receiver's clerk would then fill in blank rentebrieven with the amounts, and the names of each buyer and beneficiary (the two may or may not have been the same). A great wooden chest containing these documents, sometimes heavy enough to require two draft horses to pull the wagon, would be transported from city to city until the necessary number of seals were affixed to each *brief* (if a seal broke in the process of unpacking or repacking, the certificate in question had to be returned for a new seal). Only then were the rentebrieven ready for delivery to buyers upon payment of the purchase price.[103] As in 1482, however, Amsterdam demanded the right to "seal

---

[102]In HTR and LTR, these were called *gemeen lands renten* to distinguish them from renten that cities issued for their own purposes; the same term was later applied to renten sold by the States but funded by the beden. The word *body* (Latin *corpus*, Dutch *lichaem*) connoted that the States were acting in a corporate capacity, on behalf of the whole province. For example, on one occasion when the nobles rejected a new form of taxation in which they would have to contribute, Amsterdam's deputies said they would not consent to any grant of money until they received clarification as to "wye aan tlichaem oft corpus van hollant behooren oft niet/ en oft de adelen een lit vant voors. corpus zyn oft niet" (AJ 27 May 1524: "who belongs to the body or corpus of Holland and not; and if the nobles are a member of the aforesaid corpus or not").

[103]SH 2280: 129v–130.

apart," that is, to sell renten under its own name and seal only. This aloofness may have been more palatable to other cities because Amsterdam eventually placed or found buyers for more than a sixth of the total; it sold renten with a capital value of 9,200 pounds, whereas the other five cities had agreed to a total sale of 22,400.[104]

The 1515 sale was the first of many issues, all of which were for erfrenten, or heritable annuities, at the usual rate of 1 : 16, or 6.25 percent. At first, renten of this kind were sold only against future receipts of a current ordinaris bede. For example, if an ordinary subsidy had three years to run, renten might be sold during the first year with the stipulation that the principal be redeemed from monies collected for the last four semiannual terms. Lest "the Emperor have nothing to thank" the States for in regard to the sale of renten—in other words, so that a sale of renten would be something more than a mere anticipation of future subsidy revenues—the States sometimes agreed to assume responsibility for interest payments during the first three years.[105] These payments were made through the omslagen, or special levies, based on the schiltal, which the States periodically decreed and collected to cover their own expenses.[106] The understanding was that if the principal was not in fact retired within three years, any subsequent payments of interest would be the responsibility of the emperor; that is, they would come from ordinaris bede receipts. By 1530, renten were also being sold against the receipts of extraordinaris beden—for example, a sum of 120,000 pounds over six years to which the States consented in 1529 as Holland's portion of a special subsidy for the Emperor's upcoming coronation in Bologna.[107] All told, there were fourteen issues of renten between 1515 and 1534 secured

---

[104]Under "interest payments," GRK 3418 (ordinaris bede, St. John's day term, 1519) lists only the sum total for Amsterdam (since holders of its renten for this issue were paid directly by the city treasurer), but names and amounts for individual buyers for renten issued collectively by the five other cities.

[105]AJ 25 October 1523. For items listed in table 3, the States agreed to pay three years' interest for E, F, G, H, I, and J; all interest for A, B, C, D, K, L, and N was to be paid from the bede, while all interest for M was to be paid by the States.

[106]Accounts for the omslagen are inventoried in Meilink, nos. 1762–1798.

[107]GRK 3435.

by bede receipts in Holland, as can be seen in table 4.[108] To distinguish them from a later series discussed in chapter 3, for which numerals will be used, these issues are labeled A through N. It will be noted that items B and N are not properly provincial renten, since it was not the States of Holland as a corporate entity which issued them. They represent the more traditional procedure by which an individual town sold renten against its own bede quota, but they are included here nonetheless because interest payments stemming from the unredeemed portion of these sales were part of a growing annual burden on Holland's ordinaris bede.

The sale of these renten was a major source of revenue for the central government, particularly during the wars of the 1520s. Between 1522 and 1530, the States of Holland raised 446,400 in this manner (items C through L), a sum nearly comparable to what was collected during the same period from ordinaris beden (533,453, after subtraction for gratiën); meanwhile, the States raised another 453,821 (after subtraction for gratiën) from extraordinaris beden levied according to the same assessment, or schiltal, that was used for the ordinary subsidies.[109] The large total of renten in 1528 (items F through J = 176,000) is particularly worthy of note, since it corresponds to the Utrecht war of 1527–1528, in which this ecclesiastical principality was annexed to the Habsburg dominions by agreement of its prince-bishop, thus providing Holland with a buffer between its eastern border and the lands of the marauding Duke of Guelders. Commissioners sent by the regent were not slow in acquainting the States of Holland with this strategic reality, but the deputies could doubtless read maps well enough for themselves. Holland seems to have contributed a bit more than its share in financ-

---

[108]The following accounts list names of buyers and purchase amounts for renten issued by the five cities (items A, and C through M), but only total amounts for all the renten which Amsterdam issued in conjunction with those of the five cities, and for the two issues in which the cities acted as independent agents (items B and N): A, GRK 3418; B, GRK 3424 (cf. 3427); C-D-E, GRK 3424; F-G-H-I-J, GRK 3432; K-L, GRK 3435; M-N, GRK 3437.

[109]Figures from Tracy, "The System of Taxation in the County of Holland under the Reigns of Charles V and Philip II," forthcoming in *Economisch- en Sociaal-Historisch Jaarboek.*

TABLE 4

HOLLAND RENTEN SECURED BY THE BEDEN, 1515–1534

Item	Date	Issued by	Principal	Interest	Security
A	1515	5 cities + Amsterdam	31,600	1,975	Ordinary bede
B	1522	A'dam, Dort., R'dam, Hoorn	16,000	1,000	Ordinary bede
C	1522	5 cities + Amsterdam	32,000	2,000	Ordinary bede
D	1523	5 cities + Amsterdam	48,000	3,000	Ordinary bede
E	1523	5 cities + Amsterdam	80,000	5,000	Ordinary bede
F	1528	5 cities + Amsterdam	80,000	5,000	Ordinary bede
G	1528	5 cities + Amsterdam	40,000	2,500	Ordinary bede
H	1528	5 cities + Amsterdam	16,000	1,000	Ordinary bede
I	1528	5 cities + Amsterdam	20,000	1,125	Ordinary bede
J	1528	5 cities + Amsterdam	20,000	1,125	Ordinary bede
K	1530	5 cities + Amsterdam	62,400	3,900	Extraordinary bede
L	1530	5 cities + Amsterdam	48,000	3,000	Ordinary bede
M	1532	5 cities + Amsterdam	28,000	1,750	Extraordinary bede
N	1534	Amsterdam	16,000	1,000	Ordinary bede
Totals			538,000	33,625	

ing the wars of this decade, and it is unlikely the province would have been able to raise so much had not some alternative been found to the traditional way of levying beden according to the schiltal.[110] The renten have a double aspect, which makes them a bit difficult to classify. Though they were presented to and approved by the States as extraordinaris beden, which implies that they were seen as a new and distinct source of cash for the government, principal and (often) interest were to be paid out of future bede receipts, which means they might just as well be regarded as "anticipations," and not as an additional source of income. N. Maddens, author of a recent and richly detailed study of the beden in Flanders during the reign of Charles V, seems to have chosen the latter alternative, since he asserts that renten were "not taxes."[111] There are, however, two reasons for counting the renten as new income for the government. First, contemporary accounting practice clearly viewed the renten in this way. Receipts are always entered under "income" in the accounts of Holland's receiver for the beden. In contrast, the sums which the receiver sometimes

---

[110]Both in Friesland (across the Zuider Zee from Holland) and in Utrecht, the Duke of Guelders was attempting to expand his influence, but was thwarted by Habsburg victories in the 1520s: see Struik, *Gelre en Habsburg,* and B. Munier, "Kardinaal Willem van Enckenvoirt, 1464–1534, en de Overdracht van de Temporaliteiten van het Bisdom Utrecht," *Mededelingen van het Nederlands Historisch Instituut te Rome,* 3e Series, VII (1953): 122–168. AJ 9 February 1528. The following figures suggest that Hollanders increased their contributions somewhat, in keeping with the special significance that these wars had for their province:

PERCENTAGE OF GOVERNMENT'S NET BEDE
INCOME FROM EACH PROVINCE

	1521–1530 (Aud. 873:33–51, 57–123v)	1531–1534 (Aud. 868:3–18)
Holland	17.47	14.48
Brabant	26.5	32.78
Flanders	27.17	29.4

[111]Maddens, xvi.

had to borrow in Antwerp to realize his receipts more quickly are seldom found under income; usually, they are mentioned only under expenditures, where it is noted that the Receiver-General has authorized the Holland receiver to make interest payments on these loans.[112] Although both loans and renten are methods of anticipating income, they are treated differently in the accounts, perhaps because interest charges were 6.25 percent for the latter, and between 12 and 22 percent for the former. Secondly and more importantly, the greater portion of the money raised through selling renten was never actually paid back. Had the debts incurred through these sales been paid back as quickly as the States were promised they would be, Margaret of Austria and her advisers might well claim to have found a formula for dispelling the demons of insolvency. Unfortunately, however, government expenditures outran income even during years of peace, and revenues allocated to the repayment of debt principal had to be diverted time and again to more urgent purposes, with the approval of the States.[113] Thus in Flanders, according to Maddens's figures, 57.24 percent of the capital for renten which individual castleries sold against their bede quotas between 1515 and 1556 was still unredeemed in 1558 (332,424 of 582,448). In Holland, as of 1560, 66.27 percent of the capital for renten secured by the beden, and sold between 1515 and 1534, was still outstanding (356,612 of 538,000, the total for items A through N of table 4).[114] This unredeemed portion of

---

[112]Sums raised by loan are sometimes entered as income: 20,000 against the receipts of a not very successful "new impost" in 1523 (GRK 3425; see also AJ 3 December 1523), and 1,457 to make up what was lacking in the *blijde inkomst* gift for Prince Philip in 1549 (SH 1792); note that neither of these cases involved a routine bede. Conversely, there are numerous loans reported in other sources which leave no trace in the income columns of the corresponding bede accounts: loans of 20,000, 25,400, and 50,000 against the proceeds of sales of renten in 1524 (AJ April 1524, see also GRK 3424), 1531 (AJ 6 November 1531, see also GRK 3437), and 1542 (RSH 28 November 1542, SH 2208); and 16,000 and 17,000 against the receipts from extraordinaris beden by schiltal in 1528 (AJ 6 September 1528, see also GRK 3431) and 1530 (AJ 18 February 1530, GRK 3434).

[113]For example, AJ 1–4 October 1527; Hoogstraten to the Council of Holland, 28 June 1533 (Aud. 1446:2b).

[114]Maddens, 356–361; for redemptions of principal on Holland renten, see the articles cited in note 109, table 1, column 13.

the money raised by selling renten must surely count as income for the prince, even though carrying charges for this unpaid debt have to be deducted from disposable bede receipts in subsequent years.[115] The full burden of this ongoing, long-term debt came to rest on the ordinaris bede. In many instances interest payments were charged to the ordinaris bede from the outset, and in others they were transferred to the ordinaris bede after the three-year period during which the States agreed to pay interest had elapsed, or (see items K and M) after an extraordinaris bede on which renten were sold had expired without full repayment of the principal. From about 1530 on, treasurers of Holland's six great cities were deducting some 22,000 from what they owed on the ordinaris bede each year, in order to make interest payments to holders of provincial renten. When this sum is added to what was already lost through gratiën, it becomes apparent that the ordinaris bede, hitherto the crown's most valuable fiscal resource, was steadily dwindling in value. The summary for the year 1531 (see table 5) was made by the Council of Finance.

In addition, certain other charges were regularly assigned to ordinaris bede receipts. These included recurring military expenses (for example, the Habsburgs built a fortress in newly acquired Utrecht, and the annual wages for its garrison were assigned to Holland's ordinaris bede)[116] and interest charges for the "floating debt" contracted with Antwerp bankers. When back wages of mercenary companies, salaries and pensions for officials, and sums requested by the emperor in Germany were counted in along with other expenses for 1531, the net result was a deficit for the year of 415,878.[117]

---

[115]The article cited in note 109 distinguishes between the portion of bede income that went for debt service (interest payments, and occasional redemptions of capital), and the portion that remained at the disposal of the prince and his officials, thus avoiding the problem of double-counting; that is, counting as income both the proceeds of a sale of renten and the bede payments by which the renten were (sometimes) redeemed.

[116]Lille B 23386, "Aides de la Hollande," 5,745 for the garrison at Vredensburg castle in Utrecht; see GRK 3437 *et seq.* under "Betalingen aan officiers."

[117]Aud. 875:1–40.

TABLE 5
DEDUCTIONS FROM THE ORDINARIS BEDE IN 1531

	Nominal sum	Gratiën	Renten interest	Remainder (amount and %)
Brabant	200,000	65,807	42,092	92,101 = 46.1
Flanders	200,000	64,659	3,000	132,141 = 66.2
Holland	80,000	28,193	22,310	29,947 = 36.9
Zeeland	30,000		(gratie for floods, plus renten = 0)	
Hainaut	29,000	4,404	1,900	22,696 = 78.3
Lille, Douai, Orchies	16,000	2,000	1,566	12,434 = 77.7
Totals	555,000	165,063 + ?	70,866 + ?	289,071 = 52.1

The extent to which the ordinaris bede was indebted owing to renten interest was a matter for concern in The Hague as well as in Brussels. Not counting other assignations (like the Utrecht garrison) or administrative costs, Holland's receiver for the beden would have less than 30,000 in ordinary subsidy income at his disposal during a given year. For deputies to the provincial States, this meant there was precious little on hand for military or naval expenditures in time of emergency.[118] For the regent and her officials, it meant the government's most important and reliable source of income from Holland had shrunk to barely a third of its nominal value. By common consent, it seems, there was no talk after the early 1530s of further burdening the ordinaris bede with sales of renten.

As mentioned earlier, it was in 1531, at the end of a several months' stay in Brussels, that Charles V instructed his officials to make strenuous efforts to wipe off the books war debts from the previous decade. For example, loans for which the city of Antwerp had stood surety, totaling 400,000, were to be amortized by domain income over the next five years. Meanwhile, expenditures were to be strictly limited to anticipated income, according to budgets drawn up several years in advance. But the beleaguered Council of Finance had to report to the emperor in 1533 that their plans for that year had been upset by 364,500 in expenditures "not in the budget." Unexpected conflicts in the Baltic and in the Bishopric of Münster were partly responsible, but the main culprit was an excess of 150,000 in carrying charges for short-term debt.[119] Since both the domain revenue and the ordinaris bede (at least in Brabant and Holland) were heavily pledged already, there was little room for expansion of the long-term debt, and further military expenses—as in 1536 and 1537— could only be met by borrowing on the Antwerp exchange as money from various extraordinaris beden slowly trickled in. In a budget (called *état* in French, or *staat* in Dutch) drawn up for 1539, so much of the expected income for that year

[118]See above, note 37.
[119]Aud. 868:1–2v; cf. Aud. 868:19–44, a list of sums in the 1534 budget (état), but not to be paid.

Gross revenue for the beden ('Aydes') of various provinces, from financial summary for 1521–1530 prepared by the Council of Finance (see p. 30). Reproduced by courtesy of the Algemeen Rijkarchief/Archives Genereaux du Royaume, Brussels.

had already been pledged to creditors, and expenses, counting arrears on military pay, were so great that the projected deficit was a staggering 1,421,836 pounds, far in excess of the total income for any previous year.[120] More than once financial officials exclaimed that there was no hope of becoming solvent unless there was a prolonged period of peace.[121] But during the Habsburg-Valois wars, who could expect that peace would be anything but an interlude during which each side husbanded its resources for another contest?

Perhaps the shrewdest member of the Council of Finance at this time was Meester Vincent Corneliszoon van Mierop, scion of a noble family in Holland, who had served previously in the Chamber of Accounts in The Hague. In a memo dating from about 1540, Meester Vincent rightly observed that the government needed new sources of revenue, since the ordinaris beden were of little help in reducing the debt, and domain revenues were already overpledged. He suggested explaining the problem to the provincial States and asking them to approve a new kind of extraordinaris bede that would consist of imposts, instead of being based on the usual quota systems (like the Holland schiltal) by which ordinary subsidies were collected. For example, there might be an impost of 1 percent on the capital wealth of all subjects, or a higher levy on annual income, or a tax on "the great and excessive monopolies which merchants practice every day."[122] In Meester Vincent's comments there lay a germ of hope for the future, but it could only be brought to fruition after new political circumstances in the Low Countries, to be discussed in the next chapter, gave the government more leverage in its dealings with the provincial States.

[120]Aud. 868:115–119v.

[121]Aud. 868:44–46, minute of deliberations by Mary of Hungary "in Council" [of State: the signature is by Pensart, on whom see Baelde, 294], dated Mechelen, 17 July 1534, and intended for Charles V.

[122]Aud. 868:120–128 (for Meester Vincent's hand, with signature, see Aud.1646:1, near page 110 in an unpaginated dossier); see under "Mierop" in Jacob vander Aa, *Biographisch Woordenboek*, and Baelde, 97, 248. The previous document in this dossier (Aud. 868:115–119v) is the projection of a 1,421,836 deficit for the year 1539, cited in note 120. It too is in Meester Vincent's hand, dated 25 February 1539, and identified as having been prepared by Mary of Hungary and "messieurs de la Finance" in order to be shown to the emperor.

A page from AJ, reporting (third paragraph) consent by the States of Holland to a sale of renten (item D of table 4). Reproduced by courtesy of the Gemeentearchief, Amsterdam.

III

The "Novel Expedients"
of 1542

The foregoing discussion has shown that towns represented in the provincial States in the Netherlands were able to bargain with their government on more or less equal terms. The secret of their success, it might be argued, lay in an absentee sovereign, for Charles V had made Castile his home ever since setting sail from the Netherlands in 1517. Though the majesty of his appearances in the Low Countries may have been enhanced by their infrequency, the emperor in person certainly commanded obedience in a way no regent could match. In 1531, for example, when the States of Holland were in their usual manner insisting on certain conditions in return for their consent to a bede, they were brusquely told to assent, simply and unconditionally, leaving their stated wishes to the emperor's good pleasure, since it was not meet for subjects to "bargain like merchants" (*comenscepen*) with their sovereign.[1] Charles never asserted his authority as natural prince of the Low Countries more forcefully than in 1540, when he stamped out incipient rebellion in the great city of Ghent. Beginning in 1537, Ghent had caused difficulty for Mary of Hungary's government by refusing its contribution to a bede that had been approved by the other three "members" of the States of Flanders. The example of Ghent was perhaps especially dangerous from the government's point of view, since this proud and populous weaving town had been for two centuries and more the most potent symbol of resistance to Burgundian and Habsburg centralization. Moreover, its recalcitrance in this case must have been particularly galling, since, owing to an unusually generous level of gratie, Ghent would not have been liable for more than a small fraction of its bede quota in any event.[2] By 1540 Charles V decided negotiation was no longer the way to deal with such behavior. Sailing from Castile en route to Germany, he gathered an armed force, occupied Ghent, and suspended all its privileges, thus providing other towns with a salutary illustration of how the mighty could be brought low.[3] The emperor then moved on to more urgent business in Germany—he was then promoting religious reconciliation of Catholics and Lutherans through theological colloquies at successive imperial diets—where he spent most of his time for the next four years.[4]

Meanwhile, though the emperor was no longer present in the Netherlands, direction of the Privy Council and the Council of State had fallen (1540) to Lodewijk van Schore, a doctor of laws from the University of Leuven, who was perhaps the

[1]RSH 29 March 1531, quoting the emperor: "Ick betrout wil zyn sonder geconstringeert te worden, ofte te comenscepen mit mynen ondersaten." Cf. AJ 23 March 1531.

[2]Maddens, 66, 220–222 (Ghent and Bruges regularly enjoyed gratiën of 80% or more); see Lodewijk van Vlaanderen, lord of Praet, to Mary of Hungary, 8 October 1545 (Aud. 1661:3).

[3]Most recent treatment by Maddens, "De Opstandige Houding van Gent tijdens de Regering van Keizer Karel, 1515–1540," *Appeltjes uit het Meetjesland* XXVIII (1977): 203–239.

[4]Karl Brandi, *Emperor Charles V* (London: 1939), 420–522.

ablest domestic statesman ever to serve Charles V or Philip II in this part of their dominions.[5] It was customary for the president of the Privy Council to preside over the Council of State as well, but Schore's distinctive hand appears also in the margins of documents prepared by the Council of Finance for deliberation in the other bodies. It is probably no accident that the draft proposal, which lies behind the fiscal changes to be discussed in this chapter, is found in a dossier apparently kept by Schore and by his successor as president of the Privy Council.[6] Schore had a high conception of sovereignty, and he was fortunate to be at the center of affairs during a rare and brief interval when, thanks to Charles V's intervention in Ghent, the regent of the Netherlands was able to behave like a sovereign.

In what follows, it will first be necessary to describe how, in the fall of 1542, the States of various provinces were induced to accept "new expedients" (*nieuwe middelen*) to finance a war with France: (a) provincewide excise and land taxes paid to the central government as extraordinary subsidies, and (b) a new series of renten funded by these same provincial excise and land taxes, which for this purpose were collected and disbursed by the States themselves. Taken together, these two changes would, in the course of time, make it

---

[5]Baelde, 59–60. For a signed example of Schore's hand, Aud. 1642:3a, no. 6.

[6]Aud. 650, a dossier of 548 folios numbered in sequence: folios 1–292 deal with fiscal negotiations with the States General from 1564 back to 1557, with documents generally in reverse chronological order; folios 293–404 contain various summaries of income and expenditure during and shortly after the 1542–1544 war with France, with marginal annotations by Schore visible in a number of instances (e.g., 295–298, a comment that the value of beden, as stated for budget purposes, must be reduced by deducting gratiën); folios 405–548 are a miscellany of documents pertinent to fiscal negotiations, such as a copy of the provincial quotas used by Duke Charles the Bold for a bede in 1475. Many of the documents in the last group are identified, corrected, or otherwise annotated in the hand of Viglius Zuichemius van Aytta (Baelde 324–325; for a signed example of his hand, Aud. 325, folio 210), who succeeded Schore as president of the Privy Council (1549) and later became president of the Council of State as well (1554). There are, however, two documents in Schore's hand in the final section, including an undated Latin memo providing legal justification for the taxation of clerical wealth (527–528). It seems reasonable to think that this dossier—put together by Schore and passed on to Viglius—represents a file for conducting fiscal discussions with the States.

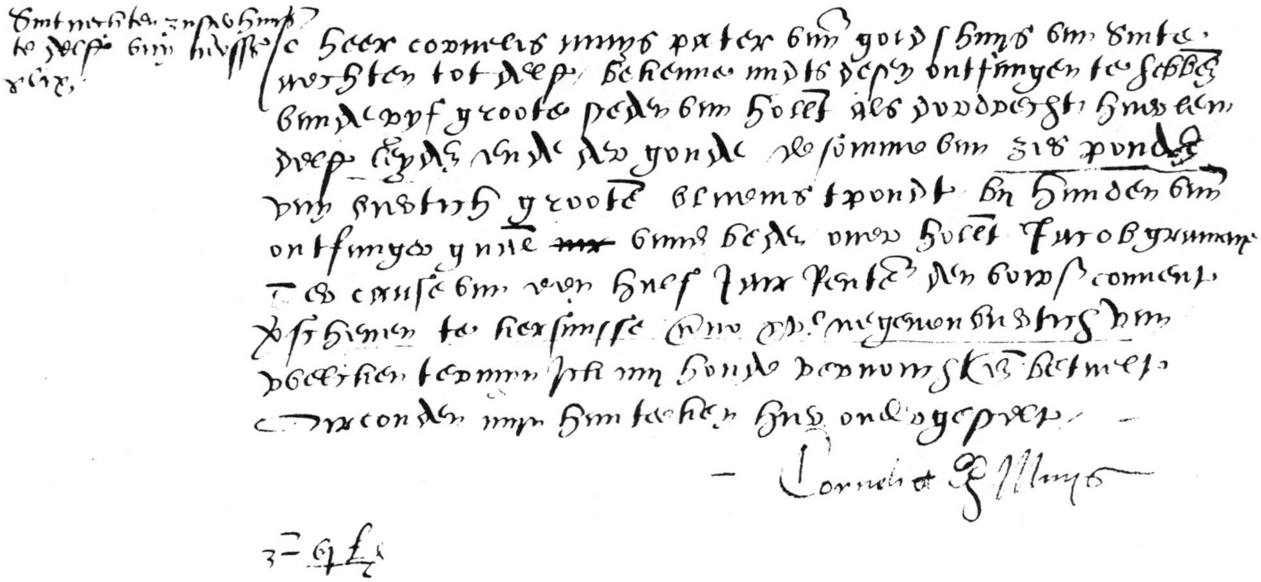

When auditing committees reviewed renten accounts, they approved only those payments of interest verified by receipts of the kind shown here. In this case, the rentenbuyer is Meester Cornelis Muys (Musius), chaplain (Pater) of St. Agatha's convent in Delft, a humanist and friend of Erasmus. Reproduced by courtesy of the Rijksarchief van Zuid-Holland, The Hague.

possible for the provincial States to create a new type of long-term debt, resting on sure foundations, and capable of vast expansion (I). Next, it can be shown how these "new expedients" became the principal source of revenue for a government driven to the brink of insolvency by the last and longest of the Habsburg-Valois wars, 1552–1559. In return for raising unprecedented sums, however, the States demanded and got nearly total control over the collection and disbursement of tax revenue, which meant that the provinces (here again the focus will be on Holland) made steady progress during the 1560s towards retiring the huge renten debts they had accumulated during the previous decade (II). Having thus lost control of its own revenues, the central government fell deeper than ever into penury, marking a poignant contrast with its creditworthy provinces, and a prelude to the coming Revolt of the Netherlands (III).

I. By January 1542 Charles V could see war clouds on the horizon.[7] Accordingly, Mary of Hungary was instructed to ask the States for an extraordinary subsidy whose proceeds were to be held ready for military use if war with France broke out; if it did not, the bede would go to arrears and current wages for the permanent companies of cavalry (*compagnies d'ordonnance*) commanded by various provincial governors, and for garrison wages and the repair of fortifications. From early February through the end of May, Mary reported to her brother on the progress of these negotiations. Deputies at first claimed it was not possible to raise more money through the traditional assessments, like the Holland schiltal, since the peasants carried the brunt of such levies, and could not be made to pay anything more. In view of the memorandum by Meester Vincent Corneliszoon, quoted at the end of the last chapter, it appears the government may have been waiting to hear such arguments. Mary instructed her commissioners to propose that, instead of resorting once more to the usual assessments, each province should decree an "impost" on wine and beer, "which each person makes use of, and the

[7]H. Lemonnier, *Histoire de la France*, E. Lavisse, ed., vol. 5:2 (Paris: 1911), 92–94, 107–111.

rich more than the poor." Though clerical and noble deputies (who could expect to be exempt) were receptive to the idea, Mary explained to her brother that town deputies rejected it "because of the large imposts which they are already collecting, and which they cannot easily increase."[8] Urban oligarchies in the Low Countries understood quite well that the treasured *bieraccijns* (beer tax) was also an explosive political issue, especially when combined with resentment of the privileged few (notably the clergy) who did not pay, as had been shown by a popular outbreak at 's Hertogenbosch in northern Brabant as recently as 1525.[9] Moreover, the states had rejected a government proposal for provincewide excise taxes a few years earlier (1536), and the one occasion when some of the provinces had agreed to such a tax (1523) was not a hopeful precedent since, in Holland at least, it had brought in barely a third of what was expected.[10] Not surprisingly, then, Artois was the only province that now consented to an "impost" on wine and beer. Flanders, Brabant, Holland, and Hainaut all chose as the lesser of two evils an extraordinary subsidy levied, after all, according to the traditional assessments.[11]

By this time (May 1542) war had actually broken out. The emperor was concerned for the safety of his Netherlands patrimony, not merely because of the long frontier with France but also because Maarten van Rossum, a feared and experienced commander, was raising troops for the new Duke of Guelders.[12] In keeping with instructions from her brother,

[8]Mary of Hungary to Charles V, 4 February 1542 (Aud. 53). The slow progress of negotiations is described in many of the regent's subsequent letters to her brother: 23 February, 23 March, 31 May, 24 September, and 28 November, 1542 (Aud. 53), 4 January, 7 March, and 7 June, 1543 (Aud. 54).

[9]Albertus Cuperinus, *Chronicke*, C. R. Hermans, *Verzameling van Kronyken, Charters, en Oorkonden betreffende de Stad en Meierij van 's Hertogenbosch* (3 vols., 's Hertogenbosch: 1847–1848), I, 79–81, 90–91.

[10]Grapperhaus, *Alva en de Tiende Penning*, 28, 46. GRK 3425: of an expected 81,067, the 1523 Holland impost on "beer, wine and beasts" yielded only 37,291, so that the remainder had to be collected by levies based on the customary schiltal. For the unpopularity of this novel tax and the difficulties of collecting it, AJ 7, 13 April, 28 May, 2 June, 9, 17 July, 5 August, 1523.

[11]Mary of Hungary to Charles V, 23 February, 23 March, 31 May, 1542 (Aud. 53).

[12]J. C. van der Does, *Maarten van Rossum* (Utrecht: 1943).

Mary of Hungary put 40,000 troops into the field in defense of the Netherlands, and maintained them in their positions during the three summer months, the favored time for campaigning, but at great cost. The special subsidy granted "in case of war" was quickly exhausted, receipts for the ordinary subsidies through the end of 1544 were "anticipated," as were those for a clerical subsidy authorized by the pope, and a further 300,000 had been borrowed on the Antwerp exchange.[13] Clearly, this government needed new sources of revenue.

Early in July, deputies from the various States were summoned to Brussels to hear a proposal: each province was asked to raise an extraordinary subsidy through a sale of renten to be funded not, as in the past, by the ordinaris bede, but by means to be determined by each issuing body. What these means might be was not specified, but it seems to have been expected that excise taxes would be involved.[14] In a broad sense the idea of funding renten by excise taxes was familiar to everyone, since town governments in the Netherlands had been doing it for centuries. A more useful precedent was provided by the Franc of Bruges, the rural "member" of the States of Flanders and a corporate body in its own right, which in 1536 (if not earlier) began issuing renten funded by a tax on land.[15] Despite this example, however, the States of Flanders rejected the government's proposal. As mentioned earlier, this provincial parliament had never agreed to assume collective responsibility for an issue of renten secured by the bede, and two years would pass before its deputies consented to begin issuing renten funded

---

[13]Mary of Hungary to Charles V, 18, 24 September, 28 November, 1542 (Aud. 53); the regent had also spent 50,000 sent to Antwerp by the emperor via letter of exchange in September.

[14]RSH 5 July, 11, 18 September, 1542.

[15]Aud. 650 (see above, note 6): 484–493, here 489v. This important document, labeled "correction," lays out the strategy to be pursued in presenting a request to the States (November 1542) for a new kind of taxation. The practice of selling renten backed by a special land tax may have been of fairly recent vintage in the Franc of Bruges: see the octroi, or permission, by Charles V, dated 24 September 1536, in Baelde, "Onuitgegeven Dokumenten," 152–157.

in the new way, through taxes devised by the States.[16] Other provinces were more cooperative. By September 1542, Brabant agreed to raise 150,000, Hainaut 35,000, and Artois 20,000.[17]

Meanwhile, Holland had been asked to raise 60,000 in the same way, but its deputies persisted in refusing to agree to yet another extraordinary subsidy, no matter by what means the money was to be gotten.[18] Schore and his colleagues in Brussels now detected a weak spot in Holland's defensive armor. Amsterdam was currently in ill favor with the regent owing to an incident the previous fall (2 October 1541), when a commissioner sent from Brussels provoked a riot by attempting to begin collection of an unpopular tax on grain exports, and had to be let out the town gates at night in peril of his life. Letters drafted by Schore threatened to invoke penalties which the law provided for lèse majesté, and even a large fine of 25,000 pounds was not sufficient to regain for Amsterdam its normal influence in political and fiscal affairs.[19] At the same time, officials in Brussels were doubtless aware that at least two of Holland's great cities (Dordrecht and Gouda) had in the past begrudged the proud isolation that permitted Amsterdam to shield its merchants from reprisals occasioned by nonpayment of interest on renten issued by the other five great cities.[20] Hence the States agreed in October to drop their opposition to the desired sale of renten, in

---

[16]Maddens, "De Invoering van de 'Nieuwe Middelen' in het Graafschap Vlaanderen tijdens de Regering van Keizer Karel," *Belgische Tijdschrift voor Filologie en Geschiedenis/ Revue Belge de Philologie et d'Histoire* 57 (1979): 882–893.

[17]Aud. 650:295–298: "aides accorded by sale of rentes, August–September 1542," 150,000 in Brabant, 60,000 in Holland, 25,000 in Artois, 35,000 in Hainaut. A 160,000 bede approved by the States of Flanders is also included here, but this sum was in fact collected via a levy according to the usual transport rather than by a sale of renten: Maddens, 224, 427 (Bijlage II, item 34).

[18]See above, note 14.

[19]The incident and its aftermath are discussed in Tracy, "Habsburg Grain Policy and Amsterdam Politics: The Career of Sheriff Willem Dirkszoon Baerdes, 1542–1566," *Sixteenth Century Journal* XVII (1983): 283–319.

[20]Assendelft to Mary of Hungary, 19, 22 October 1542 (Aud. 1646:3). According to an entry in ASR for 6 October 1542 (under "travel expenses," 66) all five of the other great cities had requested that Amsterdam join with them in selling renten.

return for intervention by the government compelling Amsterdam to abandon its independent posture, and merge its credit with that of the States at large for this new issue. Amsterdam protested the arrangement strenuously and for several weeks, but yielded in the end "to avoid the wrath of the Queen."[21]

By this time, however, the regent had in effect already spent whatever was to be realized through these sales of renten, and there were no further revenues in sight to cover the 300,000 in loans, plus interest, that was due in Antwerp within twelve months. Hence the provincial States were once more summoned to send their delegates to Brussels, on November 28. In a memo dated in the same month and obviously prior to this meeting of the States General, an unknown official works out some implications of the "impost" strategy previously suggested by Meester Vincent, and in Mary of Hungary's discussions with the States. Since there was little hope for a quick end to the war with France, it was first necessary to draw up a total budget of military expenses ("et de tout faire une masse") for the coming year to be shown to the deputies. Once anticipated income (less gratiën and renten interest) was subtracted from this sum, the remainder would equal the war deficit, here estimated at 2,400,000 pounds, which had to be covered by a new, and gigantic, extraordinary subsidy. Since this amount was roughly four or five times what the combined provincial States usually agreed to by way of an aide extraordinaire, there could be no question of raising it by means of the customary assessments. Hence it was not possible to maintain the Netherlands intact ("garder le pays") without new sources of revenue, specifically an impost, which might take one of several forms. One would be the proposal already presented by deputies from

[21]RSH 10 October 1542; "Vroedschapsresolutiën," Gemeentearchief, Amsterdam, vol. 1, entries for 17, 21, 29 October and 27 November, 1542. In his 29 October report to the vroedschap, Meester Hendrik Dirkszoon, one of the burgomasters, stated that (contrary to what Assendelft had reported to the regent about Gouda and Dordrecht in his October 22 letter) all the other cities were willing to let Amsterdam continue its traditional practice of selling renten "apart," but "this time only." If this be true, it may have been the regent herself who forced the issue.

First page of the memo (see p. 81) proposing a new tax strategy to be presented to the States General in November 1542. Reproduced by courtesy of the Algemeen Rijkarchief/Archives Genereaux du Royaume, Brussels.

Artois, Brabant, Hainaut, and Lille, which here is not further described. The fairest way would be a capital assessment ("assiette capitale") on the "value and puissance" of the goods of each subject, but such a tax would be "very difficult to manage," presumably because it required subjects to let the government know how much they were worth. It would seem best, then, to levy imposts on commercial goods and on victuals commonly consumed, and also a "10th penny" on the income from real property.[22]

This memo contains the nucleus of what was proposed to the States General on November 28: a 100th penny tax on the value of all exports from the major provinces; a 10th penny on commercial profits; and a 10th penny on income from "real property," understood as including all losrenten and lijfrenten except for those which had been issued by one of the provincial States as part of an extraordinary subsidy.[23] According to projections by the Council of Finance, the 100th penny was expected to yield 200,000, while the two 10th pennies combined were to bring in 400,000 in Brabant, 300,000 in Flanders, and 120,000 in Holland—altogether, nearly 1,000,000 of what was needed to cover the anticipated war deficit of 2,400,000[24] (further sums were sought from new renten sales, to be discussed shortly). But few things work as well as expected, and these new imposts were no exception. The States of Holland stoutly resisted the 100th penny, even after collection had begun in other provinces, alleging, with some justification, that "Easterling" merchants would bypass the Low Countries rather than submit to such a novelty, and thus jeopardize Holland's middleman role in the Baltic trade. In the end Mary of Hungary simply declared that export duties were a matter touching the sovereignty of the prince, and that collection was therefore to begin in Holland without benefit of consent by the States, "by virtue of the Emperor's absolute power" ("ex potestate absoluta imperatoris").[25] Even so, the 100th

[22]See above, note 15.

[23]RSH 28 November–2 December 1542; the government's proposals to the deputies from various provinces assembled in Brussels were read by Schore.

[24]See below, note 26; Aud. 650:295–298.

[25]RSH 25 February 1543; for evidence that the Easterlings were indeed sensitive to new impositions in the Low Countries, see the testimony col-

Lodewijk van Schore's summary (see p. 89 n. 48) of war finances for the 1542–1544 war with France. Reproduced by courtesy of the Algemeen Rijksarchief/Archives Genereaux du Royaume, Brussels.

penny tax had to be prolonged more than two years in order to bring in the 200,000 which Gasparo Ducci had advanced in exchange for the right to collect it.[26] The States of Holland also objected to the 10th penny on commercial profits, insisting, this time successfully, that it be collected in Holland as a 10th penny only on the profit (reckoned at 6%) from all mercantile inventories whose total value exceeded 1,000 pounds. But government concessions did not necessarily bring cooperation from taxpayers. Officials in Brussels subsequently accused the Hollanders of "laziness" in collecting this 10th penny, as well they might, since it brought in only 1,200.[27] The 10th penny tax on renten and real property income was more fruitful, though proceeds still fell short of expectations; according to calculations by the Council of Finance, it yielded 248,933 in Brabant, 290,000 in Flanders, and 91,482 in Holland.[28]

Once the States accepted the principle of collecting an extraordinary subsidy by way of imposts, the government could resort to it again. Thus in October 1543 the States of Brabant agreed to collect a provincewide excise on beer and wine over six years, so that the anticipated revenue (400,000) could be

---

lected on occasion by order of the States of Holland, and published in P. A. Meilink, "Rapporten en Betoogen nopens het Congiegeld op Granen, 1530–1541," *Bijdragen en Mededelingen van het Historisch Genootschap te Utrecht* XLIV (1923): 1–124.

[26]Ducci seems to have advanced a total of 206,000, some of which came from Sebastian Neidhardt, Jean Caroli, and "Bartholomaeus Welser," that is, his son-in-law and the Augsburg firm's Antwerp factor, Hieronymus Sailer. After total gross receipts of 198,441, Ducci was left with unpaid claims, including collection expenses, in excess of 51,000: CC 23357, 683–692v; 23360, 1824–1840; 23362, 1767–1769; and 23364, 2287–2288, together with a loose folio labeled (in pencil) 1021, but which ought to precede folio 2287 of volume 23364. Cf. Lille B 2442, 429v.

[27]P. A. Meilink, "Gegevens aangaande Bedrijfskapitalen in den Hollandschen en Zeeuwschen Handel in 1543," *Economisch-Historisch Jaarboek* 8 (1922): 263–277; the combined total for Amsterdam, Leiden, and Delft, the only Holland cities listed, was 185,216. This figure agrees fairly closely with the statement in RSH 5 August 1545 (see 16 October 1544) that the yield for the 100th penny in Holland was 1,200 pounds (10% of 6% of 185,216 = 1,111).

[28]Aud. 650:352, 355, 382; the figure for Holland includes only 91,482 for the 10th penny on renten and real property income, to which 1,200 for the 10th penny on commercial profits (above, note 27) is added here.

used at once as security for a loan on the Antwerp exchange.[29] In 1544 Brabant and Flanders (but not Holland, where resistance to any kind of taxes on commerce appears to have been especially strong) consented to renew the 10th penny tax on mercantile profits.[30] In the same year Brabant also agreed to an uncommonly large extraordinary subsidy of 600,000, one-third to be raised through a "10th and a 20th penny" on the income from urban real property, two-thirds through a tax on land in the countryside.[31] Holland was asked at this time for a *morgental*, which was a flat tax per land unit (one morgen = 2¼ acres) outside town and village limits, but the States preferred a renewal of the 10th penny tax on renten and real property income, to which the government agreed.[32]

Revenues from these new sources were welcome indeed but, as the war dragged on for two years more, the government naturally sought other novel ways of boosting its income. One possibility was simply to eliminate the gratiën, which (as is emphasized by Schore in one of his marginal comments on fiscal summaries) so diminished the value of beden levied according to the traditional assessments.[33] But on this point the vested interests of the great cities, at least those in Holland, were strong enough to deflect all the pressure that Brussels could bring to bear. The line of least resistance was to allow the cities to keep their gratie, but still collect the full nominal sum of a bede by having someone

---

[29]Aud. 650:406–408.

[30]Aud. 650:406–408, 429; Maddens, 427 (Bijlage II, item 38). In 1544, the two 10th penny levies to which the States of Brabant agreed were expected to yield 248,934, while the income for two 10th penny levies in Flanders was projected at 600,000 crowns, or 500,000 pounds of 40 groats. Instead of agreeing to new 10th penny levies, Holland raised its extraordinaris bede of 150,000 pounds half through a new sale of renten (below, note 38) and half through a morgental, or flat tax per unit of arable land: RSH 9 April 1544. Flanders approved two 10th pennies yet again in 1545: Maddens, 427, Bijlage II, item 39.

[31]Aud. 650:335–339 (May 1544).

[32]RSH 16 October, 21 November, 1, 4, 20–26 December, 1544. Apropos of the morgental, Assendelft pointed out to the regent that much of Holland's acreage was swampy, hence it would be great inequity ("groot ongelycheyt") to tax it at the same rate as more productive land: to Mary of Hungary, 23 February 1544 (Aud. 1646:3).

[33]Aud. 650:295.

else make up the difference. For an extraordinary subsidy of 75,000 levied by schiltal in 1543, the States of Holland agreed to have the cities' gratie made good by a levy (for which a special permission from the regent was necessary) on the normally exempt towns and villages in Holland which lay "outside the schiltal."[34] For a similar 75,000 bede the following year, the missing amount was found by raising the quota for rural areas "under the schiltal," with a special wrinkle: so that the cities could receive the extra gratie to which they would be entitled for a bede whose nominal sum was 100,000, villages had to be assessed at the rate for which they would have been liable had the total been 135,000.[35] While nobles in the States of Holland were outraged by this scheme, and angry villagers demanded explanations from town regents who professed not to understand what was happening,[36] the salient point is that Schore and the regent had found a way of squeezing out additional funds without damaging the interests of the great cities.

[34]GRK 3443, RSH 19 August 1543. SH 2278 (the *akkord*, or consent, to this bede is found in GRK 3453) lists receipts for a 10th penny on renten and real property income for all places "outside" as well as "inside" the schiltal; comparison with ordinaris bede accounts (GRK 3441), listing only places "inside" the schiltal, shows that thirty-seven villages or parts of villages lay "outside" the assessment, together with the towns of Asperen, Heukelom, Ijsselsteyn, Leerdam, Woudrichem, and Zevenbergen.

[35]GRK 3445. A few examples may illustrate what this arrangement meant for some of the wealthier villages:

	Extraordinaris bede, 1536–1537 Nominal sum 100,000	Extraordinaris bede, 1544 Nominal sum 75,000
Ablas	267p = 0.267% of total	360 = 0.48% of total
Assendelft	467p = 0.467% of total	616 = 0.82% of total
Wormer & Gisp	750p = 0.75% of total	1,012 = 1.35% of total

The figures in the right-hand column are appropriate for a hypothetical bede of about 135,000 (e.g., 1,012 divided by 0.75%, the regular quota for Wormer and Gisp, is 134,933).

[36]Council of Holland to Mary of Hungary, 26 May, 20 June, 1544 (Aud. 1646:1).

More promising was the prospect of further sales of renten which, like the 1542 issue, would be funded not from the ordinaris bede, but from new revenues to be raised by the States. Along with several other provinces, Holland consented to a second such issue in 1543, for a capital value in excess of 76,000.[37] The one question that still remained to be settled was precisely how the new renten of 1542 and 1543 were to be funded. By October 1543, a year's interest was falling due on the 60,000 issue to which the States of Holland had consented the previous year. To help the discussion along, Mary of Hungary sent, unsolicited, permissions for provincewide excises on beer, wine, and woolen cloths. The States were ready in principle to fund the new renten by some kind of impost, but wanted assurances that exempt places and persons would be made to contribute in whatever ways were found to fund the renten; it was not an idle request, since the powerful Count of Buren had petitioned the regent to have his towns and villages left as free of any new taxes as they were of the customary beden. By early 1544 the queen was instructing her commissioners to insist that Holland back its renten by the same kind of beverage excise that was already being collected for this purpose in other provinces. But Hollanders countered that, in a province whose every point was accessible by water, it was not practicable to collect a beer and wine tax except in the cities;[38] instead, rural areas should do their part by way of a land tax, or morgental. After further discussions with Schore in Brussels, the Hollanders won acceptance of their plan for funding the renten, partly because they made it a condition for agreeing to the desperately needed 75,000 bede just mentioned.[39] What remained problematic was the actual collection of the new excise and land taxes in areas of private jurisdiction that lay

[37]SH 2276, the account for this sale of renten, is "ernstig beschadigd" and thus not for use in the reading room at the Rijksarchief voor Zuid-Holland in The Hague, but names and amounts for each purchase are listed under interest payments in SH 2208.

[38]RSH 2 October, 6–12 November, 28 December, 1543, 5, 21–22 February, 5–6 March, 1544; Mary of Hungary to Assendelft, 1, 14 March 1544 (Aud. 1646:3).

[39]RSH 19, 26 March, 5–7 April, 1544.

"outside the schiltal." Mary of Hungary duly provided the requisite orders overriding all privileges of the clergy and other persons normally exempt from taxation, but men like the Count of Buren did not readily submit to rulings by a mere regent.[40]

The "novel expedients" of 1542–1544 were accompanied by a rather technical change in the manner of collecting taxes, the significance of which would not become apparent until the following decade. The Hague was the seat of two distinct tax-gathering bureaucracies, one headed by the emperor's receiver for the beden, the other by the receiver for the Common Territory (*gemeen land*). The former was appointed by the regent, and was responsible to the Council of Finance for disposition of whatever bede income he collected. The latter was an appointee of the States, and his duties had until now been confined to collecting the small levies—apportioned according to the schiltal, but called omslagen to distinguish them from the beden—which the States used to pay for their administrative expenses.[41] During the 1542–1544 war, however, provincial assemblies were particularly anxious that tax monies be kept available to protect their home ground; both Brabant and Holland, for example, were threatened by Maarten van Rossum's army. Hence, in return for their willingness to accept the government's "novel expedients," the States demanded equally novel procedures by which they themselves would control the funds raised.[42] In Holland, the re-

[40]Rather than submit to the 10th penny on real property income from his lands, the Count of Buren presented himself for detention (*gijzeling*) in The Hague, along with the treasurer for his town of Leerdam: Council of Holland to Mary of Hungary, 3 February 1544 (Aud. 1646:1). With other exempt personages, he also made difficulty about the excise and land taxes that were now to be collected to fund renten sold in 1542 and 1543: RSH 6, 15 November, 14 December, 1544, and 1545, pp. 1–7. Maximiliaan van Egmont, Count of Buren (d. 1548: see Baelde, 258–259) was named Knight of the Golden Fleece and Member of the Council of State in 1540; he later gained fame by leading a Netherlands army through Protestant Germany (1546) to provide safety for Charles V at Ingolstadt, just prior to the outbreak of the First Schmalkaldic War.

[41]Accounts for the omslagen are listed in Meilink, nos. 1762–1798.

[42]RSH 5 March 1544: the Stadtholder (Reynier van Nassau, Prince of Orange) requested on behalf of the regent a new bede of 100,000, to be kept for use in case Holland was invaded; see above, note 12. Similarly, the States

ceiver for the Common Territory now found himself entrusted with collection of the proceeds from the two renten sales of 1542 and 1543, the two 10th pennies of 1543, and a 10th penny in 1544 on renten and real property income, all of which counted as extraordinaris beden, and which therefore would normally have been collected by the receiver for the beden.[43] In addition, it was to be expected that the States would designate their own revenue agent, not the emperor's, as the collector for the provincial excise and land tax by which the renten were funded. Though the proceeds from these taxes were intended for a definite purpose, they were in some measure at the disposal of the States; already in 1544 the deputies decided to postpone repayment of some renten principal, and use the money instead to make up Holland's arrears in a recent extraordinaris bede.[44]

The importance of these fiscal changes was first recognized by Verhofstad, although the one element in the package which he rightly acclaimed as the most novel—the 10th penny on commercial profits—was also the one which was least widely used in subsequent years.[45] More recently, Baelde has

of Artois insisted on keeping money to be raised by a new excise tax there, for use in case of war: States of Artois to Mary of Hungary, 24 July 1542, Baelde, "Onuitgegeven Dokumenten," 177–179. In Namur, however, the States did not become involved in controlling or disbursing receipts until 1579, and there was no provincial excise until 1580: P. Brouwers, *Les Aides et Subsides dans le Conté de Namur au XVIe Siècle* (Namur: 1934), xii–xv, xlix–lvii.

[43]Hence the accounts for these two sales of renten were kept by the Receiver for the Common Territory (SH 2275, 2276), not by the emperor's receiver for the beden (GRK). The regent objected to the Receiver for the Common Territory's manner of collecting the two 10th pennies. Unlike officials answerable to the Council of Finance, he refused to sign a promissory note against his future receipts, which meant the government had no security for raising cash in Antwerp straightaway; eventually, the regent succeeded in having him replaced as collector for the 10th pennies by the receiver for the beden: Mary of Hungary to the Council of Holland, 5 May, 20 September, 1543 (Aud. 1646:3), and 12 May 1544 (Aud. 1646:1).

[44]SH 2208: Vrank van der Hove, Receiver for the Common Territory and thus collector for the new excise and land tax, transferred 52,650 to Pieter Moens Willemszoon, receiver for the beden, as partial payment for an extraordinaris bede of 120,000 to which the States of Holland had consented in 1542. Cf. RSH 5 February 1544.

[45]Verhofstad, 58–59; cf. Maddens, "De Invoering van de 'Nieuwe Middelen' in Vlaanderen."

noted that the fiscal reforms of the early 1540s achieved the
not inconsiderable feat of carrying the Netherlands through
a major war without plunging the government further into
debt than it already was.[46] Of the 730,788 in net bede revenue
which Holland raised between the beginning of 1542 and the
end of 1544, roughly half (365,433) came from imposts of one
kind or another, and from the sale of renten funded by the
States[47] (the rest came from ordinaris or extraordinaris beden
raised according to the schiltal). Some time after the war had
been concluded, Schore himself calculated that total military
expenses for 1542–1544 exceeded total bede receipts for the
same period by 1,103,802; but this figure compares rather
favorably with the peacetime deficit of 1,421,836 recorded for
the year 1539.[48] Moreover, the creation of a new basis for
selling renten meant that the government could raise capital
at favorable rates (1 : 16 or 6.25%) without further burdening
the ordinaris bede. Finally, contrary to all past experience,
the new renten debt was quickly retired (see table 6).

TABLE 6
RENTEN FUNDED BY THE STATES OF HOLLAND
DURING THE 1540s[49]

No. in series	Emission date	Capital	Rate	Annual interest	Retired
1	1543	61,266	1:16	3,829	1547
2	1544	76,186	1:16	4,762	1548
3	1549	20,808	1:16	1,300	1550

[46]Baelde, "Financiële Politiek en Domaniale Evolutie in de Nederlanden
onder Karel V en Filips II," *Tijdschrift voor Geschiedenis* LXXVI (1963), 25, 30.

[47]Figures from Tracy, "The System of Taxation in the County of Holland
under Charles V and Philip II," forthcoming in *Economisch- en Sociaal-
Historisch Jaarboek* (1985).

[48]Aud. 650:533–534 (summary in Schore's hand of income and outgo for
1542–1544); Aud. 868:115–119v, summary for 1539 in the hand of Meester
Vincent Corneliszoon van Mierop (see chapter 2, note 122). For 1538, the
shortage was 1,356,382: Aud. 868:110–114.

[49]SH 2275, 2276, 1792 (accounts for these three sales: but see above, note
37); SH 2208, 2210, 2211, and 1793–1795 (accounts for payments of interest
and redemptions).

The new system worked so well it was used to raise part of what was needed for a special gift for Prince Philip, the future Philip II, on the occasion of his visit to the Netherlands in 1549 (item 3 in table 6). The government had thus apparently found a better way of raising funds, and private investors could now count on recovering their capital without having to sell at a discount on the secondary market.[50] The whole process would be tested more severely in the following decade.

In sum, the "novel expedients" adopted during the 1542–1544 war with France included several different elements: (1) taxes on mercantile wealth (the 100th penny on exports and the 10th penny on commercial profits); (2) provincewide excises on beer and wine; (3) a 10th penny on the income from renten and real property; and (4) a new series of provincial renten, funded by some combination of (2) and (3). Some of these innovations would prove more important than others in the subsequent fiscal history of the Low Countries. After 1545, there were no global taxes on exports (like the 100th penny) and no more 10th pennies on commercial profits, at least not until the Duke of Alba's ill-fated 10th penny of 1572. For this reason, the fiscal reforms of 1542 have sometimes been regarded as a failure.[51] But provincial excises did become a regular feature of taxation in the Low Countries, not as part of an extraordinary subsidy paid directly to the central government, but rather to fund the new series of renten; the proceeds thus ended up in the pockets of investors, not in the government's badly depleted coffers.[52] The 10th penny

---

[50]Sales in the secondary market are indicated in GRK and SH (under the sections for payment of interest on renten) by notations that so-and-so is now the beneficiary "bij transport van" (by transfer from) the original buyer or a previous owner, but the sale price is of no importance for these accounts (it did not change the amount of interest due) and is not recorded. The only reference I have found to a sale price is GVR lxx (24 April 1530): a "gemeen lands rente" with an annual interest of 90 pounds, meaning at 1 : 16 a capital of 1,440, belonging to a burgher of Gouda whose property had been confiscated, was at the city's request sold in Bruges for 1,242, or 86.25 percent of par.

[51]Grapperhaus, Alva en de Tiende Penning, 43–51.

[52]SH 2278, 2280, 2281, 2282, 2284.

tax on renten and real property income was used at least occasionally in later decades, both as an extraordinary subsidy and to help reduce renten debt. Neither the provincial excise nor the tax on real property income was intended primarily as a means of funding the new renten but, as things turned out, that was the chief purpose they in fact served. Using these means of tapping into urban as well as rural wealth, whole provinces could now begin to do what hitherto only wealthy cities like Antwerp or Amsterdam could do; they could provide themselves with a secure annual income, large enough to serve as the basis for public indebtedness of an unprecedented magnitude. Seen from the vantage point of later decades, this combination of changes can be seen to have laid the groundwork for a financial revolution.

II. The enormous costs of the 1552–1559 war have been alluded to more than once in the foregoing discussion. This was the conflict in which the Netherlands military budget for a campaigning season roughly doubled the previous highs reached between 1542 and 1544, and had to be sustained at that level over seven years instead of three. It was during this war too that the king of France defaulted on the Grand Parti of Lyons, while Philip II avoided bankruptcy in 1557 only by a forcible conversion of short-term loans into new juros.[53] In 1558 the same Philip II, with the consent of the States General of the Netherlands, decreed a reduction of the interest rate for loans by foreign bankers in Antwerp from 12 percent to 5 percent.[54] It was not a case of revenues remaining stagnant, but of expenditures rising even faster than a rather remarkable increase in revenues, largely made possible by the "novel expedients" of the 1540s. In Holland, the average annual net bede income for the period 1519–1566 was 159,545; for the nine years from 1552 through 1560, the figure rose to 338,351. In other words, roughly 40 percent of the net bede income over a forty-eight-year stretch was collected during these nine

[53]Henri Hauser, "La Crise de 1557–1559 et le boulversement des fortunes," *Melanges offerts à M. Abel Lefranc* (Paris: 1936), 307–319; Modesto Ulloa, *La Hacienda Real de Castilla en el Reinado de Felipe II* (Madrid: 1977), 759–831.
[54]Verhofstad, 137–139.

years. If one breaks this income down according to the various ways in which a bede could be raised, it is apparent that sums collected on the basis of the traditional schiltal were not appreciably higher than they were in former decades. The ordinaris bede remained at the same nominal sum, and was reduced by approximately the same level of gratie, as during the 1540s. Extraordinaris beden levied by schiltal brought in a net sum of 611,996 for 1552–1560, as compared with 449,779 during the period 1522–1530. But over the same forty-eight-year stretch, the lion's share of income collected by way of taxes on real property (the 10th penny and the morgental) was brought in between 1552 and 1560: 572,032, or about 70 percent, of the total. Similarly, the States responded to additional requests for extraordinaris beden between 1552 and 1560 by issuing 1,236,401 in renten funded, as in the 1540s, by a provincial excise and land tax, whereas the total capital raised during the somewhat longer period when renten had been secured by the bede (1515–1534) was only 538,000.[55] Issues of renten during the 1550s must now be examined more closely.

Credit conditions were apparently tight in the Netherlands even as the armies were mobilizing for battle in 1552. Hollanders were chided by the regent for even attempting to place the erfrenten, or heritable annuities, the States had agreed to sell at the traditional rate of 1 : 16; as it turned out, the regent was right—buyers could not be found for less than 1 : 12, or 8.33 percent.[56] As the war progressed, even this rate was not high enough. Adopting another precedent developed in the inventive credit markets of Flanders, the States of Holland consented to issue a special kind of lijfrenten. Life-term annuities always carried a higher rate than the erfrenten that might be passed on from generation to generation,[57] but, from the standpoint of the issuer, they had the great advan-

[55]Figures from table 1 of the article cited above, note 47.

[56]Mary of Hungary to the Council of Holland, 15 March 1552 (Aud. 1646:2); this letter was discussed in the States of Holland four days afterwards (RSH 19 March 1552).

[57]For example, Leiden (1520) sold losrenten at 1 : 16, lijfrenten for "two lives" (i.e., the beneficiary and his or her heir) at 1 : 10, and for "one life" at 1 : 8: LTR 1520.

tage of being extinguished by the death of the beneficiary.[58] To raise yet more capital in difficult times, Flemings had devised the expedient of issuing lijfrenten that had a higher than normal rate, but could also be redeemed at any time.[59] The States of Holland now followed this practice, issuing redeemable lijfrenten at 1 : 6 or 16.67 percent.[60] By 1556, however, it was found that sufficient capital could be raised at the 1 : 12 rate, so that the expensive lijfrenten were no longer needed; by 1559 there was some movement back toward the traditional rate for erfrenten (1 : 16), as may be seen in table 7.[61]

How was a debt of this size to be funded? As in the 1540s, the States took some time to reach a decision; the receiver for the Common Territory was directed to use part of what he had collected for an extraordinaris bede to make the first interest payments falling due for renten sold in 1552, with the resulting arrears to be made up later.[62] During the course of 1553 the States determined on a levy of two groats per morgen of land, plus a beer-and-wine excise at half the rate

[58]Many cities still followed the old custom of paying a small reward to whomever brought the happy news that a holder of a lijfrente had died, meaning that interest for the current year need not be paid beyond that date.

[59]RSH 23 August 1553.

[60]SH 2279–2282.

[61]SH 2277–2287, 2289.

[62]By this time, the Receiver for the Common Territory, not the emperor's receiver for the beden, was responsible for collecting all extraordinaris beden of whatever type: see below, note 82. RSH 2 September 1553: Aert Coebel, Receiver for the Common Territory, was instructed to pay a total of 5,262 in interest "falling due soon" from his receipts for a 300,000 extraordinaris bede to which the States had consented the previous April. In fact, no interest payments are debited to the account for this bede (SH 2278), perhaps because Coebel was short 38,338 at the close of the account. Instead, interest for the first and second years on renten sold in 1552 was debited to the first year's account for the new excise and land tax, collection for which did not begin until February 1554 (SH 2293). That renteniers were not paid any interest until receipts were available from the revenues to which these payments were assigned is possible, but not likely. Instead, Coebel probably paid the first year's interest out of receipts for the 300,000 bede, as he had been instructed to do, but did not show this transaction in his account for the bede; had he done so, the emperor's auditors, from The Hague's Chamber of Accounts, would surely have disallowed the expenditure. See below, note 82.

TABLE 7

RENTEN FUNDED BY THE STATES OF HOLLAND, 1552–1565

No. in series	Issue date	Capital	Interest rate(s)	Annual interest
4	1552	58,808	1:12	4,901
5	1553	91,215	1:12	7,601
6	1553	26,584	1:12	2,215
		74,521	1:6	12,420
7	1554	56,192	1:12	4,683
		109,273	1:6	18,212
8	1554	2,400	1:16	150
		57,522	1:12	4,793
		40,622	1:6	6,770
9	1555	70,768	1:12	5,897
		59,198	1:6	9,866
10	1556	111,673	1:12	9,306
11	1557	9,420	1:12	785
12	1557	19,902	1:12	1,658
14	1558	1,200	1:16	75
		279,757	1:12	23,313
15	1559	49,192	1:16	3,074
		139,794	1:12	11,649
Totals for 1552–1559		1,258,041		127,368
17	1565	107,408	1:16	6,713
Grand totals		1,365,449		134,081

Note: For items 13 and 16, see table 9.

used to retire renten during the 1540s. As the burden of debt
mounted, it was of course necessary to increase the levels of
both taxes. The land tax rose to five groats per morgen, then

seven, and in 1557 was converted to a schiltal affecting rural areas only, with the rate per unit of assessed valuation set so as to bring in the same amount previously yielded by a seven-groat morgental (the reason for this change was that a tax which took the value of land into account was felt to be more equitable). The excise rose to three, four, and eventually seven groats per vat of beer, and thirty-six, forty-eight and then sixty groats per *aem* of Rhine wine, with higher tariffs for French and Spanish wines.[63] Several other kinds of imposts were discussed in the States as early as 1555, but none was adopted save for an excise on the sale of turf, beginning in 1560.[64] With these changes, the combined income that might be expected from the excise and land taxes reached a level roughly triple what it had been initially. As in the case of the beden, however, the expected income which the Receiver entered into his ledgers—from individual villages for the land tax, and from tax farmers who contracted to collect the excise in each city[65]—was not necessarily collected on time. As a result, substantial arrears in interest payments were passed on from year to year, presumably by withholding payment from renten-holders domiciled in Holland, who were not likely to cause trouble by seeking reprisals against Holland merchants.[66] Nonetheless, the province had made substantial progress toward reducing its debt by 1566, as shown in table 8.[67]

These figures indicate that, although there were years when the receiver for the Common Territory had great difficulty collecting enough revenue to pay renten interest, the arrears were soon made up, and Holland's annual obligation declined

[63]For adjustments in the land tax rates, RSH 10 July, 2 September, 29 December, 1553, 21 March, 11 October, 1554, 31 March, 9 August, 14, 25 November, 4 December, 1555, 26 February, 20 March, 1 May, 22 August, 7 September, 1556, 11, 13 April 1557.

[64]RSH 14 November 1555, 17–19 January 1560; SH 2299, account for the excise and land taxes, 1 May 1560–30 April 1561.

[65]RSH 5–13 December 1555, the decision to farm out collection of the beer and wine excise; urban excise taxes were usually collected the same way.

[66]For continuing reprisals by renten-holders outside the province, and fear of further such incidents, RSH 28 July 1557, 6 September 1559, 4 July 1561, 14 November 1562.

[67]SH 2293–2305.

TABLE 8

EXCISE AND LAND TAXES BY WHICH THE
RENTEN WERE FUNDED, 1554–1567

Year	Receipts	Renten interest paid	Arrears for year	Redemptions
1554/1555	34,056	17,360	16,116	
1555/1556	75,157	121,862		
1556/1557	95,283	65,850	27,238	
1557/1558	88,496	66,069	18,998	
1558/1559	86,516	40,742	43,020	
1559/1560	92,565	77,689	12,511	
1560/1561	98,139	74,032	18,167	
1561/1562	101,482	113,682		
1562/1563	96,983	90,430		
1563/1564	106,620	74,238	24,353	
1564/1565	104,151	72,753		12,078
1565/1566	105,261	66,594		33,160
1566/1567	105,700	59,685		12,192

from a high of somewhere around 100,000 to about 60,000.
One reason for this improvement was that the States adopted
a method of debt reduction long in use by individual cities
like Amsterdam. "Conversion" meant selling renten at low
rates and using the proceeds to redeem older, more costly
issues.[68] In 1556 and again in 1560 the States obtained permission from the central government to issue what were called
"conversion renten," each time at a lower rate; in both cases
holders of existing renten had a choice between accepting

[68]J. H. Kernkamp, *Vijftiende-Eeuwse Rentebrieven van Noord-Nederlandse Steden* (Groningen: 1961), 11–15.

conversion of their investments to the new, lower rate, or having the original capital paid back (see table 9).[69]

TABLE 9
CONVERSION RENTEN FUNDED BY THE STATES OF
HOLLAND, 1556–1564

No. in series	Emission dates	Capital	Rate	Interest	Used in redemption
13	1556–1558	4,808	1:16	300	
		295,523	1:12	24,637	283,654 at 1:6
16	1562–1564	374,548	1:16	23,409	344,799 at 1:12

Note: It makes no sense to add these figures together, nor to add them to the totals in table 7, since the proceeds were used to cancel debts outstanding from previous sales.

Another, almost equally important means of reducing indebtedness employed by the States, again with the permission of the central government, was to levy a 10th penny tax on the income from renten (excepting those issued by the States) and real property. In this way, 218,655 was raised in 1561, and 228,499 in 1565, almost all of which was used for further redemptions of renten.[70] It should be noted that once the war with France had ended no 10th pennies were levied in Holland for the benefit of the central government. Hence the most enduring of the "novel expedients" of 1542—sales of renten funded by the States, and the 10th penny—were both being used to improve the solvency not of the government, but of its provinces.

By the mid-1560s, interest charges had been brought to a level comfortably below annual income from the combined excise and land tax. The "mighty lords" (for so they were beginning to call themselves) who sat as deputies to the States thus had considerable sums at their disposal for such purposes as they might devise, whether for promising quick

[69]SH 2347, 2348; RSH 8–9 July, 17 October, 8 December, 1556, 5 March, 7 April, 1560, 28 October 1561, 14 July, 7 November, 1562.
[70]SH 2343, 2344.

redemption of capital for a favored rentenier,[71] or offering an unusually large gift to their stadtholder, who now happened to be William the Silent, Prince of Orange.[72] One way of gauging the relative solvency of the States at this time is to compare their success in reducing the huge renten debt of the 1550s with what was done for the smaller debt stemming from renten sold against the beden between 1515 and 1534 (chapter 2, table 4). By 1536, 181,388 pounds of the capital for these earlier renten had been redeemed, which meant that annual interest charges were 22,282, or 66.27 percent, of what the total would have been had there been no redemptions.[73]

[71]See Appendix II*a*, no. 1; on Duke Erich von Braunschweig-Kalenberg (1528–1583), a spendthrift north German prince and Habsburg ally who spent more time in Brussels than in his own territory, see Otto von Heinemann, *Geschichte von Braunschweig und Hannover* (3 vols., Gotha: 1882), II, 311–331. In 1565, when the States of Holland agreed to raise an extraordinaris bede of 100,000 through a sale of renten, Duke Erich made several purchases totaling 64,000 (SH 2289); the fact that he was then negotiating, unsuccessfully as it turned out, for purchase of the rich barony and chateau of Gaesbeek in Brabant (Griffiths, *William of Hornes*, 11–14) probably explains why the duke had such a large amount of cash on hand for a short-term investment. Within a year, Duke Erich was paid back 32,000, plus interest on this sum and the remainder, from the next excise and land tax account. It seems likely the States were able to attract an investment of this size—far the largest purchase of Holland renten (see Appendices)—because they were able to promise prompt restitution of at least a good part of the capital.

[72]The excise and land tax account for 1566–1567 (SH 2305) records that the Prince of Orange received 10,000 as a "propyne" (gratuity), and there is mention of a further 20,000. When this account was audited (as was usual) a year or so after it was submitted by the receiver, political circumstances in the Netherlands were such that the auditors "for certain reasons" refused to allow this expenditure on behalf of William of Orange, now in exile in Germany. RSH 27 January 1566: the prince refused to accept so large a gift, saying the money could better be employed for the needs of the province; it was decided to give him the 10,000 and use the rest to redeem renten. Gifts to a new Stadtholder were common practice, but the States had never previously offered so much money at once; Hoogstraten, Stadtholder from 1522 until 1540, received 30,000, but spread out over three years (AJ 7 September 1525). See below, note 82.

[73]See above, chapter 2, table 4, and note 114. According to ordinaris bede accounts in the 1540s (e.g., GRK 3442), annual interest charges for renten secured by the beden, and sold from 1515 to 1534, were 22,282, or 66.27 percent, of what would have been owing (see table 4) had no redemptions been made. According to figures from table 1 of the article cited above, note 47, redemptions during the 1520s and 1530s totaled 181,388, against an

For renten issued by the States between 1552 and 1565, redemptions made in the ways just described reduced interest
charges to 59,685 per year (table 8), or 44.51 percent, of what
would have been due each year if no redemptions had been
made (see table 7). Although a province with an annual debt
of 60,000 pounds in interest might be excused for not regarding itself as prosperous, Holland's success in managing its
debt puts it among the relatively few sixteenth-century territories—like Venice and the Papal States—which were able
to shrink their indebtedness. An examination of the provincial
finances of Flanders and Brabant during the same period
would very likely yield similar results.[74]

III. Meanwhile, the central government labored under a
burden of debt that grew steadily larger. As noted in the
previous chapter, Lodewijk van Schore calculated that expenditures for the 1542–1544 war exceeded bede income by a little
over 1,000,000 pounds, a relatively modest sum, given the
circumstances. But by the time Charles V abdicated all his
titles in the waning months of 1555, and his son Philip II
succeeded him, the Netherlands was in a much more difficult
situation. Hopes that the Truce of Vaucelles (April 1556)
might be converted into a lasting peace with France proved
illusory,[75] and the new ruler had to prepare his lands for yet
another grueling campaign the following year. When Philip
presented his requests to the States General in November
1556, deputies were shown a statement listing the government's nonfunded debt at 3,807,000 (a total that roughly corresponds to what was owed to Antwerp bankers during the
last year or so of Charles V's reign).[76] Even though Holland

---

original capital of 538,000, meaning that 356,612, or 66.28 percent, remained
unredeemed.

[74]Verhofstad, 101: already by 1556, the capital value of the outstanding
debt of both Flanders and Brabant exceeded 2,000,000; the comparable figure
for Holland at the same time (adding items 4 through 10 of table 7) would
be 758,776. Aud. 650:232: a proposal for the nine-year bede (November 1557)
states that Brabant, Flanders, and Holland together have an outstanding debt
in excess of 10,000,000.

[75]Verhofstad, 1–19.

[76]Verhofstad, 86; chapter 2, note 49.

and other provinces were raising unprecedented sums through the "novel expedients" and by traditional taxes as well, Philip recognized that the Netherlands—rich and populous, but not marked off from its foes by any defensible frontier—could not be protected solely by its own resources. Great quantities of South American gold were brought from Spain under convoy, of which, according to information given the States, some 10,000,000 pounds was expended for military needs in the Low Countries between 1556 and 1558.[77] Still the government could not keep pace with its obligations to the merchants and bankers whose ready cash kept troops in the field. When the States General convened again in August 1557, the deficit had risen to 7,000,000.[78]

Desperate for further support from the States, Philip reverted in a sense to the plans of 1542, asking the States (March 1556) to accept a 100th penny tax on the value of real property, and a 50th penny on the value of moveable property. When this proposal was rejected, the king and his advisers embraced a political strategy which Mary of Hungary and Margaret of Austria had of set purpose avoided. Hitherto under Habsburg rule, meetings of the States General were convoked only to hear a "general proposition" from the government, while what was asked of each province was discussed only with its deputies (a "particular proposition"), and the nettlesome question of how much one province paid relative to another was avoided altogether.[79] For the States General of 1557, however, Philip resolved to leave it to the deputies of the several provinces, working together, to determine both the means for raising what was needed, and the amount due from each province. After various meetings in

[77]Aud. 650:110–114, "Proposition Generale" for the 19 August 1558 meeting of the States General: ". . . 12 millions de florins [= pounds of 40 groats] sans les frais de change"; Verhofstad, 153, reports from other sources a figure of 10,000,000 spent on the Netherlands. These transfer payments of the 1550s were small by comparison with the estimated 5,000,000 florins per year that Spain would be sending to the Netherlands once the Dutch Revolt began (Geoffrey Parker, "The Development of European Finance," in *Fontana Economic History of Europe*, vol. 2 [New York: 1977]), 582.

[78]RSH 1 September 1557; Verhofstad, 117–118, quotes a figure of 9,000,000.

[79]Grapperhaus, *Alva en de Tiende Penning*, 51–68; Maddens, "De Invoering van de 'Nieuwe Middelen' in Vlaanderen," 348–354.

which deputies from Brabant played the leading role, the States General made a proposal which the King accepted in January 1558: (1) the States General would raise at once a bede of 2,400,000 by selling renten funded separately by each province; (2) the balance of what was needed for campaigns of the coming season, another 2,400,000 would be borrowed on the Antwerp exchange; (3) to pay off this loan, and also to furnish a total of 300,000 per year for troops to be kept on garrison duty, even after the war was concluded, the States agreed to a second bede of 800,000 per year for eight years, beginning with 1559; (4) remaining payment terms for the current ordinaris bede, which began in 1555 and was scheduled to run through 1560, would be abolished; (5) to pay off debts for the sale of old renten and other charges assigned to this ordinaris bede, the States agreed to a further bede of "800,000 once," that is, for one year, to be collected during 1558. In this way, the "eight-year bede" (item 3) became a *novennale*.[80]

For present purposes, the important point about these negotiations is that the States made everything conditional on their being given complete control over collection and disbursement of the funds involved. Each province would levy its portion of the new beden through persons designated by the States (like Holland's receiver for the Common Territory), and these collectors were in turn accountable to a Receiver-General named by the States General.[81] This was the capstone of a process begun in the 1540s, by which tax collectors responsible to the regent and her Council of Finance were displaced by others whose loyalty lay with the provincial States. In Holland, the receiver for the Common Territory had gained control of the "novel expedients" when they were introduced in the 1540s. His accounts were audited by a committee of the States rather than by the prince's Chamber of Accounts in The Hague.[82] By 1553, he was also collecting

[80]Verhofstad, 112–120, 128–148.

[81]Material concerning the nine-year bede is found in Aud. 650:209–214; see also Aud. 650:215–216, commission for Antoon van Stralen, the Receiver-General chosen by the States General.

[82]RSH 6, 10 June, 5 August, 1555: the States obtained permission for the accounts for the excise and land taxes to be audited by members of the States

for extraordinaris beden levied according to the traditional schiltal, which meant that the emperor's receiver for the beden had no "receipt" whatever except for the ordinaris bede.[83] The same trend can be observed in other provinces, and indeed seems to have begun somewhat earlier in Brabant.[84] Finally, the ordinaris bede itself was abolished, at least for a time. Even when the novennale was dropped after only three years (1560) and the ordinaris bede was reinstated, Philip II's tax collector in Holland still had little to do in comparison with his counterpart in the employ of the States. Net receipts of the ordinaris bede at this time amounted to about 50,000 pounds, while the receiver for the Common Territory collected roughly 100,000 per year for excise and

---

deputed ("gecommideerden") for that purpose, plus one auditor from the emperor's Chamber of Accounts in The Hague. Unlike ordinaris bede accounts, which were heard in the office of the Chamber of Accounts (see GRK 3451, "ten burele") by one or more auditors, these accounts were heard in the Dominican cloister in The Hague (SH 2295). Accounts for all extraordinaris beden collected by the Receiver for the Common Territory were heard in the same manner as those for the excise and land taxes. In addition, the Receiver for the Common Territory sometimes received instructions from the States that were not meant to come to the attention of the one or two auditors from the Chamber of Accounts who sat on the auditing commissions to which he was accountable. RSH 13 December 1555, the Receiver was ordered to use excise and land tax receipts to pay off an obligatie, or bond, which the States had given to bankers in Antwerp; receipts for the bede by which this bond was secured were not coming in fast enough to make the payment on time. The receiver doubtless did as he was told, but there is no entry for such an expense in the excise and land tax accounts. RSH 5 May 1557, the receiver was explicitly instructed to account separately to the States (thus not to any member of the Chamber of Accounts) for certain "gratuities" paid to the president of the Council of State (Viglius) and other high officials in Brussels; no such payments appear in the excise or land tax accounts, all of which are extant for this period.

[83]Above, notes 45, 51, 61. When the States consented to an extraordinaris bede of 200,000 falling due in April and October 1552, the 100,000 collected according to the schiltal was collected by the receiver for the beden (GRK 3452), while 100,000 coming from a hearth tax and a sale of renten was collected by the Receiver for the Common Territory (SH 2277). But for a 300,000 extraordinaris bede the following year the latter official collected the schiltal portion as well as what came from a morgental and a 10th penny on renten and real property; henceforth the only accounts in GRK are for ordinaris beden.

[84]Verhofstad, 159.

land taxes, plus all proceeds from the sale of renten and 10th pennies.[85] Historically, sums collected by the receiver for the Common Territory, and thus technically at the disposition of the States, had never been more than a fraction of the bede income that was at the disposal of the prince and his officials. During the 1560s, this relationship was clearly reversed.[86]

These changes are reflected in the character of discussions within the States of Holland, as recorded in the official journal kept by successive Advocates of the States,[87] and in the still-extant travel diaries of two of Amsterdam's paid officials.[88] In one respect these documents suggest a decline in the level of political debate in Holland during the course of Charles V's reign. Sources for the 1520s and 1530s have the appearance of being written by statesmen, those for the 1540s and 1550s by mere bureaucrats. Discussions from the earlier period are sometimes enlivened by a well-articulated conception of the common good of the province, in contradistinction to both the private good of individual cities and the alleged general good of all the Netherlands provinces. As time goes on, however, the pages of the *Resolutiën van de Staten van Holland* are filled more and more with special pleading, from deputies who think they were not properly reimbursed for their travel costs, or from villages seeking a change in their quota for the provincial morgental. Yet from another point of view, this very process, in which the precious coin of political ideas is driven out by a multitude of petty interests, is a sign of

---

[85]Compare (for example) GRK 3457, the ordinaris bede account for two terms falling due Christmas 1560 and St. John's day 1561, with SH 2299, the excise and land tax account for 1 May 1560–30 April 1561. Subtracting for gratiën, interest on renten sold prior to 1534, and collection costs, the net disposable income from a 100,000 bede was 48,997. Meanwhile, the land tax (which like the ordinaris bede was now collected according to the schiltal) alone resulted in an income entry of 48,391, and the excise brought in somewhat more. From the standpoint of the central government, it was not even worth having a separate receiver for the beden; beginning in 1560, Aert Coebel, who had served for some years as Receiver for the Common Territory, was also named receiver for the beden.

[86]See figure H of the article cited above, note 47.

[87]Volume 1 of RSH was compiled by Aert van der Goes, Advocate of the States of Holland from 1524 until his death in 1543; volumes 2–6 were compiled by his son and successor, Adriaan van der Goes.

[88]AJ (1522–1538) and Sandelijn (1548–1564).

institutional maturity. It betokens the fact that the States were more and more replacing the central government as the principal collector and disburser of tax receipts.

After the nine-year bede had been in force only two years, the government decided to scrap it and return to the old system, whereby an ordinaris bede could be expected annually from each of the hereditary provinces.[89] Since the provinces were straining their resources to pay back the huge renten debt accumulated during the last war, additional extraordinaris beden for the central government, although theoretically possible, were not easily obtained.[90] Moreover, the disposable portion of the ordinaris bede in Holland—that is, the portion not lost to the government through gratiën or through interest payments still being made on old renten (1515–1534) secured by the bede—was only about half as much as the provincial States collected each year through provincial excise and land taxes[91] which, as noted above, were more than sufficient to pay interest on the new renten (1552–1564). The States were in a position to use their surplus income to offer gratuities for special favors by high officials in Brussels, making sure the payments were handled in such a way as to prevent the King's auditors from finding out.[92] Meanwhile, the central government could not even pay the regular salaries of its most important local officials; the Council of Holland, whose wages were assigned to domain receipts from the revenue district (North Holland) in which The Hague was located, went nearly three years without receiving a groat.[93] Thus while Holland and, presumably, other provinces improved their creditworthiness in the minds of potential investors by making timely payments on their debt, even

[89]The ordinaris bede in Holland resumed with the Christmas term, 1560, GRK 3457.

[90]After 1560, there was no extraordinaris bede in Holland until 100,000 was raised through a sale of renten in 1565 (SH 2289).

[91]See above, note 85.

[92]See above, note 82.

[93]Cornelis Suys, president of the Council of Holland after the death of Assendelft, to Viglius, 12 May 1563 (Aud. 1417:11): ". . . conqueruntur [Suys's fellow councilors] non solvi stipendia annua, quae iam nobis pro toto biennio debentur tertio quoque anno . . . pene affluxo." For the revenue to which these salaries were assigned, Aud. 867:116–123.

reducing the principal appreciably, the government of the new regent, Margaret of Parma, was more and more dependent on the mercies of financiers who had been burned by its partial repudiation of short-term debt in 1557.[94] As Verhofstad rightly points out, there was in the Netherlands a genuine fiscal crisis that preceded, and does much to explain, the political crisis which Margaret of Parma faced in the 1560s.[95]

Verhofstad's carefully detailed argument did not have quite the scholarly impact one might expect, probably because it ran counter to the dominant tendency of traditional Netherlands historiography. In the 1930s, when Verhofstad wrote, it was common for scholars to interpret domestic political conflicts of the sixteenth century in light of what has been called the "new monarchy thesis," which portrayed the prince as representing the true interests of the nation, while parliamentary bodies, dominated by their privileged orders, fought a rearguard action in defense of more selfish concerns. For the Low Countries, the two volumes of Henri Pirenne's *Histoire de Belgique* devoted to the Burgundian and Habsburg periods are a brilliant illustration of this interpretative genre.[96] But Dutch historians were (and occasionally still are) exponents of a patriotic myth, in which brave Protestant burghers who challenged the power of the Spanish tyrant were seen as heirs to a freedom-loving tradition distinctive to the northern Netherlands.[97] Verhofstad was professor of history at the new (1922) Catholic university of Nijmegen, and thus im-

[94]A potentially important document for this question, which to my knowledge no one has used, is the account drawn up by Melchior Schetz (son of the founder of one of Antwerp's greatest merchant-banking houses) for the period (1555–1558) when he served as factor or financial broker for the government in Antwerp: Stadsarchief Antwerp, see "Inventaris van de Tresorij," 60.

[95]Verhofstad, 51–56.

[96]Pirenne, *Histoire de Belgique* (7 vols., Brussels: 1902–1932), vols. 2, 3; A. J. Slavin, ed., *The New Monarchies* (New York: 1959).

[97]For Netherlands historiography of the Revolt, see J. M. Romein, "Spieghel Historiael: De geschiedschrijving van de Tachtigjarige oorlog," *Tijdschrift voor Geschiedenis* 56 (1941): 225–257, and Pieter Geyl, "The National State and the Writers of Netherlands History," in his *Debates with Historians* (The Hague: 1955), 179–197.

plicitly a spokesman for the Netherlands' large but historically underprivileged Catholic minority; it was natural for a scholar of his background to view with a certain skepticism patriotic conceptions nurtured among the dominant Protestant majority. The deputies to the States General of 1558 he saw not as statesmen defending the public interest against an alien tyranny but as men of wealth determined to shield their constituents' riches from the tax collector's ken, even if it meant imperiling in time of war the common welfare of the Netherlands, as it was rightly understood by the central government.[98]

But if Verhofstad's description of the government's fiscal predicament and its significance for the coming Revolt remains valid, he nonetheless neglects the other side of the coin, that is, the growing fiscal strength of provinces that would soon be competing against their erstwhile sovereign in the credit markets as well as on the field of battle. Similarly, while there is no denying that protecting the interests of property was a high priority for the men who represented Holland's town oligarchies in various deliberative assemblies, the full story also requires some admixture of the patriotic version of Dutch history. Deputies who represented individual towns in the States of Holland were capable of rising to a vision of the common good which embraced the province as a whole,[99] and there were areas—for example, taxation of

[98]Verhofstad, 64–65, 74–75, 102–105, 125–129, 171–176; for Dutch Catholicism and its transformations, P. Brachin, L. J. Rogier, *Histoire du Catholicisme Hollandais depuis le XVIIe Siècle* (Paris: 1974); J. M. J. Thurlings, *De Wankele Zuil* (Nijmegen: 1971).

[99]On matters that threatened Amsterdam's position as an entrepôt for Baltic merchants, like the 100th penny of 1543 or the export tax on grain, government officials were surprised to find Amsterdam's views supported by a cloth town like Leiden (AJ 11 February 1530: the men of Leiden pointed out that, if Easterlings went to London in place of Amsterdam, they would bring home cloths from England, not Holland) and by the nobles (Mary of Hungary to Assendelft, 11 March 1544, Aud. 1646:3). Cf. Andries Jacobszoon's complaints that agreements by the States could be broken down when government commissioners met with deputies from each city individually: this "hearing apart" he called "auricular confession," while the favors dispensed to cooperative towns were "holy water" (AJ 5 March 1530, 28 March 1531). It would appear the government's interest did indeed lie in exploiting the traditional jealousies of Holland's towns, rather than in fostering among them a common sense of purpose.

the grain trade—in which what may have been good for the Netherlands as a whole was clearly contrary to the well-being of Holland.[100] The great Revolt which began in 1572 was, among other things, a contest between rival conceptions of the common good. Holland, which had ranked a poor third in wealth and influence among the seventeen Habsburg provinces, immediately assumed a dominant role among the seven northern provinces as they entered upon a struggle against their former sovereign that would last, intermittently, until the Peace of Westphalia in 1648. There will be occasion for comment later (chapter 6) on the continuity of fiscal institutions in Holland, from the Habsburg era to the republican period. For the present, it has been shown in this chapter that Holland established, by the 1550s, a pattern of debt management that demonstrated to wealthy individuals within Holland and also in neighboring northern provinces that renten backed by the States of Holland were worthy of trust. But even a carefully managed public debt is not capable of expansion unless investors are found willing to entrust their funds to state securities voluntarily. In the next chapter it will be shown how investor confidence of this kind, previously lacking among wealthy Hollanders as regards provincial renten, was also created during the 1550s.

[100]On this dispute, see Tracy, "Habsburg Grain Policy and Amsterdam Politics."

IV

The Emergence of a Free Market
for Provincial Renten in Holland

Like the Habsburg monarchy in Spain, the Netherlands government "defaulted" during the great war of the 1550s by compelling bankers to accept a conversion of their loans into long-term obligations at lower rates of interest. For a government to carry out such conversions without losing its credit altogether, it must have instruments of long-term debt that have a reputation for reliability. In fact, despite all the financial difficulties of the Spanish crown, interest on royal juros seems to have been paid without fail, at least during the sixteenth century.[1] Lacking a comprehen-

[1] There is at least no mention of any default or suspension of payments during the sixteenth century in the literature on the juros cited in chapter 1, note 41.

sive study of the question, one hesitates to make the same claim for all the various kinds of rentes secured by revenues of the central government in the Netherlands, whether based on domain income or on provincial subsidies.[2] In the case of Holland, there were, prior to the Revolt, no suspensions of payment on any of the renten issued by the States, either for the first series, secured by the beden, or for the second series, secured by the provincial excise and land taxes. Temporary shortages in revenue seem to have been handled by paying "foreigners" first,[3] and asking residents of Holland to be patient for a few months. This record of fiscal probity in sixteenth-century Spain and the Netherlands contrasts strikingly with the eventual failure of the rentes sur l'hôtel de ville which the French monarchy was issuing during roughly the same period; these instruments enjoyed a certain vogue among wealthy subjects of the crown during the 1550s, but by the 1570s interest payments were irregular, and thereafter new rentes were sold mainly to the king's creditors and at a 50 percent discount. Meanwhile, on the secondary market, these rentes traded at a fraction of their face value, like shares of forced-loan debt in Italian city-states such as Florence and Venice. The French monarchy, like the Italian republics, relied on coercion for obtaining its funds; wealthy bourgeois were protected from forced buying of rentes by the *parlement* of Paris as late as 1554, but Henri II's subsequent conversion of banker's loans into rentes apparently opened the way for a more general policy of constraint. By the time France's civil wars began in 1562, the distinction between rentes sold on the open market and forced loans occasionally imposed on

<hr>

[2]A list of rentes on domain revenues could be put together from the appropriate items under "dépenses" for each collection district in the 1559 summary of domain finances edited by Michel Baelde, *De Domeingoederen van de Vorst in de Nederlanden omstreeks het midden van de zestiende eeuw (1551–1559)* (Brussels: 1971); see also 352–365.

[3]RSH 30 July 1544: for renten interest falling due at Christmas, Vrank van der Hove, Receiver for the Common Territory, was instructed to pay "outlanders" first, to avoid arrests on Hollanders' goods. Hoogstraten once floated the idea of delaying interest payments, but the Council of Holland opposed it, and sent Willem Goudt, receiver for the beden, to discuss the matter with the "lords of finance" in Brussels: Assendelft to Hoogstraten, 11 July 1536 (Aud. 1530).

the wealthy inhabitants of major towns had become purely theoretical.[4]

Compulsory investment in the public debt and irregular payment of interest would appear to have a more than incidental connection. A government which, in effect, taxes its subjects by making them allocate a fraction of their wealth to its needs can easily enough tax them again by withholding the interest in a given year, without itself suffering any ill effects. Conversely, where governments are scrupulous about meeting annual payments, as they seem to have been in Spain, the Netherlands, and (later) the Papal States, it is because they are conscious of being dependent for their future credit needs on the voluntary cooperation of investors. In Spain there are at least no references to forced buying in any of the literature on royal juros.[5] For the Netherlands no general conclusion will be possible until each of the major provinces has been studied separately. In keeping with the limited focus of this study, discussion in this chapter will be limited to characteristics of the market for renten issued by the States of Holland. It will be useful to look first at the market outside the boundaries of the province, where the States of Holland obviously had no authority to coerce anyone to buy (I). Within Holland, it will be seen that most of the funds that were obtained came from individuals and corporate entities that were obliged to invest, not only during the period when renten were secured by the ordinaris bede but as late as 1552 (II). Beginning in 1553, however, the domestic market was deliberately freed from constraint and, allowance being made for the fact that Holland was less wealthy, quickly came to resemble "foreign" markets in Flanders and Brabant (III).

I. As noted in chapter 1, towns in the Netherlands went looking for foreign buyers as soon as they began issuing renten to raise capital.[6] In the southern part of Holland, towns like Delft and Gouda were accustomed to place some of their renten in Bruges, the commercial and financial center of

[4]Chapter 1, note 3.
[5]Chapter 1, note 41.
[6]Chapter 1, note 113.

nearby Flanders, and in some of the smaller cities along the Flemish coast,[7] a region that provided both a market for Holland beer and a granary for the barley it required.[8] When the States of Holland began issuing provincial renten, it was natural for Willem Goudt, the emperor's receiver for the beden, to follow the path that had been blazed by the city treasurers of Delft and Gouda.[9] After all, as one deputy remarked, there were more "renteniers in [Bruges] than in all of the six cities" of Holland combined. Bruges was indeed much larger than any of the Holland towns, but its perceived preeminence as a market for renten rested not merely on size and wealth but also on the fact that techniques of public and commercial borrowing were much more advanced here than in Holland.[10] In any event the debtor-creditor relationship between Holland and Flanders was accompanied by considerable ill will on the part of the debtors. If Holland fought several wars against Lübeck to establish and maintain its Baltic trade, Bruges, the traditional Netherlands "staple" for the Hanseatic League, was at the very least a welcome haven for Lübeck merchants.[11] If Holland insisted on free export of the Baltic grain brought in via Amsterdam, leading political figures associated with Flanders and Artois demanded governmental

[7]GVR 23 October 1523; AJ 1–6 December 1527.

[8]GVR 20 February 1509, 4 July, 4 November, 1524, 9 April 1537; RSH 5 May, 28 November 1530, 6 November 1531; cf. Aud. 1441:3, no. 6, an undated memo (1536?) complaining that Flemish "brewing grain" dealers were withholding their stocks from market.

[9]GVR 9 November 1522; AJ 9 October 1523: it was understood in the States that Gouda and Delft were the cities at risk when Holland renten were placed in Flanders, presumably because shipments of their beer, or of brewing grain destined for their industries, were the Holland assets most easily seized in Flanders.

[10]AJ 29 December 1523: the city actually named is Ghent, where no Holland renten were sold, which suggests that an Amsterdammer's concept of "Flanders" may have been rather vague.

[11]Flemings were suspected, and not only in the States of Holland, of abetting Lübeck in its intermittent conflicts with Holland shipping in the Baltic: AJ 31 December 1531, 29 June 1535, 11 April 1536; RSH 29 May, 13 July, 2 August, 1533, 7 April 1536; cf. a minute of a meeting of the Council of State, [June] 1533, and Council of Holland to Hoogstraten, 4 November 1533 (Aud. 1446:2b). In general, see Rudolf Häpke, *Die Regierung Karls V und der Europäische Norden* (Lübeck: 1914).

controls in the interest of the more populous southern provinces.[12] The English wool for Leiden's cloth industry, purchased at Calais, was often held up by toll disputes at
Gravelines (Grevelingen) in Flanders,[13] while Holland beer
exporters complained of new exactions on "foreign" beer
along the Flemish coast,[14] and Holland's herring fishermen
feuded with their Flemish counterparts about such issues as
the opening date of the annual sailing season, and how best
to protect the fleet.[15] As one Hollander commented when
Flemish deputies failed to appear for a meeting on fisheries
disputes, "Thanks be to God, for they are always against
us."[16] More pertinent to renten, past experience gave the
States of Holland reason to expect that Flemish renteniers
would unleash the full power of the law against any Holland
merchants who chanced within their grasp whenever interest
payments were not made in timely fashion.[17]

It was doubtless for this reason that those responsible for
placing Holland renten made a conscious effort not to become
too dependent on Flemish markets. Notices of sale were on
an average posted in Bruges for every other issue, not for
every issue.[18] Alternative foreign markets were also sought.

[12]Meilink, "Rapporten en Betoogen nopens het Congiegeld op Granen"·
AJ 12 January 1527, 7 January 1536. See also below, note 13.

[13]During the last two decades of the fifteenth century, Leiden had become
indebted to the tollmaster of Gravelines: N. W. Posthumus, *Geschiedenis van
de Leidsche Lakenindustrie*, I, 197–199. A remonstrance of Holland cities against
a grain-export ban dated in Bruges 12 May 1532 (Aud. 1441:3, no. 5) mentions
that grain owned by Hollanders was being held up at Gravelines.

[14]GVR 9 April 1537.

[15]Council of Holland to Mary of Hungary, 30 May 1533 (Aud. 1446:2b).
Another cause of dispute between fishermen of the two provinces was that
while Hollanders preferred to deal with threats of piracy by letting herring
busses sail "at their own risk" (GVR 28 June 1524; AJ 8, 25 June 1524),
Flanders had a history of convoy service for its herring fleet: Rogier De Gryse,
"De Gemeenschappelijke Groote Visscherij van de Nederlanden in de XVIe
Eeuw," *Bijdragen voor de Geschiedenis van de Nederlanden* 7 (1952): 32–54, and
"De Konvooieering van de Vlaamse Vissersvloot in de 15e en 16e Eeuwen,"
Bijdragen voor de Geschiedenis van de Nederlanden 2 (1948): 1–24.

[16]AJ 14 February 1524.

[17]See chapter 2, note 100.

[18]Of twelve Holland renten issues secured by the bede (items A and C
through M in table 4), sales were made in Bruges or other Flemish towns for
items E, F, G, J, K, L, and M (SH 3424, 3432, 3435, 3437).

'S Hertogenbosch, a city in northern Brabant that often made common cause with southern Holland during the Guelders wars, was one possibility, though its wealth could not match that of Bruges.[19] More promising was Mechelen, situated halfway between Antwerp and Brussels but technically not part of the Duchy of Brabant.[20] Mechelen (Malines) was a particularly likely market for public renten of all kinds because of its role as a government center. Since 1504 it had been home to the high court of the Netherlands, the Grand Council and, during the regency of Margaret of Austria (1506–1514, 1519–1530), it temporarily supplanted Brussels as administrative capital of the Netherlands, which meant that the councilors and great lords who frequented the court had residences here.

By long tradition, those who would serve the prince in the Netherlands were expected to place a portion of their wealth at his service. One who did so seemingly without stint was Antoine de Lalaing, lord of Montigny, Count of Hoogstraten by marriage, head of the Council of Finance, chief confidant of Margaret of Austria, and also Stadtholder of Holland from 1522 until his death in 1540. In 1523 Hoogstraten pawned his jewels to raise 16,000 pounds to relieve fortresses in Friesland, which were under attack from Guelders. Ten years later, when the emperor insisted on arming a fleet for action against Denmark, while Holland refused to fund a campaign that might cut off its access to the Baltic, Hoogstraten undertook to find the needed 35,000 on his personal bond or obligation, provided that other members of the Council of State joined him in sharing the risk. Though Hoogstraten evidently received recompense in both of these cases, he complained of coming out the loser in other transactions. Certainly in his case, it would appear that the great families of the Netherlands fell into debt[21] partly through service to the crown, and

[19]During the campaigning season of 1528, two of the four great cities that voted in the States of Brabant, Antwerp and 's Hertogenbosch, agreed to join with Holland in a "Union" to pay for an army that would carry the war to Guelders (the other two great cities of Brabant, Brussels and Leuven, which lay farther south and were thus less exposed to attack from Guelders, refused to participate): RSH 17, 27–29 May, 17 August, 6 September 1528.

[20]Mechelen was treated as a separate province for purposes of the beden (e.g., Aud. 650: 24–25, 33–34).

[21]AJ 2, 20 October, 29, 31 December 1523, 28 January, 10, 14 February, 9

not merely through conspicuous consumption. It was the "great lords" like Hoogstraten—Knights of the Golden Fleece, provincial governors, and members of the Council of State— who set the tone for political life. If they routinely interposed their own wealth between the prince and the chasm of debt that yawned wider as years passed, those at lower levels of the official hierarchy understood very well what was expected of them, even if there was no formal system for the purchase of office.[22]

April, 1524 (it was only after much persuasion that the States of Holland agreed to allocate 16,000 from the income for an 80,000 sale of renten to repay Hoogstraten); the minute of a Council of State meeting, cited above, note 11, accompanied by a letter patent from Charles V outlining terms of security to cover Hoogstraten's obligation for 35,685. For indications that the Stadtholder suffered personal losses in such transactions, Margaret of Austria to Charles V, 5 April 1530 (Lanz, I, 380–384); Hoogstraten to Assendelft, 23 February 1532 (Aud. 1525); GVR 27 August 1534; Assendelft to Hoogstraten, 28 January 1537 (Aud. 1523). On noble indebtedness, see chapter 2, note 44; on the great families of the Netherlands, Paul Rosenfeld, "The Provincial Governors from the Minority of Charles V to the Revolt," *Standen en Landen: Anciens Pays et Assemblées d'Etat* XVII (Leuven: 1959): 1–63.

[22]The County of Holland had 105 judicial officers (schouten, or sheriffs, for the cities, *baljuwen*, or bailiffs, for rural districts) responsible for local posting of government ordinances, or *plakkaten:* Council of Holland to Mary of Hungary, 15 January 1552 (Aud. 1646:2). With rare exceptions (see the article cited in chapter 2, note 41), they were appointed by the Stadtholder, upon recommendation of the Council of Holland, on the basis of a three-year *pacht,* or farm-contract. One who offered the government a higher annual sum but was bidding against a reliable incumbent did not necessarily get the post: Assendelft to Hoogstraten, 26 October 1536 (Aud. 1530). On the organization of the Hof van Holland in The Hague, see the introduction to Blécourt; annual salaries for its major officials in the 1550s are given under expenditures on domain receipts for the district of North Holland in Baelde, *De Domeingoederen van de Vorst in de Nederlanden,* 272–273. The judicial section of the Hof (that is, excluding the Chamber of Accounts, with its five masters of accounts and two auditors and their subordinate personnel) included the Council of Holland, with a president or First Councilor and seven other salaried Councilors Ordinary, a Procurator-General (representing the emperor) and his Substitute, a Receiver of Fines and Confiscations, a legal maximum of eight Secretaries Ordinary, sixteen Procurators, twenty bailiffs, or *deurwarders,* and thirty messengers: note by Jan de Jonge, Griffier (scribe) of the Hof, 28 September 1535 (Aud. 1532). In addition, there were non-salaried officials, living on fees from special commissions but eager to move up a notch to salaried posts—the Councilors Extraordinary (see Assendelft

It is not surprising, then, that many of the largest purchasers of Holland renten were found in Mechelen, and particularly at Margaret of Austria's court. (Here, and in subsequent discussions, "total purchase" means the sum of all purchases by the same individual or corporation; since some redemptions were made, the amount a given buyer had tied up in renten at any one time would normally be less than his total purchase.) Hoogstraten himself led the way with a total purchase of 40,806 pounds, including two single purchases of 8,000.[23] Four other persons associated with the court made purchases totaling 37,408, including the Marquise of Aerschot; Jean Micaut, Receiver-General for All Finances; and Count Wilhelm von Rennenberg, a Rhenish nobleman who made his purchase a few months after the States of Holland induced Hoogstraten to accept him as commander of forces in Holland during the 1528 Guelders campaign[24] (see Appen-

---

to Lodewijk van Schore, 19 March 1543, Aud. 1646:3) and the Secretaries Extraordinary—while the Procurators were nudged from below by a group of Procurator-Postulants (Council of Holland to Mary of Hungary, 11 June 1548, Aud. 1646:2). Thus Charles V as Count of Holland had roughly a hundred officials scattered through the various localities, and perhaps two hundred more at the Hof van Holland. Officials sometimes tried to resign their posts in favor of designated successors, but Assendelft thought this practice was contrary to "the honor of the Emperor," even though it would have been profitable: to Hoogstraten, 6 May 1533 (Aud. 1446:2b), and to Schore, 19 March 1543 (Aud. 1646:3).

[23]Hoogstraten invested 1,600 for item A of table 4 (SH 3418), 8,000 for item E (SH 3424), 4,665 for item I (SH 3432), and 4,320 and 4,488 for item L (SH 3435), for a total of 23,073 in renten issued by the five cities acting jointly; in addition, he made purchases of 6,400 for item A (ASR 1535, 1554), 3,333 for item I (ASR 1554), and a further 8,000, unspecified as to issue (RSH 9 October 1530, cf. AJ 2 October 1530), in Holland renten issued by Amsterdam under its own seal. The last reference (8,000) is doubtless to item D or L, since Receiver-General Jean Ruffault was the buyer on the only other occasion when Amsterdam sold 8,000 (item B: see below, note 24).

[24]"Vrouwe Marie van Hamale, Margravinne van Aerschot," 13,008 in behalf of the convent of the Annuncianten in Leuven, item L (SH 3435); Count Wilhelm von Rennenberg, 10,000, item I (SH 3432); on Rennenberg, see Leo Peters, *Wilhelm von Rennenberg, ein Rheinischer Edelherr zwischen den konfessionelen Fronten* (Kempen: 1979); cf. Ter Gouw, IV, 72–85, and AJ 23–25 September 1527, 22–23 March, 14–17 April, and 12 October, 1528: unable to force the States to accept the commander of his choice, Hoogstraten reluctantly agreed

dix I*a*). It may be noted that Hoogstraten on two occasions, and Micaut on one other, bought up the entire quota (8,000 pounds) of Holland renten issued by Amsterdam under its own seal;[25] if men of such rank were expected to put their money to good use, nothing prevented them from using their expert knowledge to make the soundest investments possible. Buyers could also be found among government officials at a lower level. Apart from what was sold to persons connected with the court, another 12,932 pounds' worth was placed in Mechelen, of which roughly half (6,432) was bought by members of the Grand Council or their heirs.[26]

Even so, Mechelen and the court together did not surpass Bruges as a market for Holland renten during the 1520s, as may be seen from the first column of table 10.[27]

If Bruges was the paramount market while Holland renten were secured by the bede (column 1), there was a dramatic change when renten were funded by the provincial excise and land taxes (columns 2, 3), especially during the 1550s (column 3). To be sure, there were also some continuities. The Habsburg court, relocated in Brussels under Mary of Hungary, continued to be important, even though there was no other stadtholder who invested nearly so much in Holland

---

to Rennenberg's appointment); GRK 3430 mentions that the 500-pound rente (capital 8,000) sold by Amsterdam in 1522 (item B) had been bought by Micaut; "Jacques de Marseilles, Voorsuyer van de keizerlijke Majesteit," 6,400, item K (GRK 3435).

[25]Above, notes 23, 24.

[26]Leading purchasers were two men identified in the accounts as members of the Grand Council, Meester Jan van Amerongen and Meester Jan Rousseau, and the heirs of a deceased member, Jerome Busleiden (GRK 3418, 1,600 each).

[27]The 64,000 purchase by Duke Erich von Braunschweig-Kalenberg (chapter 3, note 71) is included here under "Brussels" rather than "the court," since he held no office. For present purposes, the court includes officials connected with the provincial administration of Brabant, also located in Brussels, as well as officials of the central government. Leading purchasers of renten at the court include Lodewijk van Vlaanderen, lord of Praet, member of the Council of State and (1544–1555) Stadtholder of Holland, 12,000 (SH 2282); Meester Philips Lang van Wellenbach, Secretary of the Camere van Brabant, 7,800 (SH 2280, 2281); and Meester Joest Ban, Keeper of the Great Seal, 6,400 (SH 2348): see Appendix II*a*.

TABLE 10

"FOREIGN" MARKETS FOR HOLLAND RENTEN, 1515–1565
(in Holland pounds)

	(1) Issues A–N	(2) Issues 1–4	(3) Issues 5–17*	(4) Issues 1–17
Court	78,214	0	54,468	54,468
Bruges	94,053	10,018	0	10,018
Flanders	15,516	5,074	0	5,074
Mechelen	12,932	21,326	160,092	181,418
Ten Bosch	15,448	0	15,116	15,116
Brussels	6,000	0	106,386	106,386
Antwerp	0	2,400	91,018	93,418
Brabant	0	0	26,900	26,900
Middelburg	0	9,268	193,909	203,127
Zierikzee	0	0	152,315	152,315
Utrecht	0	1,452	44,076	45,528
Other	4,960	0	33,151	33,151
Totals	227,113	49,538	877,431	926,969

Note: Ten Bosch = 's Hertogenbosch.
Flanders = Flemish towns other than Bruges.
Brabant = Brabant towns other than Antwerp, Brussels.
*See note 27.

renten as Hoogstraten had done.[28] Burghers of Brussels seem to have picked up the habit of investing in state securities from the many government officials now domiciled among them, much as Bennassar has suggested for Valladolid during

[28]The totals in column 3 for "Antwerp" and "Other" include two large sales mentioned in RSH, but not recorded in the appropriate accounts: 12,000 to the Antwerp merchant-banker Arent van Daele, RSH 10 March 1558 (see also SH 2286, 2347), and 18,000 to Diderik Heer van der Lippe, Heer van Blyen-

the period when it was administrative capital of Castile.[29] The same might be said for Mechelen, which blossomed as a major source of demand for Holland renten in the 1550s. Personnel of the Grand Council and advocates accredited to plead before it were likely buyers, as their predecessors had been already in the 1520s, but the city itself now boasted veritable dynasties of investors, like the widow and three daughters of one Joest Snellincx (purchaser of a large Holland rente in Bruges in his own lifetime), who between them entrusted 7,920 to the States of Holland.[30]

Unlike Brussels and Mechelen, where Holland renten were sold in the 1520s, Antwerp, their neighbor to the north, was approached for the first time in 1552, and then only for two purchases of 1,200 each. Accounts for subsequent sales give the impression that agents of the States, on their circuit of potential markets, seem to have called at Antwerp for almost every issue, but never accepted more than a few purchases, though often for large amounts.[31] Such behavior may seem odd, since Antwerp was of course Europe's greatest capital market. Yet the very magnitude of Antwerp's "great purses" was intimidating to merchants who, like the Hollanders, operated on a far smaller scale and with less sophisticated techniques. Amsterdam's grain dealers had good reason to be nervous about the growing prominence of Antwerp firms in the Baltic trade,[32] and the States were probably wary of

---

beek, RSH 2 November 1564 (this rente had been purchased at 1 : 12, at a date not given, and was now being converted to 1 : 16, but there is no such entry in the accounts for sales of losrenten at 1 : 12, SH 2277–2287 and 2347).

[29]Bennassar, *Valladolid au Siècle d'Or*, 250–259.

[30]Joest Snellincx and his wife, Anna Verleyen (no domicile given, but listed after four buyers from Bruges), purchased a large Holland rente in 1533 (item M, GRK 3437). In Mechelen, "Anna Verleyen, widow of Joest Snellincx," made two purchases of 1,200 each in 1552 and 1553 (SH 2277, 2278); in subsequent years purchases were made by "Cathalina Snellincx Joestendochter" (1,800, SH 2347), "Clara Snellincx Joestendochter" (1,800, SH 2286, 2347, 2348), and "Johanna Snellincx Joestendochter" (1,920, SH 2286, 2347).

[31]SH 2277, two buyers for a total of 2,400; SH 2278, two for 2,400; SH 2279, three for 2,100; SH 2280, six for 8,862; SH 2281, eight for 15,516 at 1 : 12, four for 1,380 at 1 : 6; SH 2286, three for 19,000; SH 2287, two for 10,300; SH 2347, nine for 10,860; SH 2348, one for 2,000.

[32]See the article cited in chapter 2, note 41.

becoming too dependent on Antwerp capital. At the same time, the convenience of dealing with a few buyers instead of many could hardly be overlooked, as is evident in the case of the van Daele family, one of Antwerp's premier banking houses. When merchant-banker Arent van Daele purchased a large Holland rente on the secondary market (1557), the States took the unusual step of requiring sworn statements as to how the price was paid before authorizing payment of interest to the new owner. Within a few months, however, the receiver for the Common Territory was instructed to sell van Daele a new rente for 12,000, and also to inquire whether he knew of other persons willing to buy at a "notable" (*merckelyke*) price. His daughter, Lady Josyna, whose husband was Receiver-General for All Finances, then purchased a rente for 18,000. Some months later, when it was discovered that some 10,000 was still lacking for an extraordinaris bede to be raised through the sale of renten, the needed sum was found by approaching Lady Josyna's brother, Meester Pieter van Daele, dean of Aalst and canon of Our Lady church in Antwerp.[33]

The most striking change shown in column 3 of table 10 is the emergence of two cities in Zeeland—Middelburg and Zierikzee—as major markets for Holland annuities. The province of Zeeland, a group of islands astride the Maas estuary, shared a common history with Holland, lying just to the north and west, and had similar economic interests. Goods coming from Holland and bound for southwestern France or Iberia were typically shipped by way of Middelburg.[34] Though

[33]RSH 19 August, 29 September, 7, 25 October, 1557, 10 March 1558 (Arent van Daele); SH 2286 (Lady Josyna, wife of Gerard Sterk, Receiver-General); SH 2287 (Meester Pieter van Daele). For details on family relationships, I am indebted to a communication from G. De Gueldre, adjunct-bibliothecaris of the Antwerp Stadsarchief.

[34]For example, the trade in Haarlem cloths to Iberia was routed by way of Zeeland. In the 1520s the city subsidized exports to Spain through an arrangement apparently worked out between burgomaster Frans De Wet and his son-in-law, Gregorio de Ayala, a Spanish merchant based in Middelburg (HTR 1520–1521–1527–1528, under miscellaneous expenditures). Cf. CC 23358, 735–764, accounts for the 100th penny tax on exports from Middelburg (10 August–1 November 1543) and Arnemuiden (18 July 1543–10 February 1544: Arnemuiden was the small Zeeland port through which goods from

Zeeland had its own provincial States and fiscal institutions,[35] long association of the two counties under successive medieval dynasties was reflected in the fact that the Council of Holland in The Hague served as a court of appeal for lesser jurisdictions in Zeeland as well; according to a privilege granted by Mary of Burgundy in 1477, the council was always to have among its members two men from the island province, who presumably resided in Zeeland and attended to its affairs.[36] It was apparently by way of this administrative connection that the habit of investing in Holland renten was transmitted to Zeeland. One of those representing Zeeland on the council during the 1520s was Meester Jasper Lievenszoon van Hoogelande, who, like his colleagues, was a notable buyer of provincial renten (1,164). Of two brothers accredited to plead before the council as advocates, Meester Balthasar van Hoogelande invested 1,500, and Meester Eewout van Hoogelande, 2,016. All three resided in Middelburg.[37] After Meester Eewout's death, his widow, Lady Margriet Jacobsdochter de Connincx, like many officeholder widows,[38] con-

---

Antwerp bound for Iberia were shipped): while the previous section of this account, for exports from Holland, contains no entries whatever for Haarlem, eighteen merchants exported 336 Haarlem cloths from Middelburg, and six others shipped 333 from Arnemuiden, all bound for Spain.

[35]F. H. J. Lemmink, *Het Ontstaan van de Staten van Zeeland en hun Geschiedenis tot 1555* (Rozendaal: 1951); G. Taal, "Het Graafschap Zeeland en zijn Verhouding tot Holland in de landsheerlijke tijd," *Archief van de Zeewsch Genootschap* V (1965): 51–96.

[36]Lemmink, *Het Ontstaan van de Staten*, 132; Taal, "Het Graafschap Zeeland," 79. See Mary of Hungary to the Council of Holland, 4 June 1552 (Aud. 1646:2): the Council was neglecting Zeeland's affairs.

[37]Meester Jaspar made six purchases totaling 1,164 (GRK 3424, 3432); Meester Eewout's 2,016 was invested all at once (GRK 3435), and Meester Balthasar made two purchases for 1,600 (GRK 3424, 3432). For details about family relationships I am indebted to a communication from Drs. R. C. Hol of the Rijksarchief van Zeeland in Middelburg.

[38]See above, note 30. Other official widows in The Hague who invested in Holland renten included "the widow and heirs of Meester Nicholas Coebel" (GRK 3432, 400 pounds; according to the inventory for GRK at the Rijksarchief van Zuid-Holland in The Hague, Meester Nicholas Coebel was collector of domain receipts for the district of South Holland, 1506–1528), and "Juffrouw Dieuwer Cranebrouk, widow of Albrecht van Loo" (GRK 3423, 3432, two purchases totaling 350; Albrecht van Loo preceded Aert van der Goes

tinued her late husband's practice of investing in State securities. In 1533, when the States of Holland needed cash in a hurry to raise a mercenary contingent of 600 men, Lady Margriet was found willing to purchase a rente for 4,800, secured by certain of the emperor's domain revenues in Holland. In the following decade, when the States began issuing the new series of renten funded by the provincial excise and land tax, she made purchases of 2,348 and 800 pounds.[39] Eventually, with six of her kinsfolk, Lady Margriet was to account for purchases of 20,886 between 1542 and 1565.[40] The example set by this family needed only to be followed by a few other persons of comparable standing—like Meester Roelant Pottere, pensionary of the States of Zeeland, who invested 1,200, or Meester Adriaan de Proost, town secretary of Middelburg, who invested 14,400[41]—to acquire a certain momentum among wealthy burghers in Middelburg, Zierikzee, and lesser towns like Veere and Vlissingen (Flushing).[42]

Taken in conjunction with the more modest but equally novel interest in Holland renten in the city and province of Utrecht, Holland's neighbor to the east, Zeeland's avid par-

---

as Advocate of the States of Holland, but was dismissed by the States because he had accepted a position in the Emperor's service: AJ 22 January, 7–8 March, 1523).

[39]RSH 18 March 1533, and Lille B 2386, under "Vendicions des rentes"; SH 2275, 2208.

[40]Additional purchases of 2,352 by Lady Margriet (SH 2277, 2280, the latter counting 432 in Mechelen as well as 1,200 in Middelburg); "Collart Gilliszoon Tsoggaert as *rentmeester* (administrator) for the orphans of Jaspar Eewoutszoon van Hoogelande," 2,106 (SH 2281, 2347); "Lady Johanna Herlin, widow of Jacob Eewouts van Hoogelande," 3,600 (SH 2277); "Lady Marie van Hoogelande, widow of Jacob van Vallydolyt," 7,016 (SH 2280, 2282, 2286, 2347, 2348); "Lady Marie de Vallydolyt," 1,800 (SH 2286); "Cornelis Jacobszoon de Vallydolyt," 648 (SH 2347); and "Jonge Jacob de Vallydolyt," 216 (SH 2347). A communication from R. C. Hol, Rijksarchief van Zeeland, Middelburg, identifies Jacob van Vallydolyt as a merchant and magistrate (much local archival material was destroyed in 1940). The names suggest that Jacob Eewouts was the son of Eewout Lievenszoon van Hoogelande, and Jacob van Vallydolyt may have been a son-in-law of Eewout Lievenszoon, or one of his brothers.

[41]SH 1792, 2278, 2286, 2347, 2348.

[42]Of the total listed under Middelburg in column 3 of table 10, 22,024 was bought by burghers of Veere, 27,756 by burghers of Vlissingen.

ticipation in Holland's money-raising plans has important implications for the long view of Netherlands history. On the one hand, demand for these securities was now evident in enough other places to make it possible for the Hollanders to sever their connection with the renteniers of Bruges; small amounts were sold in Bruges and other Flemish towns in 1542 and 1552, but none after that.[43] There is nothing in the sources about avoiding Flanders, but the previous history of Holland's relationship with the largest and perhaps most influential of its southern neighbors suggests a conscious decision to this effect. On the other hand, Hollanders recognized their close community of interests with regions immediately adjacent to their own—Zeeland, Utrecht, and northern Brabant—and on two occasions expressed the wish to be joined in a "Union" with these areas (and no others) to fight the Guelders wars.[44] No one dreamed in the 1550s that the smaller, less populous northern provinces would one day eclipse their prosperous and sophisticated neighbors to the south. Yet it was at this time, well in advance of events leading to the Dutch Revolt, that Holland began drawing to itself the capital that was available in the northern provinces for state investments.

II. Even at a glance, the accounts for renten sold inside Holland are strikingly different from those for "foreign" buyers. For one thing, the average purchase in Holland was less than one-fifth as large during the 1520s (see table 11).

It should not be thought that table 11 represents the relative wealth of Holland and, say, Flanders or Brabant; for purposes of such comparisons, the ordinaris bede quotas of the various provinces (in the 1520s, 200,000 for Flanders and Brabant, 80,000 for Holland) are doubtless a much better gauge. One circumstance that helps to account for the difference is that investing in State securities was, at the outset of Charles V's reign, evidently less common in the northern provinces. Renten accounts for 1515–1534 give two important indices of a relative lack of interest on the part of individual buyers in

[43]SH 2275, 2277.
[44]RSH 8 July, 23 August, 1534; AJ 29 June 1535.

TABLE 11

(RENTEN A–N ONLY)
RENTEN PURCHASES BY INDIVIDUALS (EXCLUDING
CORPORATE BUYERS), 1515–1534

	Total purchases	Buyers	Average purchase
Outside Holland	227,123	160	1,420
Inside Holland	133,334	532	251

Holland. First, while purchase amounts for Bruges or Mechelen vary almost at random among large numbers that are multiples of sixteen (since the rate was 1 : 16), lists of buyers within Holland are punctuated by series of repetitive numbers, whether it be rural landholders who all make purchases of 100 or 200 pounds (item D), or burghers of Rotterdam who each invest exactly 96 pounds.[45] Second, corporate buyers are rare outside the province, but of great importance within Holland. In the "foreign" category, six religious communities made purchases totaling 7,602, led by the Charterhouse of Cologne with 4,160.[46] Inside Holland, sixty-nine religious corporations, mostly convents and monasteries, purchased a total of 29,370, while town and village governments, each acting in a corporate capacity, accounted for an even larger share of the domestic market.[47] The obvious explanation for both of these circumstances is that individuals and corporate entities within Holland, unlike those outside, could be and were assessed amounts of purchase by the States, in the same way that towns imposed forced loans on their citizens,[48] or

[45]Rotterdam burghers figure in only two renten accounts between 1515 and 1534 (GRK 3424 and 3432).
[46]GRK 3435.
[47]See table 12, column 1, "Towns, villages," and "Cloisters."
[48]Mary of Hungary to the Council of Holland, 6 July 1544, and Council of Holland to Mary of Hungary, 19 July 1544 (Aud. 1646:1): the regent chided the council for authorizing the town of Gorinchem, without her permission, to levy a forced loan on its burghers to pay for its bede quota; the council replied it had always been its practice to authorize an "asiette capitale" to further the beden, without seeking higher approval.

the central government on its subjects.[49] In other words, the accounts confirm what is already known from the record of discussions within the States. Meester Floris Oem van Wijngaerden, a deputy from Dordrecht, put the matter succinctly: Hollanders would not invest in such renten unless they were compelled to, partly because (he asserted) gold at the official rate was undervalued relative to silver, and partly because "people have no confidence of being paid back by the prince or by the province, but (so said he) I should find money enough by means of renten if I wanted to have it."[50]

Since the central government was more than willing to furnish the necessary *octroi*, or permission, to compel inhabitants of Holland to purchase renten, it fell to the States to decide whom to coerce. As often happened the issue turned on the disparity between urban deputies' claim to represent the interests of the province as a whole, and the fact that their constituencies were formed by men of wealth in the six great cities. It was one thing to lay claim in this way to the capital of wealthy peasants, but something else again to subject one of Amsterdam's leading politicians, who was a member of the landowners' board for the drainage district of Amstelland, to the same constraint.[51] The sticking point was not the principle of coercion, but who was to be coerced, and by whom. Gouda, which had no compunction about forcing its burghers to buy renten issued by the city, stoutly protected them from

[49]According to letters exchanged between the Duke of Savoy and Maximiliaan van Bergen, lord of Beveren and Stadtholder of Holland (1555–1560), on 24, 28 February, 3, 8, and (?) March, and 11, 16 April, 1557 (Aud. 321 for the second letter, Aud. 325 for the rest), a forced loan in Holland in 1557 brought in 100,000. For references to another forced loan in 1552, see below, note 67.

[50]AJ 28 January 1524.

[51]AJ 11 March 1523: "Ruysch Janss als heemrade/ mr Jan Hubrechts als scout/Symon Claes Scol als rentmeester van Goylant zyn geconstringeert geweest omme rente te copen by brieven van Willem Goud dair op antwordde gescreven omme tselffe affgedaen te hebben in date den xxven dach aprilis anno 1522 sed nihil profuerunt." On Ruysch Jan Bethszoon, B. J. M. De Bont, "De Onze Lieve Vrouwe of Nieuwe Kerk te Amsterdam," *Bijdragen voor de Geschiedenis van het Bisdom Haarlem* 31 (1908): 215–219. On Meester Jan Hubrechtszoon, Schout (sheriff) of Amsterdam from 1518 to 1534, see Elias, I, 218. On drainage boards (*heemraadschappen*), see chapter 5, note 88.

similar coercion by the States.[52] Amsterdam publicly objected to the principle of constraint, but on one occasion secretly agreed to "find" buyers for a stated amount, in return for a letter from the regent permitting its government to force local cloisters to buy.[53]

In these circumstances, the States followed the line of least resistance, aiming by turns at practically every group of wealth-holders in the province, except for the burghers of the six great cities. In 1523, prosperous villagers were assessed for purchases of (usually) 96 or 100 pounds each.[54] In 1528 towns (including the great cities) were obliged to purchase renten as corporate entities.[55] For the same issue (80,000), cloisters throughout the province were also compelled to make purchases.[56] As may be seen from the first column of table 12, involuntary purchases by rural folk, or wealthy peasants (39,013), towns and villages (48,804), and cloisters (36,629) amount to 124,446, or 57 percent, of the total sold within the province between 1515 and 1534. In addition, some form of pressure, if not coercion, may be assumed for purchases by members of noble families (9,158), whose names are often grouped together in the accounts.

The same is true for personnel of the Hof van Holland in The Hague, consisting of the Council of Holland, the Chamber of Accounts, and all attendant functionaries. Like government officials at a higher level in Brussels or Mechelen, these men were expected to invest a portion of their wealth where it would do the prince some good; advocates who

[52]GVR 10 February 1523, 20 February, 15, 24, 26 March, 1528.

[53]AJ 25 October 1523, 25 January 1524, 31 March 1528.

[54]GRK 3424 (item D, 48,000 capital); cf. AJ 11 March 1523.

[55]GRK 3432 (item F, capital 80,000). There are occasional references to apportioning renten to be sold in Holland "by the schiltal" (GVR 3, 20 February 1524), but this could only have meant that each of the traditional collection districts (Zuid-Holland, Noord-Holland, Rijnland, Kenemerland and Westfriesland, Amstelland, Delfland, and Gouda) was assessed as a whole to purchase a sum equivalent to its bede quota. When renten are purchased by towns and villages as corporate entities, as in this account, the purchase amounts are in no way proportional to their individual ordinaris bede quotas.

[56]GRK 3432 (item F, 80,000 capital), 19,318 purchased by cloisters in Holland.

pleaded before the council, and who were often kinsmen of council members or other officials, were perhaps bound, albeit more loosely, by the same code.[57] For example, members of the council and the Chamber of Accounts were prominent among Hollanders who bought renten on the prince's domain revenues in Holland in the 1520s and 1530s.[58] If there was at times a glimmer of the modern notion of conflict of interest, there was no doubt where the government's real priorities lay. When Mary of Hungary chided council members for their heavy involvement in the emperor's domain income, Assendelft laid the matter to rest by pointing out that he and his colleagues had been invited in no uncertain terms to make just such investments.[59] It is not surprising, then, if the same men and their subalterns figure prominently among purchasers of renten issued by the States. Between 1515 and 1534, the only persons in Holland whose total purchases exceeded 2,000 pounds were the just-mentioned Assendelft, the superiors of two wealthy religious houses, Meester Eewout Lievenszoon van Hoogeland (the advocate whose widow helped popularize Holland renten in Middelburg), and a widow from an office-holding family (see Appendix I*b*).

Keeping still to the first column of table 12, one also finds that purchases by town dwellers were low, save in The Hague.[60] Like Mechelen and Brussels on a smaller scale, Hol-

[57]Ten men named as advocates before the Hof van Holland bought 4,944 in renten between 1515 and 1533, including the two Hoogelande brothers (above, note 37), and Meester Willem Willemszoon van Alkmaar, who became Procurator-General in 1536. See Appendix I*a*, no. 13.

[58]Lille B 2380, 2386, 2392, 2398, 2404, 2418, 2436, under "Vendicions des rentes," total purchases by the following members of the Council of Holland: Andries van der Bronkhorst, 6,491; Lord Gerrit, lord of Assendelft, 4,634; Jan van Duvenvoorde, lord of Warmond, 1,300; Joest Sasbout, 1,610; Meester Geleyn Zeghers, 3,425; Abel Coulster, 330 (for identification of Council members, see Blécourt).

[59]Assendelft to Hoogstraten, 23 January 1540 (Aud. 1532); see Mary of Hungary to Assendelft, 19 November 1539 (Aud. 1528).

[60]Renten issued apart by Amsterdam are not recorded in GRK, which mentions only the lump sum deducted each year from Amsterdam's bede quota to pay current interest. Amsterdam sold renten with a total capital value of 112,266, of which 25,733 came from purchases by Hoogstraten and Micaut (above, notes 23, 24: these purchases are included under "Court" in table 10), leaving 86,573 from unknown investors. If this figure is added to

TABLE 12

DOMESTIC MARKETS FOR HOLLAND RENTEN, 1515–1565

	(1) Issues A–N	(2) Issues 1–4	(3) Issues 5–17	(4) Issues 1–17
Amsterdam	?*	9,835	451,889	461,724
Delft	14,012	10,492	147,915	158,407
Dordrecht	6,910	5,728	95,284	101,012
Gouda	1,560	2,332	82,988	85,320
Haarlem	5,146	4,890	76,182	81,072
Leiden	4,052	3,610	33,428	37,038
The Hague	23,690	12,638	129,082	141,720
Hof van Holl.	14,602	0	63,512	63,512
Rotterdam	5,672	4,528	40,166	44,694
Small cities	9,009	6,644	3,180	9,824
Towns, villages	48,804	59,370	0	59,370
Rural folk	39,013	8,005	0	8,005
Cloisters	36,629	12,676	824	13,500
Nobles	9,158	9,880	0	9,880
Totals	218,257	150,628	1,124,450	1,275,078

*See note 60.

land's administrative capital was unusual in that many of its burghers (physicians, widows of government officials, and so forth) had a precocious taste for investing in state securities

purchases by known investors outside Holland (table 10: 227,113) and inside Holland (table 12: 218,257), the result is 531,953, which is 6,047, or 1.12 percent, short of the official total of 538,000 given in table 4. About a third of this shortage results from the fact that actual sales recorded in each account are slightly more or less than what the States agreed to, with a net deficit for all issues (A–N) of 2,115.

of one kind or another, and did not require coercion.[61] Otherwise, not counting Rotterdam and the other small cities, the five great cities that voted in the States accounted for only 31,680, or 14.52 percent, of the total sold in the province (in contrast, the same cities accounted for 33.97 percent of Holland's wealth as assessed in the 1515 schiltal).[62] There are indications that great cities did occasionally assess their own burghers for purchases; for example, in 1528 nine men and women of Dordrecht bought renten for exactly 48 pounds each.[63] By and large, however, the magistrates who represented these cities in the States seem to have spared their constituents the inconvenience of forced purchase, not only by shifting the burden to other groups, but also by purchasing renten in good quantities themselves, lest it be said their cities were not contributing anything to the cause.

Printed lists of magistrates are available for three of the five cities that joined together to issue renten in the name of the States. On this basis, purchases by individuals can be broken down to show the importance of magistrates (see table 13).

That town officials—occupying the lowest rung of the political hierarchy in the Netherlands—resembled their social betters in showing a certain proclivity to invest in government securities is in itself not surprising. Their names too, along with personnel of the Hof van Holland, may be found among buyers of renten on domain revenues on Holland.[64] That city fathers in Delft seemed particularly willing to invest their

[61]See above, note 38, and Appendix I*b*, no. 2.

[62]Percentages for the great cities' schiltal quota are most easily obtained from an ordinaris bede account for 100,000 pounds (e.g., GRK 3441).

[63]GRK 3432 (item H, capital 16,000); at the same time, renten for 96 pounds were purchased by Jan Drenkwaert, Sheriff of Dordrecht, and the city's Heylige Geest Meesteren, or curators of the poor chest, while one widow bought a rente for a little over 85 pounds.

[64]See the accounts cited above, note 58: magistrate-purchasers of domain renten include Dirk Duyst Hendrikszoon (2,312) and Jan de Heuter (432) from Delft, Ruysch Jan Bethszoon (300), Meester Hendrik Dirkszoon (1,353), Jan Hollesloot (1,030) and Meester Jan Teyng M. D. (432) from Amsterdam, Wouter Bekesteyn (592) from Haarlem, and Damas Philips and Jan Drenkwaert (200 each) from Dordrecht. Of these men, de Heuter, Drenkwaert and, later, Bekesteyn were sheriffs of their respective cities, and thus appointees of the emperor; Duyst seems to have made a business of investing in the emperor's domain incomes (see Aud. 1441:4, no. 5).

TABLE 13

PURCHASES BY URBAN MAGISTRATES (RENTEN A–N)

Total purchase (number of buyers) average purchase		
	Magistrates	Others
Delft	8,472 (8) 1,059	5,970 (22) 263
Dordrecht	3,152 (6) 525	1,327 (14) 95
Gouda	100 (1) 100	1,460 (7) 209
Totals	11,724 (15) 782	8,577 (43) 199

money in this way is worthy of note, but comment will be reserved until the following chapter.[65] What matters here is that the magistrates' purchases made it all the easier for other wealthy inhabitants of the great cities to escape obligation in connection with the sale of renten.

From the standpoint of the central government, the fact that a substantial portion of the province's wealth could not be tapped for this purpose was doubtless another good reason for discontinuing the practice of having the States issue renten secured by the ordinaris bede. Some renten had to be sold within the province, particularly since incidents like the seizure of Holland ships at Sluys in Flanders in 1530[66] made the States reluctant to continue their usual recourse to the renteniers of Bruges. But just as there was resistance to the idea of being asked twice for the sacrifice of a forced loan, at least within a short span of time, there seems to have been a similar feeling in regard to the forced purchase of renten.[67]

[65]See chapter 5, notes 41–43.

[66]AJ 31 December 1530.

[67]RSH 28 September 1552, to find buyers for renten the States agreed to constrain those who had not already been made to subscribe to a forced loan the same year (see the Receiver-General's account for 1552, Lille B 2493, 257–539, "Deniers prestz," a total of 1,052,598 raised throughout the Netherlands). See GVR 6 October 1523, for a sale of 5,000 in renten (item E, capital 80,000), the States agreed not to use constraint on nobles, small cities, and the countryside; these were the groups—especially wealthy peasants—that had been compelled to contribute heavily in two previous sales (items B and D, capital 32,000 and 48,000). When the five cities were ordered to find

Once nobles, cloisters, towns and villages, wealthy peasants, and personnel of the Hof van Holland had been compelled to buy once or twice, there was nowhere else to turn, since the burghers of the great cities were, for political reasons, beyond reach. In 1530, when first 62,400 and then 48,000 was to be raised through two new issues, the States made it a condition of their consent that there was to be no "constraint." As a result, only nine buyers were found for both issues in the entire province, all in The Hague, and for a total of only 6,352; to make up what was lacking for the second issue, Stadtholder Hoogstraten had to make two last-minute purchases for a total of 8,748 pounds.[68] For a further issue of 28,000 in 1533 the States reverted to constraint, largely by once more assigning quotas to towns and villages as corporate entities, but for the final issue of this series, in 1534, the government went back to the old system of asking a single wealthy town (Amsterdam) to sell renten against its own bede quota.[69]

Meester Floris Oem van Wijngaerden had pointed to a way out of the impasse by suggesting that the sale of renten be reorganized to ensure that the principal was retired in timely fashion, and thereby gain the confidence of investors. In fact, unless the Habsburg government were somehow to create an absolute monarchy in the Low Countries, it was not possible to mobilize urban capital for state investments except by voluntary means. But deputies to the States of Holland had no incentive to change the existing system, so long as it was not

---

buyers "by the schiltal" for item E, Gouda's city council determined that those wealthy burghers who had been "commanded" to buy town renten "last time," yet had not done so, should do so now (GVR 24 February 1524).

[68]Accounts for both issues are in GVR 3435, and terms of consent are spelled out in copies of the two "Acceptatiën" at the head of the account; in both cases most of the money was raised by sales in Bruges, although by 1530 it was recognized that Holland had a serious problem with arrears to "foreign" renteniers (AJ 31 December 1530, 6 January 1531).

[69]For the 28,000 issue (item M), GRK 3437, and Assendelft and Meester Vincent Corneliszoon to Hoogstraten, 16 September 1532 (Aud. 1525); in extant ordinaris bede accounts, the 16,000 issue by Amsterdam (item N) is first mentioned in GRK 3440, where it is said the money was used to pay back loans by Amsterdam burghers for the war with Lübeck in 1533 (see Lille B 2386, "Vendicions des rentes").

their constituents who were being inconvenienced by repeated failures to redeem the principal out of bede revenues. Change would have to await the day, in 1542, when the central government was momentarily strong enough to push through a new initiative.

III. The new series of renten, funded by the excise and land tax, began in 1542. At the time of the first two issues, it had not yet been determined exactly how they would be funded, except that it would not be from the bede. Potential buyers within Holland were not expected to display any more confidence in some untried new system than they had shown previously. The account for the first of these issues (61,227 in 1542) contains the first explicit reference to a ledger (*cohier*) of those in Holland who were "assessed to buy" (*geset te copen*), with separate categories for cloisters, officials and minor functionaries of the Hof van Holland, barons and knights, and a miscellaneous group of "others in the cohier," mostly domiciled in The Hague.[70] Even so, there were important changes in the nature of urban participation in these issues. Since Amsterdam was forced to abandon its isolation and join with the other five cities that made up "the common body of the territory," names of buyers within its walls appear in the accounts for the first time. Amsterdammers were not such lavish investors in the 1540s as they would be a decade later, but it is worth noting that purchase amounts here vary randomly, as they did at Bruges and Mechelen, suggesting there was no constraint. In other cities the pattern was the same as it had been in the 1520s, with purchases either by officeholders and their kin, or by lists of burghers buying identical amounts, like the thirty-six men and women of Leiden who each invested 96 pounds in 1543.[71] Burghers of the six great cities taken together accounted for an unusually high percentage of sales in Holland for the 1542 issue (47.98%), but

[70]SH 2275.
[71]SH 2208; there were also two purchases in Leiden for smaller amounts. In the same account there were twenty-one purchases in Rotterdam each for 96 pounds, twenty-three purchases of 96 pounds in Dordrecht (plus one for 270 by the city), and four by convents for 192, or 288), and twenty-nine purchases for 96 pounds each in Gouda (plus three for 192, or 528).

for subsequent issues in 1543 and again in 1549 most of the "domestic" capital was found by having towns and villages make corporate purchases proportionate to their schiltal quotas.[72] Contrary to all experience with renten secured by the bede, the new issues of 1542 and 1543 were fully retired within a few years, as was the smaller amount for 1549.[73] But one swallow does not a summer make, nor do even two or three. The expectation that public debts, whether of the government or the States, would never be repaid persisted, and with it the conviction that Hollanders would only buy provincial renten under compulsion. In 1552, when renewed war with France prompted new and larger issues, the States of Holland were not fully persuaded that "constraint" was necessary, perhaps because current interest rates (1 : 12 for losrenten, or heritable annuities, instead of the usual 1 : 16) were thought to make such investment more attractive. But the regent insisted it was only right for the wealthy to be compelled in this way to assist in the defense of the land, and the States agreed to obligatory purchase by those who had not already contributed to a forced loan levied by the government the previous year—a juxtaposition that neatly illustrates the kinship of forced loans and compulsory renten purchases.[74] For another large sale at the 1 : 12 rate the following year, urban deputies, rejecting a proposal from their noble colleagues, stipulated there would be no constraint. They were evidently right in judging that coercion was no longer necessary, since the account for this issue (item 5 of table 7) shows unprecedented total purchases, in random amounts, by the burghers of individual cities (12,956 for Amsterdam, 8,344 for The Hague).[75] The free market for Holland renten

[72]See table 10, column 2, "Towns and villages"; all of these collective purchases were made in 1543 and 1549 (SH 2208, 1792), none in 1542 (SH 2275).

[73]SH 2208, 2210, 2211, the debt of 137,452 accumulated in 1542 and 1543 (table 6, items 1 and 2) was retired by means of provincial excise and land taxes, while the 20,808 debt from 1549 (table 6, item 3) was paid off with two levies by schiltal (SH 1793, 1794).

[74]Above, note 67. RSH 27–28 February 1552.

[75]RSH 14–16 March, 23 August, 1553; SH 2278. Between February 1552 and August 1553, the States considered yet another sale of renten, but their

may thus be dated from this sale, even though the real explosion of interest among buyers in Holland first appears with the following issue (item 6 of table 7) somewhat later in 1553. It was at this time that the governments, desperate for funds, induced Holland and other provinces to begin offering redeemable lijfrenten at the rate of 16.67 percent (1 : 6) as well as the losrenten at 1 : 12 (see table 7, items 6–9). Lijfrenten had long been favored even among the not so wealthy as a means of providing for their offspring (children quite young, but old enough to have survived the rigors of infancy, were the ideal beneficiaries).[76] In Amsterdam, the demand for life annuities was so great that the city fathers would occasionally authorize an issue not for any urgent civic need, but merely "to satisfy the community"; often there was a one-to-a-customer rule, with a limit of 10 or 12 pounds per year in interest income.[77] In contrast to the lijfrenten now being issued by the States, urban life annuities were not redeemable—they were extinguished only by the death of the beneficiary—but they also carried lower rates of interest, 1 : 8 or 1 : 10. The popularity of the new lijfrenten in Holland, as compared with the losrenten at 1 : 12, is evident from table 14.

If total sales for both kinds of annuities are added together, the amounts sold inside (256,657) and outside (235,052) the province are roughly equal, which is true for other issues during the 1550s as well. But more than two-thirds of the lijfrenten were bought up by Hollanders, while about the same proportion of losrenten went to foreign buyers. Though there is nothing in the sources to document such a supposi-

request for permission to coerce Hollanders to buy was rejected by Mary of Hungary and Viglius: Sandelijn 2, 9 August, 22 October, 1552.

[76]For lijfrenten issued by the States (items 6–9 of table 7, SH 2279–2282), ages of the beneficiary are given; children younger than one year old are rare, and there are none less than six months old.

[77]ASR 1552: to raise its portion of a 100,000 extraordinaris bede levied by schiltal (Amsterdam's quota = 8,017), the city issued 8,015 in lijfrenten at the rate of 1 : 9 for one life, with buying restricted to burghers of Amsterdam, and a limit of 6 pounds interest per year per life, "so that everyone might be satisfied"; the limit had been 3 pounds two years earlier, and appears to have been 12 pounds in 1554 (ASR 1550, 1554).

TABLE 14

SALES OF LIJFRENTEN AND LOSRENTEN, 1553–1556

(Items 6 through 9 from table 7)				
	Item 6	Item 7	Item 8	Item 9	Totals
In Holland, 1:12	13,856	15,718	9,300	22,504	61,370
In Holland, 1:6	66,960	72,867	18,426	37,034	195,287
Outside Holland 1:12	10,116	40,232	48,222	48,264	146,834
Outside Holland 1:6	6,034	36,794	22,230	22,560	88,218

tion, it looks as though domestic buyers were given preferential access to this highly favorable investment opportunity. More importantly, though the lijfrenten were all redeemed within a few years, mostly through the "conversion" sale of 1556–1558, the habit of investing in such instruments, once acquired, was apparently strong enough to survive the transition back to lower rates. Thus in the two "conversion" issues of 1556–1558 and 1560–1562, in which outstanding lijfrenten debt at 1 : 6 was converted first to losrenten at 1 : 12, then 1 : 16, Hollanders bought 395,987, or 58.6 percent, of the total.[78]

Changes associated with the removal of constraint are evident in the third column of table 12. Column 2 represents the period when Hollanders were still being forced to buy, even though renten were no longer funded by the bede, and column 3 represents the period of the free market (1553–1565). Several previously important categories of buyers wholly disappear from the accounts beginning in 1553— towns and villages, rural folk, and nobles—while cloisters become insignificant in this respect. Once in a while the accounts mention buyers who live in villages, but these transactions are made in cities, and there is no suggestion of a capital levy on prosperous peasants.[79] Noble titles occur

[78]SH 2347, 2348.
[79]In the accounts that are examined in detail here (see chapter 5, note 7), there were only eleven such buyers in Holland, with a total purchase of 2,176 pounds.

among purchasers in The Hague, also in Haarlem and Leiden, but such names are never grouped together, and if they were subjected to any pressure to buy it had to be by town governments, not by agents of the provincial States. Although over sixty Holland cloisters had bought renten between 1542 and 1552, only two such communities made purchases during the following period, for a total of 824 pounds. The opposite was true for the urban religious and charitable foundations—like parish vestries and hospitals—which town councils controlled through appointed boards. Though represented here and there in earlier transactions, corporations of this kind made much larger purchases during the 1550s. In other words, if convents and monasteries bought Holland renten only when they had to, burghers charged with responsibility for the town's widows and orphans were more than willing to entrust endowed funds to these annuities, once rates were favorable and there was a reasonable assurance that capital would be redeemed in a timely fashion. In Amsterdam, only one cloister purchased a rente between 1553 and 1565 (for 176 pounds), while twelve institutions controlled by lay boards, none of which had invested in renten during the 1540s, made purchases totaling 14,421 pounds.[80]

In recognition of the far greater importance of urban markets, beginning in 1553 the accounts list sales of renten under the names of the six great cities plus The Hague, not, as previously, under the names of traditional domain-revenue collecting districts, which were more rural than urban.[81] This shift is visible in huge increases for the six great cities in

[80]In 1542–1543 three Amsterdam cloisters made purchases totaling 768. Purchases (1553–1565) by lay boards of religious corporations included the church wardens of the Nieuwe Kerk (1,600) and the Oude Kerk (1,648), the city's two parish churches, and of two chapels, the Heilige Stede (672) and St. Jacobscapelle (276), and the Getijdemeesteren of the Oude Kerk (572). The city's two hospitals had male and female boards, all of which bought renten: St. Pieter's Gasthuismeesteren (2,368) and Gasthuismoeders (1,280), and Onze Lieve Vrouwe Gasthuismeesteren (2,025) and Gasthuismoeders (576). There were, finally, investments by the two poor relief foundations, the Huissittenmeesteren on the New Side (1,600) and the Old Side (904), and by the Orphan Bureau (900). During the 1540s, trustees of the Orphan Bureau and the Old Side Huissittenmeesteren made purchases of city renten (ASR 1541, 1545, 1547), but no Holland renten.
[81]SH 2278; see above, note 55.

Page from one of the receiver for the common territory's accounts for renten interest payments, grouped by city; here, Meester Gerrit Hendrikszoon van Ravensberg (p. 153) heads the list for Haarlem. Reproduced by courtesy of the Rijksarchief voor Zuid-Holland, The Hague.

column 3 of table 12, as contrasted with the first two columns. (Small cities in Holland, save for Rotterdam, are under-represented in column 3, since most of their burghers who purchased renten now did so in one of the great cities; most of the "nonresident" buyers in the great cities—see table 15*a*, column 3—were from small cities in Holland.) The role of the great cities in placing renten within their walls can be conveniently expressed as a percentage of the total sold in Holland during each of the three periods under discussion here:

	1515–1534 Issues A–N	1542–1552 Issues 1–4	1553–1565 Issues 5–17
Percent sold in great cities	13.67 (5 cities)	28.11 (6 cities)	77.6 (6 cities)

The same relationship can be expressed differently by noting how much of the total in column 4 of table 12 (that is, for all renten funded by the excise and land tax) was sold between 1553 and 1565, when the practice of forced buying had been abandoned:

	All Holland	Six great cities	Amster-dam	Leiden
Column 3 as % of column 4 (table 12)	86.99	94.85	97.28	80.64

The two extremes among the great cities are represented by prosperous Amsterdam and by Leiden, the only city whose economy was almost wholly dependent on an afflicted industry—that of the production of heavy woolen cloth.[82] In be-

[82]For difficulties Leiden wool merchants had in maintaining their credit in the early decades of the century, Posthumus, *Geschiedenis van de Leidsche Lakenindustrie*, I, 197–199, and AJ 10 September, 19 December, 1523, 28 January 1524. The dismal state of the industry in the 1540s is indicated by a

tween, Delft, Dordrecht, Haarlem, and even Gouda, despite the problems of its brewers, all show extraordinary increases in the volume of renten purchases for the 1550s, and the same is true for The Hague.

In sum, the combination of initially high rates, freedom from constraint, and some assurance of repayment led to an explosion of interest in provincial renten among urban wealth-holders in Holland. Together with the opening of new markets, particularly in Zeeland, it was this extraordinary expansion of "domestic" urban markets which enabled the States of Holland to raise unprecedented sums through the sale of renten during the 1550s. Urban renten-buyers were thus the key to a major turning point in Holland's fiscal history; in the following chapter it will be useful to take a closer look at who they were.

---

report drawn up by two Leiden schepenen, or aldermen, on the basis of testimony from the heads of the weavers' and fullers' guilds, dated 8 October 1547 (Aud. 1656:1), according to which three-fourths of Leiden's fulling capacity had been idled during the previous year.

V

The Renteniers

Investment in public debt is one aspect of a larger problem that has occupied historians of early modern Europe in recent decades. Scholars have noticed that, at one time or another during the sixteenth or seventeenth century, in several different countries there was an important shift of urban capital away from trade and industry into agriculture and other forms of investment where profits were perhaps less spectacular but more certain. Some historians, employing phrases like "treason of the bourgeoisie" or "rearistocratization of society," have seen this process of disinvestment in productive enterprise as prompted by the social aspirations of townsfolk, the desire to "live nobly." Others contend that prudent urban investors were simply responding to the fact that opportunities in trade and industry were not what they once were.[1] Whichever interpretation of the phenomenon one prefers, it is clear that investment in State debt could have the same function as investment in agriculture. In this chapter, no attempt will be made to resolve, even for the single province of Holland, the complicated questions that are latent in the interpretation of such fluid social categories as "bourgeoisie" or "nobility." Such larger issues will, however, be kept in view as this study proceeds with more manageable questions.

To date, scholars have not devoted much effort to determining exactly what sorts of people did invest in early modern public or royal debts. Lists of subscribers to forced loans in the Italian city-states are available here and there,[2] but such lists merely indicate who was wealthy, not who freely chose to entrust money to State securities. For those realms which had long-term debts based on voluntary subscription, the available literature, at least for the sixteenth and seventeenth centuries, offers impressionistic comments, but no systematic studies. In Castile, royal juros seem to have enjoyed an initial popularity among noble families, wealthy clerics, and religious houses, but by the 1570s prosperous townsmen began shifting their funds to these State securities, and eventually did so to such an extent that the kingdom's commercial economy was thereby deprived of needed capital.[3] In France, where royal officials and great nobles were apparently the chief investors, the bourgeoisie of Paris also had some interest in rentes sur l'hotel de ville as late as the 1550s, but not after Charles IX's government began to apply constraint to support the large issues of the 1560s. In the following decade there

[1]See the references in H. Soly, "Het "Verrad" der 16e Eeuwse Burgerij: een Mythe? Enkele Beschouwingen betreffende het Gedragspatroon der Antwerpse Ondernemers," *Tijdschrift voor Geschiedenis* LXXXVI (1973): 262–280, translated as "The 'Treason of the Bourgeoisie': A Myth? Some Considerations on the Behavior Pattern of Antwerp Entrepreneurs," *Acta Historicae Neerlandicae* VIII (1975): 31–49.

[2]Molho, *Florentine Public Finance*, Appendix E, 214–216; lenders are occasionally named in Bowsky, *The Finances of the Commune of Siena*, Appendixes 12–13, 329–354.

[3]A. Castillo Pintado, "Dette Flottante et Dette Consolidée en Espagne, de 1557 à 1600"; see also Bennassar, *Valladolid au Siècle d'Or*, 257–258, and Philips, *Ciudad Real*, 208–210.

emerged a pattern that was to last until the financial reforms of Colbert: financial officials and syndicates of lenders, using unpaid royal debts as part of their capital, bought up new rentes at roughly half the nominal price. As if to corroborate this picture of things, social historians looking at the investment habits of the French provincial bourgeoisie in the seventeenth century have not found royal rentes worthy of comment.[4] For England, where annuities backed by Parliament first appeared in the 1690s, John Dickson provides an extensive discussion of eighteenth-century investors both domestic and foreign. Examining separately several issues over a period of about forty years, Dickson finds that, in England, individual investors predominated, though with growing participation by charitable institutions and trustees for minor children. Investors were overwhelmingly concentrated in London, and included large numbers of merchants and financiers, but few peers or members of Parliament.[5] If a broader inference may be extracted from these scattered observations, it seems that the likelihood of various groups investing in public debt depends not on some abstract conception of social structure, but on the particular makeup of each society; hence the prominence of ecclesiastical buyers in sixteenth-century Spain, royal officials in sixteenth-century France, and holders of private wealth in eighteenth-century England.

For purposes of this chapter, buyers of provincial renten in Holland will be segregated into categories largely suggested by the foregoing discussion. Institutions, meaning cloisters as well as the religious and charitable foundations controlled by lay boards, will be separated from individual buyers. To facilitate comparison among individuals living in the same city, persons not domiciled in the city where they purchase renten (or under whose name the purchase is listed) will be counted separately. Among the inhabitants of a given city, the most obvious distinction (at least in the Holland renten accounts, where a good many of the buyers are women) is

[4]Chapter 1, notes 39 and 40; see also Pierre Goubert, *Beauvais et le Beauvaisis, 1600–1730* (Paris: 1960), 516–545, and Pierre Deyon, *Amiens, Capitale Provinciale* (Paris: 1967), 309–322.
[5]Dickson, *The Financial Revolution in England*, 249–340.

by sex. Moreover, since women were more likely to be in control of the family wealth during their years of widowhood, those named in the accounts as widows will be segregated out from other laywomen. Nuns and Beguines,[6] along with priests and monks, will be counted among the religious. Finally, among laymen it will be worth checking whether officeholders (meaning town magistrates as well as officials of the central government) continued to be the prominent renten-buyers they were during the years when Hollanders were being constrained to make such purchases.

In what follows, it will first be necessary to define the above categories of renten-buyers a bit more precisely (I). The discussion will then focus on the disproportionately large investments made by officeholders and their kin (II), a circumstance that will appear all the more striking when the buying habits of officeholders are compared (so far as available information permits) with those of other wealthy townsmen grouped first according to mercantile and industrial interests (III), and then according to their interests in agriculture and other "safe" investments (IV). It will then be possible to comment on the significance of officeholder investment in State debt as it pertains to larger issues in Low Countries history (V).

I. In keeping with the argument set forth in the last chapter—that there was within Holland no free market for States renten until 1553—only purchases made between 1553 and 1565 will be considered in this chapter. For present purposes, ten of the thirteen renten accounts during these years have been analyzed.[7] Buyers included in these ten accounts made

---

[6]Beguines lived a common religious life, usually in a quarter separated from the rest of the city by a wall or a moat (*begijnhof* or, in French, *beguinage*), but took no vows, and were free to leave the community and marry if they wished; see Ernest McDonnell, *Beguines and Beghards in Medieval Culture, with Special Reference to the Belgian Scene* (New Brunswick, N.J.: 1954).

[7]Utilized here are SH 2278, 2279, 2280, 2281, 2282, 2284, 2285, 2289, 2347, and 2348, corresponding to items 5–9, 11, 12, and 17 of table 7, and items 13 and 16 in table 8. For SH 2283 (item 10) only renten sold outside Holland are included, and SH 2286 and 2287 (items 14 and 15) are not included at all. Note has been taken, however, of the totals by place listed at the head of the accounts not otherwise used, which permits the tabulation given in column 1 of tables 15a and 15b. Omitted from these two tables is a total of

purchases totaling roughly 78 percent of the amount sold between 1553 and 1565, although—as can be seen by comparing columns 1 and 2 of tables 15*a* and 15*b*—locations outside Holland happen to be better represented (96%) than those within the province (69%). The samples used here are in fact rather small for two of the great cities of Holland—Leiden (57%) and especially Dordrecht (28%)—though not for the larger and more important renten markets in Amsterdam (68%), The Hague (79%), and Delft (70%).[8]

In analyzing who the buyers were, the first step (column 3 in tables 15*a* and 15*b*) is to segregate out those not domiciled in the city where renten were bought (one could easily buy renten while on a business trip to another city, or even while being kept in detention in The Hague).[9] Deciding where buyers are domiciled is not quite so easy as it may sound, but by adopting prudent rules[10] one arrives at totals for non-

---

[8]75,167 in renten sold in thirteen places not listed: Bergen-op-Zoom, Breda, Hasselt, Leuven, and Lier in Brabant; small amounts for Gorcum and Alkmaar in Holland; and, elsewhere in the northern Netherlands, Amersfoort, Deventer, Gelderland, Lingen, and Maastricht. If all figures both in the original accounts and in this book were free of error, the total by places sold (802,264 from column 1 of table 15*a*, plus 1,120,446 from column 1 of table 15*b*, plus the just-mentioned 75,167 from "other places" = 1,997,877) should equal the total sold for items 5 through 17 in tables 7 and 9 (1,981,520). Most of the actual difference (16,357) between the two sums is perhaps accounted for by an 18,000 sale (chapter 4, note 28) known from other sources, but not listed in the appropriate accounts. In any event, the totals for column 2 of Tables 15*a* and 15*b* (1,535,620) are equal to 79.87 percent of the totals for column 1 (1,922,710).

[8]With the exception of one purchase, the accounts treat Rotterdam as part of the Delft market; the roughly 44,000 listed under Delft but not analyzed here would doubtless include further purchases by Rotterdammers.

[9]SH 2347: Meester Hendrik Dirkszoon, leader of Amsterdam's ruling faction, invested 600 in renten in Amsterdam and another 600 in The Hague, where he had been detained for some time in connection with a charge (eventually dismissed) of suborning witnesses in support of the heresy charge (also dismissed) against the magistrates' great enemy, Sheriff Willem Dirkszoon Baerdes; see J. J. Woltjer, "Het Conflikt tussen Willem Baerdes en Hendrik Dirkszoon," *Bijdragen en Mededelingen betreffende de Geschiedenis van de Nederlanden,* LXXXVI (1971): 178–199.

[10]Since a place-of-origin designation (e.g., "van Monnikendam") often served as a surname for someone long domiciled in another city, persons so named in the accounts are treated as residents of the city where the renten

TABLE 15a
BUYERS OF RENTEN OUTSIDE HOLLAND, 1553–1565
(Renten 5–17)

Top number = total purchase, in pounds / (bottom number) = number of buyers

	(1) Total sold	(2) Total here	(3) Nonresidents	(4) Institutions	(5) Religious	(6) Officeholders	(7) Other lay men	(8) Widows	(9) Other lay women
Mdlbg.	193,909	184,403 (155)	60,958 (34)	2,593 (6)	0	22,868 (4)	68,080 (85)	24,168 (18)	5,736 (8)
Bsls.*	160,854	148,624 (176)	6,544 (6)	2,042 (3)	8,316 (19)	12,924 (10)	86,958 (89)	22,248 (31)	9,592 (18)
Mchln.	160,092	157,104 (163)	6,544 (6)	2,044 (2)	9,428 (19)	14,732 (11)	93,288 (85)	23,160 (25)	7,908 (15)
Zkzee.	152,315	140,587 (138)	3,472 (4)	360 (1)	96 (1)	47,496 (15)	71,387 (82)	12,230 (17)	5,546 (18)
Atwrp.	91,018	86,918 (36)	6,708 (2)	0	10,840 (2)	0	44,562 (24)	5,548 (5)	19,260 (3)
Utrct.	44,076	44,132 (93)	1,528 (7)	180 (1)	4,264 (12)	1,160 (2)	29,737 (49)	2,280 (7)	4,983 (15)
Totals	802,264	761,768 (761)	85,754 (59)	7,219 (13)	32,944 (53)	99,180 (42)	394,012 (414)	89,634 (103)	53,025 (77)
Average purchase, in pounds		1,001	1,483	555	622	2,361	952	875	689

Key: Mdlbg. = Middelburg   Mchln. = Mechelen   Atwrp. = Antwerp
Bsls.* = Brussels (* = includes the Court)   Zkzee. = Zierikzee   Utrct. = Utrecht
Foreign markets not included here (see table 10, column 3) are 's Hertogenbosch, other Brabant towns, and those included under Other.

TABLE 15b
Buyers of Renten in Holland, 1553–1565
(Renten 5–17)

Top number = total purchase, in pounds / (bottom number) = number of buyers

	(1) Total sold	(2) Total here	(3) Nonresidents	(4) Institutions	(5) Religious	(6) Officeholders	(7) Other lay men	(8) Widows	(9) Other lay women
A'dam.	451,889	305,889 (526)	24,066 (45)	17,347 (15)	4,686 (32)	61,345 (41)	125,456 (218)	30,192 (40)	42,807 (135)
Hague*	192,594	153,811 (189)	2,124 (7)	0	2,230 (3)	50,108 (36)	68,383 (75)	18,180 (24)	12,786 (44)
Delft+	147,915	103,748 (164)	3,548 (8)	5,768 (10)	6,349 (38)	55,358 (23)	20,060 (49)	9,186 (13)	3,479 (23)
Dort	95,284	26,998 (36)	3,000 (2)	360 (2)	108 (2)	11,840 (8)	9,534 (14)	1,664 (4)	492 (4)
Gouda	82,988	58,509 (207)	3,768 (9)	2,016 (3)	640 (6)	13,100 (24)	23,241 (87)	6,082 (23)	9,662 (55)
Harlm.	76,182	66,116 (57)	2,072 (6)	2,400 (1)	522 (2)	26,990 (5)	18,666 (22)	2,780 (4)	12,686 (17)
R'dam.+	40,166	39,930 (44)	0	1,032 (1)	220 (1)	8,112 (5)	19,260 (21)	9,752 (7)	1,554 (9)
Leidn.	33,428	19,351 (60)	2,772 (12)	0	666 (5)	2,736 (4)	9,180 (27)	2,536 (4)	1,461 (8)
Totals	1,120,446	774,352 (1,283)	41,350 (89)	28,923 (32)	15,421 (89)	229,589 (146)	293,780 (513)	80,372 (119)	84,927 (295)
Average purchase, in pounds		604	465	904	177	1,573	513	675	288

Key: A'dam = Amsterdam   Hague* = The Hague (* = includes Hof van Holland)   Dort = Dordrecht
      Harlm. = Haarlem   R'dam.+ = Rotterdam (+ = sales listed under Delft)   Leidn. = Leiden

resident buyers which are not very large, save for Delft in Holland and Middelburg in Zeeland. The great bulk (92%) of renten listed under Delft but bought by nonresidents is accounted for by Rotterdam. Rotterdam had been an independent market for Holland renten during the 1520s and 1530s, and probably continued to be during the 1550s. In other words, it seems likely that agents of the States posted notices in Rotterdam for each issue, and then sent collectors to Rotterdam as well as nearby Delft, and simply listed these purchases under Delft for the sake of convenience. In any case Rotterdam is treated in table 15*b* as a separate market. Nonresident purchases in Middelburg are mainly accounted for by some quite large investors in the neighboring Zeeland towns of Veere (22,366) and Vlissingen, or Flushing (27,576; see Appendix II*a*, nos. 4, 15, 16, 42, 52, and 95).

As mentioned in the last chapter, a number of purchases were made during this period in Amsterdam on behalf of religious and charitable foundations controlled by lay boards (column 4 of table 15*b*). Outside of Amsterdam and (to a lesser extent) Delft, it does not appear that such institutions invested very heavily in provincial debt.[11] Convents and monasteries in Holland bought renten only rarely during this period, which makes for a sharp contrast with the decades when forced purchase was the rule.[12] Outside of Holland institutional buyers of all kinds are but sparsely represented in the accounts, perhaps because institutions preferred, for added safety, to invest in securities issued by the States of their own province or some other body closer to home.

Identification of individual buyers (columns 5 through 9 in tables 15*a* and 15*b*) is complicated by the fact that surnames

---

purchase is made (e.g., Amsterdam), except in cases where the name includes another identifying designator (e.g., Pieter Corneliszoon *grootschipper van Monnikendam*), which would make it unnecessary for the clerk to add the place name except as an indication of where the buyer actually lived. The unambiguous indicator for place of residence is the preposition "te."

[11]See chapter 4, note 80. Lane, "Public Debt and Private Wealth in Venice," 320, mentions that in the early sixteenth century, over half the shares in the city's monte vecchio were held by benevolent foundations like the *scuole*, or religious and charitable guilds; cf. Kirshner, "Moral Problems of Discounting Genoese *Paghe*," 113–115.

[12]See chapter 4, note 47.

were still relatively uncommon in the Low Countries, though less so among the people of wealth who were the most likely investors. When a particular first-name–patronymic combination, like "Claes Pieterszoon" or "Grietken Claesdochter," occurs two or three times for the same city in the same account, there is no way of telling how many individuals are involved. Here it is usually assumed that each repetition of a given combination refers to a different person, unless the name and patronymic are accompanied by some distinguishing feature, such as a title (*Meester* Hendrik Dirkszoon), an occupation (Claes Pieterszoon *de lootgieter*, or plumber), a surname (Dirk Hillebrandszoon *Otter*), or one of the designations from which surnames were often derived, that is, a house name (Jans Janszoon in *'t Hart*) or a place of origin (Harman Ellertszoon *van Diemen*). Women here taken for Beguines are either so named in the accounts, or are said to live at the local Beguinage (*begijnhof*). Similarly, nuns are either so identified, or reside "in" or "at" a particular convent. Priests are often so named, and may also be recognized from the title *heer*, except when the "lord" in question is further identified, as noblemen of a certain rank would be, as lord of this or that place (for example, the First Councilor of the Council of Holland is invariably referred to as *heer Gerrit, heer van Assendelft*). Members of the nobility are not made a separate category here, since their titles are not always used, and it would require an exacting knowledge of Holland genealogy to determine who was or was not a member of the noble family that called itself by the names of its ancestral seat (e.g., van Assendelft, van Warmond).[13] In any case it does not appear that nobles were major buyers during the 1550s, which means that the history of their involvement with Holland renten rather resembles that of the cloisters.[14]

[13]On Holland's nobles, see chapter 6, note 23. One would also have to deal with the fact that men whose families had been part of the nobility for centuries did not readily accept novel titles as conferring real nobility: see Assendelft's scorn for the social pretensions of his adversary within the Council of Holland, Willem Snouckaert: Assendelft to Mary of Hungary, 7 December 1555, paragraphs 6–18 (Aud. 1646:3).

[14]Among the 169 large investors for the period 1542–1565 (Appendixes II*a* and II*b*), there were only thirteen whose titles a man like Assendelft would probably have respected, eleven outside Holland (Appendix II*a*, nos. 3, 6,

Problems of a different sort are posed by the legal and social relationships between men and women. Since husbands were the legal guardians of their wives,[15] in the case of joint purchase by spouses[16] the man is here treated as the buyer. When the accounts give only the name of a woman, it need not mean she was the buyer, because the accounts do not always name the buyer when he or she is different from the beneficiary (for example, there are entries in which the only person named is a minor child). But it was also true that married women in the Low Countries had more control over their ancestral property than they did in some other parts of Europe, and it was not at all unusual here for a widow to continue her late husband's business.[17] It is thus assumed that women beneficiaries are also the buyers, unless their age is given as less than twenty-one. The unnamed buyer for a minor child or children is always assumed to be a man. Women counted as widows are so named in the accounts, except for a few cases where Elias's collective biography of the Amsterdam patriciate permits additional identifications as widows. Finally, purchases are attributed to a buyer regardless of whether or not the person in question is acting for him or herself and family, as true in the vast majority of cases, or merely as an agent for someone else, like the directors of a town orphan bureau (*weeskamer*)[18] or, occasionally,

---

10, 21, 22, 33, 34, possibly nos. 36, 47, 69, and 72), and two within the province (Appendix II*b*, no. 10 and possibly no. 39).

[15]This relationship occasionally appears in the accounts in the statement that a man is buying a rente "als man ende voogd" of his wife, that is, as her "husband and protector," and presumably as custodian of her property.

[16]For example, among purchases by "Other lay men" in The Hague (table 15*b*, column 7, seventy-five buyers for a total of 68,383), there were ten (for a total of 7,604) who made some purchases, but not necessarily all, in conjunction with their wives.

[17]The 100th penny accounts for Amsterdam exports between 1543 and 1545 (CC 23358, 23360, 23362, 23364, 23366) list a number of women shippers, some of whom were widows presumably carrying on the businesses of their late husbands (e.g., "Douwe [Duyf] Adriaen Ockers" [widow: see Elias *sub nomine*], entry for 20 April 1544, a shipment of wine and fruit).

[18]See the purchases by no. 26, Appendix II*b*, whom the accounts identify as a member of Rotterdam's *weeskamer* board.

THE *RENTENIERS*   149

the individuals who can be identified from these accounts as financial brokers.[19]

The term *officeholder* requires special explanation. As has been mentioned, it refers both to officials of the central government, like those attached to the Hof van Holland, and to town magistrates. Also included are the permanent salaried officials who tended more and more to represent cities in their dealings with other governmental bodies (the town pensionary and the town secretary), and who supervised the operation of essential city functions like the treasury.[20] For the great cities of Holland, plus Rotterdam, those counted in table 15*b* (column 6) as officeholders were only rarely officials of the central government,[21] whereas those listed for The Hague and (in table 15*a*) outside of Holland were mostly government officials rather than locally elected magistrates. Printed lists of town magistrates for this period are available for Amsterdam, Delft, Dordrecht, and Gouda and, outside Holland, for Antwerp.[22] For Rotterdam and Zierikzee there are collective biographies of the patriciate which, although beginning at a somewhat later date, provide the names of most men who held office during the 1550s.[23] To round out

[19]For example, Appendix II*a*, no. 25, eight purchases for many different persons, including one widow and two sets of orphans; in one case the buyer is identified as *ontvanger* (administrator) of the beneficiary's estate.

[20]In addition to Aert Sandelijn (Appendix II*b*, no. 29), who was both town pensionary and a member of the vroedschap, salaried officials of Amsterdam who purchased renten include Gerrit Hagen Dirkszoon, clerk of the treasury (1,840), two other pensionaries, Meester Jan van der Nijenburch (880) and Meester Reinier Suyn van 's Hertogenbosch (864), and Jan Boel Gerritszoon, a town secretary (300); see also Appendix II*a*, no. 5.

[21]Exceptions are the sheriffs (see Appendix II*b*, nos. 16 and 48, for two large investors), the tollmaster of Gouda (Appendix II*b*, no. 71), the master of the mint in Leiden, Anthonis Carlier (1,356 pounds) and, in Amsterdam, Jan Cort Janszoon (1,685), a former clerk of the city treasury who was local collector of the 10th penny tax in 1543–1544.

[22]For Amsterdam, Ter Gouw prints lists of magistrates at the end of each volume; for Delft, Boitet; for Dordrecht, Balen; for Gouda, Walvis; and for Antwerp, Floris Prims, *Geschiedenis van Antwerpen* (28 vols., Antwerp: 1927–1949), VII:1.

[23]For Rotterdam, E. A. Engelbrecht, *De Vroedschap van Rotterdam, 1572–1795* = vol. V of *Bronnen voor de Geschiedenis van Rotterdam*, J. H. W. Unger and J. W. Bezemer, eds. (Rotterdam: 1973); for Zierikzee, P. D. De Vos, *De*

the picture, at least within Holland, partial if incomplete lists of officeholders have been compiled for Haarlem and Leiden by noting the names of those chosen to represent these cities as deputies to the States of Holland between 1553 and 1565.[24] For the Hof van Holland there is a printed list of councilors, procurators, and secretaries of the Council of Holland,[25] while those who served with the Chamber of Accounts will usually be found among the collectors of domain receipts whose names are listed elsewhere.[26] From the sources just mentioned it is clear that renten accounts—note that these are final copies drafted in The Hague for presentation to an audit committee named by the States—almost always identify as such purchasers who were officials of the Hof van Holland, but rarely do the same for town magistrates, unless they happened to be serving as burgomaster at the time of purchase. It is to be expected, then, that results presented here are reasonably accurate as regards officials of the central government, although purchases by town magistrates and salaried officials are understated. Finally, three officials for enclaves of noble jurisdiction, all of whom bought renten in The Hague, are also counted here as "officeholders."

What it means to be an urban magistrate is yet another question. In most Holland towns, daily business of the city was conducted by a college of burgomasters, assisted in judicial matters by a college of aldermen, or schepenen, not to mention a sheriff appointed by the central government. For important questions burgomasters and schepenen consulted a larger town council, often called the vroedschap, or "men of ease," membership in which was for life, and by co-option.

Vroedschap van Zierikzee van de tweede helft der XVIe Eeuw tot 1795 (Middelburg: 1931).

[24]This procedure yields a list of about thirty names for both cities, as opposed to eighty or ninety for cities for which full officeholder lists are available. There appears not to be a copy in North America of G. van Kessel, *Naamlijst der Regering van Haarlem* (Haarlem: 1733), to which there is a reference in J. C. Grayson, "The Civic Militia in Amsterdam," *Bijdragen en Mededelingen tot de Geschiedenis van de Nederlanden*, XCV (1980): 35–63, here p. 37.

[25]Blécourt, I, xxxii–lxvi.

[26]"Inventaris van de Graafelijkheidsrekenkamer," Inventory no. 61, Rijksarchief van Zuid-Holland, The Hague.

There was to some extent an informal *cursus honorum*, by which a fairly young man might be elected schepen a few times, later elevated to the vroedschap, and finally chosen to serve as burgomaster.[27] One could be a magistrate in the sense of currently holding annual office (as burgomaster, schepen, or city treasurer), or in the sense of being a member of the vroedschap, or in the still looser sense of having once served as schepen or burgomaster, and thus being counted in the pool of men deemed worthy of higher office. For present purposes it makes little sense to undertake the vast labor of correlating renten purchases with the holding of specific offices on a year-by-year basis. In cities small enough so that people knew quite well who did or did not belong to the political elite, members of the vroedschap were certainly considered "officeholders" even in years when they filled no other function. Moreover, since a man once entrusted with responsibility (for instance, by being elected schepen) could expect to be called upon sooner or later to serve in other capacities as well, it seems best to define the urban political elite broadly. Accordingly, column 6 of table 15*b* identifies as magistrates all those who served as burgomaster, schepen, or member of the vroedschap at any time between 1553 and 1565. By this definition, Amsterdam, for example, had sixty-six magistrates between 1553 and 1565, of whom thirty-six bought renten.

From the bottom lines of tables 15*a* and 15*b* (average purchases), it can be seen that the typical buyer outside Holland still had considerably more to invest than purchasers within the province, whether because Brabant and Zeeland were simply that much wealthier (which seems dubious in the latter case), or because investors in Holland knew of better

---

[27]For example, of the seventeen men who (according to Boitet) held the office of burgomaster in Delft between 1542 and 1565, five were first schepenen, then members of the Council of Forty (which here functioned like the vroedschap in other towns), then burgomaster; four were first members of the Forty, then schepenen, then burgomaster; three schepenen and one member of the Forty served as burgomaster without filling the other office at any time; two were first members of the Forty, then burgomaster, then schepenen; and two were first schepenen, then burgomaster, then members of the Forty. No one was chosen burgomaster without having first served in at least one of the other offices.

things to do with their money, or, as seems most likely, because small investors were welcome at home, but rather a nuisance in "foreign" parts. Amsterdam may serve as an illustration of how evenly divided large and small purchases were in Holland. Investors of small amounts (under 100 pounds), numbering seventy-three, accounted for only 1.4 percent of the sales; in ascending order, those investing between 100 and 500 pounds (277, by far the largest number of buyers) accounted for 21.2 percent, those investing between 500 and 1,000 (92) accounted for 20.1 percent, those investing between 1,000 and 2,000 (57) accounted for 25.6 percent, and the twenty-nine making the largest investments (over 2,000 pounds) in Amsterdam, listed in Appendix II*b*, accounted for 31.7 percent of the sales.[28] The spread approaches that of a random distribution, and contrasts sharply with purchases outside Holland, where the ninety-six major investors, listed in Appendix II*a*, account for over half of the total.

By putting their trust in these investments, men and women of moderate means were simply following the example set by their social betters. The connection between persons of high and low station is occasionally illustrated in purchases by clerks or household servants of the great men who themselves invested large sums in Holland renten. That men such as Assendelft or (outside Holland) Viglius van Aytta would knowingly give bad financial advice to their own retainers is scarcely credible,[29] and other folk doubtless concluded it would be safe for them to invest their savings in the same way. At the lower end of the scale, purchases of 36 pounds (none smaller is recorded in the accounts analyzed here, save one for 24 pounds), often made by women not otherwise identified, or (especially in Delft)[30] by nuns

[28]Based on 528 buyers for a total of 312,837 pounds for the whole period 1542–1565.

[29]"Anthonis Roelofs, servant of the lord of Assendelft," 252 pounds, SH 2278 (see Appendix I*b*, no. 1); in Brussels, "Nicholas Hoerler, clerk of President Viglius," 150 pounds (SH 2281), and "Christian Heyndricks at [the house of] President Viglius," 448 pounds (SH 2348; see Appendix II*a*, no. 37); in Mechelen, "Margriete, servant girl of Anthonis Sucquet," 36 pounds (SH 2286; see Appendix II*a*, no. 18).

[30]In Delft, twenty-one Beguines and five nuns made purchases totaling 3,793, for an average of 146 pounds each. It is curious that 108 pounds is

and Beguines, made for good public relations in Holland, but were probably thought not worth the trouble of soliciting outside the province, where the preferred method of finding capital was perhaps exhibited in negotiations with the wealthy van Daele family of Antwerp.[31] To set things in perspective, it might be noted that 36 pounds was quite a bit more than any ordinary person's annual wage;[32] thus even these small investors were in no sense poor. In any event the disparity between average purchases inside and outside the province was notably less than it had been while Hollanders were still being forced to buy, since the figure for Holland rose from 251 pounds in 1515–1534 (see table 11) to 604 in 1553–1565, while the average foreign purchase declined from 1,420 to 1,001.

Some totals for particular subcategories in tables 15*a* and 15*b* are distorted by one person making an unusually large investment. About five-sixths of the renten bought by office-holders in Haarlem are accounted for by Meester Gerrit Hendrikszoon van Ravensberg, who bought by far the largest amount in Holland (Appendix II*b*, no. 1). Meester Gerrit, who served more than once as burgomaster of Haarlem during the 1550s, was the son-in-law of Meester Vincent Corneliszoon van Mierop, the Holland fiscal official who was promoted to the Council of Finance in Brussels, and authored a memorandum on tax strategy that pointed the way towards the "novel expedients" of 1542.[33] In Brussels, the 64,000 invested by Duke Erich von Braunschweig-Kalenberg (who despite his political connections is not counted here as a

---

invested by a "poor" (*miserabele*) Beguine (Anna Matthysdochter, SH 2280), unless the purchase was made for her by an unnamed benefactor.

[31]See chapter 4, note 33, and Appendix II*a*, nos. 2, 7, and 9.

[32]See ASR 1546: Amsterdam paid 10 pounds a year to its master mason, 9 pounds to its master of artillery, 20 to its superintendent of public works (*fabriekmeester*), and 6 pounds each to the rectors of its two schools, whose income was supplemented by student fees. Only the two pensionaries (40 pounds each per year) and the *stroommeester*, or master of the current (70 pounds), received annual salaries in excess of 36 pounds (the master of the current was responsible for preventing the vital sailing channels leading out to the North Sea from silting up).

[33]Communication from Drs. J. J. Temmink, Archivaris, Gemeentearchief, Haarlem, 16 January 1984.

member of the Court, since he held no office) makes up over three-fourths of the total for "other lay men." In Antwerp, one single purchase by Lady Josyna van Daele, for 18,000, accounts for the great part of what is listed here under "other lay women."

For purchases by religious men and women outside Holland, much of the total comes from Lady Josyna's priest-brother in Antwerp, and, elsewhere, by the brother of the secretary of the Council of State, and by a scion of the leading noble family of the southern Netherlands.[34] Otherwise, the relative lack of interest in Holland renten shown by clergy and members of religious orders may seem surprising, certainly in light of the Spanish clergy's importance in the market for juros. As may be seen from column 5 of tables 15*a* and 15*b*, there were a few cities (Amsterdam and Delft) in which fair numbers of religious persons invested in renten but, as the averages indicate, the typical buyer in this category was not a wealthy priest, but a nun or "poor Beguine" whose purchases (36–144 pounds) were comparable with those of less affluent lay women.[35] Even in Utrecht, the greatest ecclesiastical center of the Netherlands, only eleven clerical buyers were found. Of Utrecht's five collegiate chapters, famed throughout the Netherlands for their wealth, power, and prestige, three are represented in the Holland renten accounts, but only by nine canons, whose purchases averaged a relatively modest 274 pounds.[36] However the clerical elite of the northern Netherlands employed its wealth, it was apparently not in the purchase of provincial renten.

That widows show purchases of higher average amounts than do lay women (columns 8 and 9, especially for Table 15*b*) is hardly surprising. Brides were typically a fair bit

[34]In addition to purchases by nos. 9 and 69, Appendix II*a*, a member of the Croy family, "Meester Gabriel Vlierden, licentiate in theology" (apparently a brother of nos. 60 and 61, Appendix II*a*) invested 1,614 (SH 2279, 2348).

[35]In addition to nuns and Beguines in Delft (above, note 30), there were ten priests who bought renten totaling 2,548, for an average of 255 pounds each.

[36]For the Utrecht chapters on the eve of the Reformation, see L. J. Rogier, *Geschiedenis van het Katholicisme in Noord-Nederland in de Zestiende en Zeventiende Eeuw* (2 vols., Amsterdam: 1947), I, 260–283.

younger than their husbands, and could thus expect to live a portion of their lives bereaved of companionship, but in control of the family fortune.[37] Yet widows with money at their disposal need not have invested in Holland renten. In this part of Europe it was quite common for a widow to carry on her late husband's business, and those who chose for one reason or another not to do so still had a variety of safe and attractive investment opportunities available, including private renten (rather like mortgages, which could be retired any time the principal was paid back) secured by urban real estate,[38] or "ship-parts," the traditional small fractions of ownership usually spread among several merchant vessels in order to minimize the risk.[39] For example, using the account for an urban real estate tax from 1553, and taking a rental income of 100 pounds per year (equivalent to an assessed value of 1,600) as a threshold, one finds in Amsterdam twenty-six women with a serious interest in urban property, not all of whom were widows. Of these women only six bought Holland renten between 1542 and 1565, for a total of 3,420 pounds.[40] Lacking a comprehensive list of women

[37]Rights of widows in north Netherlands law are discussed by Sherrin Wyntjes, "Survivors and Status: Widowhood and Family in the Early Modern Netherlands," *Journal of Family History* (1982): 396–405.

[38]I. J. G. Kam, *Waar Was dat Huis in de Warmoesstraat* (Amsterdam: 1968) gives details on some 200 houses along this prestigious street during the sixteenth century, including many instances in which rente "speaking on" (*sprekende op*) or secured by a particular house was passed on as a liability from one owner to the next.

[39]N. W. Posthumus, *De Uitvoer van Amsterdam*, 49–57: male and female members of the Kantert family (see Appendix II*b*, nos. 45, 53) were among the leading ship-part owners during the early decades of the century; see also Christensen, *Dutch Trade to the Baltic*, 105–134. Posthumus (69–84) suggests that ownership by parts was at this time declining in favor of an arrangement whereby merchant shippers simply hired vessels owned by their captains.

[40]SH 551; this and other "hearth tax" accounts are especially difficult to use because owners are seldom identified by anything more than name and patronymic (entries are arranged by street, and local clerks would always know which "Jan Claeszoon" it was who lived on Zeedijk or Kalverstraat). For example, Simon Maarten Dirkszoon van den Ruwiel (on whom see Elias *sub nomine*) is identifiable in the Holland renten accounts because he is called "Simon Maarten Dirks" in one instance, and in another only "Simon Maarts," but with the addition of his wife's name; but one cannot be sure that the

wealth-holders, it is difficult to place figures like these in a meaningful context. But the one circumstance that does seem to influence a widow's level of interest in Holland renten is whether or not her late husband or one of her sons was a member of the officeholding elite, as is indicated in table 16 for the three largest urban markets in Holland.

TABLE 16
PURCHASES OF RENTEN BY WIDOWS, 1553–1565

| | Total purchase (number of buyers) average purchase | |
Marketplace	Late husband or son an officeholder	Other widows
Amsterdam	11,100 (6) 1,850	19,902 (34) 562
The Hague	9,112 (10) 911	9,068 (14) 714
Delft	5,240 (2) 2,620	3,946 (11) 359
Totals	25,452 (18) 1,414	32,106 (57) 544

This breakdown is yet another indication that the clearest connection that emerges from the figures in table 15*b*, and which merits more extensive discussion, is that between renten-buyers and officeholders in Holland.

II. Within the six great cities of Holland, plus Rotterdam and The Hague, averages calculated from figures shown in table 15*b*, and represented on the following page (table 17),

---

"Simon Maarts" whose name recurs frequently in the hearth tax account is invariably the same person. The six women property-owners who also bought renten were: [Aef Vrankendochter de Wael], widow of Cornelis Bennink, 384 pounds; Nell Sijbrandsdochter Buyck, sister of no. 31, Appendix II*b* and widow of Claes Jeroen, 180; Weyn Cornelisdochter Vlaminck, wife or perhaps widow of Dirk Jan Lambertszoon, 792; [Bennicht Claes Walichsdochter], widow of Olfert Hendrikszoon inde Fuyck, 924; Grietken Jan Claes Korssen's widow, 600; and Nies Jansdochter, 540 pounds. Among thirteen women who declared 1,000 pounds or more in commercial inventory in 1543 (see below, note 51), there were three renten-buyers: Luduwe Arisdochter Boelens (2,340), Geert Dirk Pouwelsdochter (1,300), and Marij Jansdochter Hollesloot (400). For all of these women except Nies Jansdochter, see Elias, *sub nomine*.

TABLE 17

AVERAGE PURCHASES (IN POUNDS) BY OFFICEHOLDERS
AND OTHER LAY MEN, 1553–1565

	Officeholders	Other lay men
Amsterdam	1,496	575
The Hague	1,392	912
Delft	2,407	409
Dordrecht	1,480	681
Gouda	546	267
Haarlem	1,105	848
Rotterdam	1,622	917
Leiden	684	340
Totals	1,428	573

consistently show magistrates and salaried officials buying more than their fellow townsmen. (Haarlem's officeholder average is calculated after subtracting the huge purchases by Meester Gerrit Hendrikszoon van Ravensberg, which would otherwise distort the result.) That the burghers of Gouda and Leiden were less affluent than their social peers in other towns, as is suggested by these figures, is consistent with what is known about the difficulties of their major industries.

What stands out in table 17 is the high average amount of purchase by the magistrates of Delft, who outspent their fellow townsmen in this regard by a ratio of six to one, instead of the more usual ratio (except for Haarlem without Meester Gerrit Hendrikszoon) of two or three to one. As mentioned in chapter 3, Delft's ruling patricians were also unusually prominent as buyers of Holland renten between 1515 and 1534, and again from 1542 through 1552.[41] Since Delft's ar-

---

[41]For 1515–1534, see table 13. Between 1542 and 1552, eleven Delft magistrates bought renten totaling 6,700 (average 609), while forty-six officials in The Hague invested 6,634 (average 144), and nine Amsterdam magistrates 2,581 (average 288).

chives were devastated by a major fire in 1536, its social and political makeup for this period is uncommonly difficult to reconstruct. But two points that may be related to the special interest in Holland renten among Delft magistrates should be noted here. First, insofar as information is available about the business interests of these men, it appears that the largest purchases were often made by magistrates who were also brewers;[42] as will be explained in a later section of this chapter, Hollanders engaged in the business of brewing for export may have had special reasons for disinvestment in their own trade. Second, Delft was the only city that argued vainly, decade after decade, that Holland's tax structure needed fundamental revision so as to place the tax burden on "tall masts," instead of relying on urban excises and other levies, which struck hardest at those less able to pay.[43] Given that Delft was assessed at the highest rate in the 1515 schiltal, protests of this kind have an element of collective self-interest, but they may also express a genuine conviction that those who have wealth ought to pay for the military forces by which wealth is protected. The renten accounts suggest that Delft's city fathers practiced what they preached by investing a disproportionate amount of their own funds in State annuities.

The connection between officeholders and renten-buyers becomes even stronger as one isolates leading Hollanders at either pole of the relationship—that is, those who invested the largest sums of money, and those who served most often as sheriff, burgomaster, or schepen in the great cities. If 2,000 pounds is taken as the threshold for large investments, the seventy-one buyers in Holland (Appendix II*b*) whose purchases exceeded this limit account for 288,859 of the total for column 2 of table 15*b*; in other words, 5.6 percent of the buyers bought 37.3 percent of the renten. Of these seventy-one, the thirty-three who were government, noble, or town officials invested 153,388, or about 53 percent, of the funds

---

[42]See Appendix II*b*, nos. 8 and 28; according to De la Torre, the father of nos. 2 and 41, Jan Aper Melis van Melisdijk (Boitet: d. 1555) was also a brewer.

[43]AJ 15 October 1523, 19 May, 24 June, 10 September, 21 October, 1528; Assendelft to Mary of Hungary, 28 December 1543 (Aud. 1646:3).

that came from major investors; eight others who were members of officeholder families invested a further 22,840. Officeholders and their families thus account for some 58 percent of the major investors, and 61 percent of what all major investors bought.

Outside of Holland, officeholders as a group do not stand out among the major investors. Counting only the markets listed in table 15a, there were ninety individuals who invested over 2,000 pounds in Holland renten, for a total of 431,828 pounds (see Appendix IIa). Of these ninety, the twelve who were officials of the central government invested a total of 58,534, and the seventeen who were magistrates in Middelburg or Zierikzee invested 64,958. "Foreign" officeholders thus accounted for only 32 percent of the major investors and 29 percent of their total investments. But investors in Brabant (Antwerp or Brussels) had many kinds of state securities to choose among, including the much larger renten issues of the States of Brabant and Flanders. Zeeland, where the eagerness of investors in the 1550s suggests that opportunities of this kind may have been rare hitherto, is one province where the market for Holland renten probably offers a better indication of the investment habits of officeholders outside of Holland. The crucial test comes in Zierikzee, the one city in Zeeland for which there is something resembling a complete list of urban magistrates.[44] Here the average purchase by magistrates (3,166 pounds) outstripped that by "other lay men" (871 pounds) in proportions which in Holland are found only in Delft. While it would be rash to draw conclusions in the absence of studies of the other provinces, there is at least reason for thinking that the magistrates' inclination for investing in provincial renten was not peculiar to Holland.

For determining which magistrates were most prominent in a given city, one can obtain a rough index by selecting, from among all those who held office between 1553 and 1565, those who during their careers (which may have begun prior to 1553) were elected burgomaster at least twice, or schepen at least four times. This selection process shows that magis-

---

[44]Above, note 23.

trates thus defined as "prominent" were more likely than their colleagues to buy Holland renten.

Purely quantitative measures of political importance should also be checked against contemporary assessments of whose voices counted for most among the city fathers. For Amsterdam it is possible to do so because in 1564 the ruling faction of patricians had to face charges of nepotism and other grievances which seventy burghers submitted in a formal *Doleantie* presented to the central government. The Doleantie contended that real political authority in the city was concentrated in the hands of five men: Meester Hendrik Dirkszoon, after whom the ruling party was known as the "Hendrik Dirkisten"; Pieter Kantert Willemszoon; Dirk Hillebrandszoon Otter; Joost Sijbrandszoon Buyck; and Sijbrand Occo.[45] It happens that these same men (except for Occo, whose role as Amsterdam factor for the Fuggers made him a key figure in the city's economy) were also the ones elected burgomaster more often than anyone else.[46] As may be seen from Appendix II*b* (nos. 6, 7, 31, 45, and 55), their combined purchases of Holland renten totaled 22,840 pounds, for an average of 4,568, or more than twice the average purchase for "prominent" magistrates in Amsterdam (table 18). Finally, for a full picture of political life in Amsterdam, Delft, or any other city, one would have to look not just at individuals but at the families whose sons and sons-in-law were deemed eligible for important responsibilities generation after generation. For example, in Delft, those making the very largest purchases were young men of such families, who were just beginning their political careers, not all of whom were "prominent" in

---

[45]Quoted by Elias, I, xxxv; the 1564 Doleantie and related documents are edited by Brouwer Ancher.

[46]For Occo and his better-known father, Pompeius, or Poppius, Occo, see the references *sub nomine* in Götz Freiherr von Pölnitz, *Anton Fugger*, vols. 1–2 (Tübingen: 1958–1967). Meester Hendrik Dirkszoon and Pieter Kantert Willemszoon were each burgomaster fourteen times, Joost Buyck (between 1549 and 1565) ten times, and Dirk Hillebrandszoon Otter (between 1545 and 1566) nine times. Other men frequently chosen to this office were Claes Gerritszoon Mattheus (d. 1558: he bought no renten), eight times, and Claes Doedeszoon (Appendix II*b*, no. 18), nine times.

the sense used in table 18.[47] It appears, then, that as one comes closer to defining a political elite in Delft or Amsterdam, one comes upon men who might be expected almost as a matter of course to invest huge sums in renten.

TABLE 18

PURCHASES BY MAGISTRATES IN AMSTERDAM
AND DELFT, 1553–1565

	Group members	Buyers	Total bought	Average per buyer	Average per group member
"Prominent" in Amsterdam	26	18	36,960	2,053	1,422
Others in Amsterdam	38	16	18,464	1,154	486
"Prominent" in Delft	26	10	29,814	2,981	1,147
Others in Delft	49	10	24,644	2,464	499

Given the previous history of such investments, one might wonder whether government officials and town magistrates were not still subject to at least some informal pressure to buy, so as to demonstrate their loyalty to the prince, even though constraint was now prohibited. Although it would be foolish to exclude this possibility, there are good reasons for thinking it does not explain the phenomenon in question. First, as of 1542, when the renten began to be funded by special taxes collected by the States, the central government no longer had any means of determining who the purchasers were. The commissions that audited the renten receipts counted among their members at least one from the prince's Chamber of Accounts in The Hague (the rest were deputies to the States), but apart from this official the government had

[47]Appendix II*b*, nos. 2 and 5.

no access to the accounts, and the States were no doubt as zealous in protecting these records from official scrutiny as they were for others that contained information about the wealth of his majesty's subjects.[48] Second, average purchases by officeholders after 1553 are out of all proportion to those made during the previous decade. This relationship is clear whether one looks at officeholder buyers as a group in the three leading Holland markets, or at the few individuals in each city who bought renten in both periods (see table 19).

TABLE 19

AVERAGE OFFICEHOLDER PURCHASES, 1542–1565

(Number of buyers) / average purchase per buyer			
	Amsterdam	The Hague	Delft
All buyers, 1542–1552	(9) 287	(48) 143	(10) 640
All buyers, 1553–1565	(41) 1,496	(35) 1,377	(32) 2,407
Individuals buying in both periods, 1542–1552	(5) 423	(8) 88	(3) 160
Individuals buying in both periods, 1553–1565	(5) 3,107	(8) 2,380	(3) 1,728

That the government could compel even its own appointees in The Hague to open their purses so wide, especially while constraint was formally prohibited by the terms of the States' consent to the sale of renten, is simply not credible. Here, too, the pattern of heavy purchase by magistrates from Zierikzee is a useful indication from outside of Holland that men engaged in urban politics had reasons of their own for investing in state securities. What these reasons may have been is an appropriate subject for speculation, but it will first be

[48]For beden (including those raised by sales of renten) collected by the Receiver for the Common Territory, members of the audit committee are listed at the end of each SH account. For the strict conditions under which officials of the central government were allowed access to local 10th penny accounts (with names and amounts for each taxpayer), always with an oath of secrecy and in the presence of deputies from the States, RSH 26 March, 9 April, 9 July, 6 August, 1545, 20 February, 27 June, 1549.

useful to highlight the profile of officeholders as renten-buyers still further by comparing them with fellow townsmen, grouped according to their economic interests.

III. Surviving documentation for Amsterdam permits comparison at two different levels. First, magistrates as a group can be compared with their political opposition which, in the 1550s, crystallized around Sheriff Willem Dirkszoon Baerdes, and next found expression in the 1564 Doleantie signed by seventy burghers, one of whose aims was to prevent the ouster of Baerdes.[49] Second, tax records and other sources throw isolated shafts of light on the economic activities of Amsterdam's burghers at various points in time: exporters during the period of the 100th penny tax (1543–1545),[50] owners of mercantile inventories valued at 1,000 pounds or more in 1543,[51] holders of rye and wheat stocks during a 1551 grain census,[52] and owners of urban real estate in 1553.[53] In addition, the city treasury accounts will occasionally have reason to list persons engaged in a particular trade, like grain dealers from whom the city acquires its stockpile in times of anticipated shortage. Finally, Elias's collective biography identifies many patricians as to occupation or prime business interest, though it is in effect biased against the men who ruled Amsterdam during the 1550s and 1560s, since it begins only in 1578, when the Hendrik Dirkisten were ousted from power by a new ruling group in which former *Doleanten* (those burghers who signed the Doleantie) and their kinsmen were prominent.[54] This fragmentary information must be used with

[49]Brouwer-Ancher, 64–65, lists the seventy Doleanten. For present purposes, Sheriff Baerdes, leader of political opposition to the ruling party (see above, note 9), has been added to the list, though he was not a signatory of the Doleantie.

[50]CC 23358, 23360, 23362, 23364, and 23366, analyzed by Posthumus, *De Uitvoer van Amsterdam*.

[51]P. A. Meilink, "Gegevens aangaande Bedrijfskapitalen in den Hollandschen en Zeeuwschen Handel in 1543," *Economisch-Historisch Jaarboek* VIII (1922): 263–277.

[52]Aud. 1419:1.

[53]SH 551.

[54]See the genealogies of nos. 1–36 in Elias, the men chosen to the vroedschap just after what is known in Amsterdam history as the "Alteratie"

caution because, as will be seen, it was quite common, even normal, for a man to have his working capital invested in different areas at the same time. Moreover, since some of the more useful information is not applicable to the brief time span between 1553 and 1565, when Holland renten were being sold on the free market, it will be necessary to abandon the caution thus far exercised in this chapter and deal with the whole period from 1542 to 1565. This procedure will skew the results in favor of officeholders, since they will have been prime targets for whatever constraint was being practiced on renten-buyers in Amsterdam during the 1540s, but not appreciably, because total sales during this decade were quite small compared with total sales in the 1550s.[55] In the figures to be presented in table 20, then, the renten-buying inclinations of the Dirkist magistrates may be slightly exaggerated, while the range and variety of their business interests will be somewhat understated.

In a city that throve as an entrepôt for trade between the Baltic and southern Europe, it was natural for the same merchant to handle commodities going in both directions. Thus Jan Harmanszoon in 't Goudenberg, though known in city treasury records as a grain dealer, exported salt herring to the Baltic during the 1540s, presumably to help pay for his imports.[56] Meester Hendrik Dirkszoon, leading figure of the current ruling group, seems chiefly to have been interested in the export of French wine to the Baltic, but he was also among those who had large quantities of Baltic rye warehoused in their attics during the 1551 grain census.[57] Any

---

of 1578: nine were Doleanten, and many others were connected with Doleant families.

[55]See table 11: renten sold in Amsterdam between 1542 and 1552 were only 2.17 percent of the total sold between 1542 and 1565.

[56]CC 23358; ASR 1552, 1556; see also Elias, *sub nomine.*

[57]CC 23362; Aud. 1419:1. A further indication of Meester Hendrik's interest in *romeinij,* or French wine, is the fact that he and two members of the Hollesloot family (on whom see Elias) declared, as partners, the largest value for commercial inventories at the time of the 10th penny in 1543 (6,000 pounds: Meilink, "Gegevens aangaande Bedrijfskapitalen"); cf. wine exports by Jan Ijsbrantszoon Hollesloot, one of Meester Hendrik's partners, and his son Cornelis in CC 23362, 23364, and 23366.

classification of a man's mercantile interests must therefore be somewhat arbitrary, all the more so since "merchants" of any description might also have some of their capital tied up in Amsterdam's woolen cloth industry, or in the "inpoldering" (reclamation) of new farm land along the Maas delta in southern Holland.[58] In what follows, certain procedures are adopted to make classification consistent if not necessarily accurate. Women merchants and entrepreneurs are excluded, since they had no chance of becoming magistrates, or of signing the Doleantie. Since Baltic grain was Amsterdam's "mother trade," in which amateurs were particularly likely to dabble, mention in the 1551 grain census is not in itself sufficient grounds for classifying as "grain dealers" those for whom other interests are indicated elsewhere. Men known to be active in two different branches of commerce—for instance, as brewers and drapers—are arbitrarily assigned to whichever category has fewer representatives. Millers are counted as grain dealers, and dyers as drapers. "Baltic exporters" includes three disparate kinds of activity, which had only the Baltic market in common: herring-packing, soap-boiling, and the transshipment of French wines.[59] "Merchants" includes those so identified, without further qualification, in Elias or the renten accounts, plus dealers in a number of specialized commodities (furs, silk, chalk, flax, eels, lumber, iron . . .) and, finally, a few goldsmiths. "Professional men" are lawyers, doctors, apothecaries, and city employees and nonelected officials. "Shippers" are of course captains of seagoing vessels, but also manufacturers of prod-

[58]The land-holding interests of Gerrit Willekens (below, note 68) are mentioned by Elias.

[59]On soap-boiling, Posthumus, *De Uitvoer van Amsterdam,* 34–40. There are no studies of Amsterdam's wine trade or herring-packing industry, but in general see J. Craeybeckx, *Un Grand Commerce d'Importation: les Vins de France aux Pays Bas au XVIe Siècle* (Paris: 1958), and Rogier De Gryse, "De Gemeenschappelijke Groote Visscherij van de Nederlanden in de XVIe Eeuw." In the remarkably detailed bird's-eye view of the city drawn in 1544 by Cornelis Anthoniszoon (discussed in Ter Gouw, V, 16–83), herring-packing is indicated by barrels stacked along Nieuwendijk, towards Haarlemmerpoort, while Kam, *Waar Was dat Huis in de Warmoesstraat,* mentions a number of wine dealers living along the upper end of the street (Meester Hendrik Dirkszoon's large house was the present No. 166).

ucts used in the ship-building industry, like rope and compasses. Although most magistrates and members of the political opposition can be fitted under one or another of these categories, there are still thirty-two Dirkisten and twenty-seven Doleanten on whom little or no information is available in the sources used here.[60]

Between 1542 and 1565, 267 lay men in Amsterdam, including officeholders, invested a total of 190,721 pounds in renten as listed in the ten accounts examined here. Of this number, 136 buyers (50.9%) can be identified as to political stance, and/or as belonging to one of the economic interest categories included in table 20, and they were responsible for 62.3 percent of the purchases by lay men (118,834 pounds). In table 20, types of business activity are arranged in a sequence that reflects a rough distinction one can make between sectors of economic life in Amsterdam: those that were wholly dependent on the Baltic trade and those that were less so. Grain dealers and those here called "Baltic exporters" (wine merchants, soap-boilers, and herring-packers) represent the two sides of this vital exchange in the most obvious way. Ship captains and those with property and business facilities in Amsterdam's shipyard district were equally dependent for their livelihood on this flow of traffic, as were the "merchants" who dealt either in a great variety of goods, or in specialty items (like Westphalian ham or Baltic gunpowder), which only had a market because Amsterdam had a large concourse of foreign merchants during the sailing season. Conversely, brewing was less dependent on the Baltic connection, since Amsterdam's beer was not exported,[61] although brewers certainly profited from the city's population growth,[62]

[60]Some had interests in the land, but they are not made into a separate category in table 20 because too many of them may have had other interests that are listed in the table.

[61]Posthumus, *De Uitvoer van Amsterdam*, 32–34: apart from a weak ship's beer, the city's product could not compete in other markets with Hamburg beers or *jopenbier* from Danzig.

[62]Population growth and the frequenting of the city by foreigners are doubtless both reflected in the impressive increase in income from the groote accijns, the combined excise in which the beer tax was by far the most important component, from an average of 20,841 pounds per year in 1531–1534 to an average of 45,474 for 1561–1564.

which was made possible by its commercial prosperity. The woolen cloth industry had less connection with the Baltic than it might appear, because foreign markets were found not by sea (cloths exported to the Baltic were mostly from England, less so from Leiden and other Holland towns), but, by way of the overland route from Antwerp, in south Germany, where Sijbrand Occo's Fugger connections were doubtless of some benefit.[63] Finally, doctors and lawyers would obviously be in demand—and increasingly so[64]—regardless of how the city's merchants made their living.

The first comparison that can be made using the information in table 20 is between the magistrates as a group and their political opponents, or at least those who signed the Doleantie. The sharpest difference between the groups lies in their interest in Holland renten, high among elected officials, and very low among the Doleanten, whether one measures by average purchase per buyer or average purchase per group member. The disinclination of the Doleanten to make investments of this kind appears even more clearly from the fact that (with two exceptions) the few among them who made purchases of 600 pounds or more were closely related to leading members of the ruling faction. Pieter Boel Allertszoon (2,254) was the son-in-law of Joost Sijbrandszoon Buyck; Pieter Jacobszoon Schaep (1,624) and his brother (who was elected schepen in 1562, and was not among the Doleanten) were sons-in-law of Dirk Hillebrandszoon Otter; Jacob Claeszoon Basgen (900) was the son of Claes Hendrickszoon Basgen (d. 1563), who had been five times burgomaster and

---

[63]Tracy, "Shipments to Germany by Erasmus Schetz and other Antwerp Merchants during the Period of the 100th Penny Tax," forthcoming in *Journal of European Economic History.*

[64]On the growing importance of legal training for the careers of town magistrates and appointed officials in Brabant, see H. de Ridder-Symoens, "De Universitaire Vorming van de Brabantse Stadsmagistraten en Funktionarissen: Leuven en Antwerpen, 1430–1580," *Verslagboek van de Vijfde Colloquium "De Brabantse Stad"* ('s Hertogenbosch: 1978), 21–125. In Amsterdam, Andries Jacobszoon van Naarden functioned quite effectively as a mere town secretary (as may be seen from AJ), but the men who succeeded him in representing the city at meetings of the States and on other occasions were all "pensionaries," and had the title "Meester," which here indicates a law degree.

TABLE 20

RENTEN PURCHASES BY AMSTERDAM LAY MEN, 1542–1565
MAGISTRATES, DOLEANTEN, AND NONPOLITICAL BUSINESSMEN

	Members of group	Number of renten buyers	Total bought	Average purchase per buyer	Average purchase per group member
				(In pounds)	
Magistrates only	32	13	21,040	1,618	657
Magistrate professionals	4	3	4,532	1,511	1,133
Magistrate brewers	9	5	6,840	1,368	760
Magistrate drapers	9	4	11,744	2,936	1,305
Magistrate grain dealers	11	4	5,662	1,415	515
Magistrate Baltic exporters	7	4	4,260	1,065	609
Magistrate merchants	12	4	4,136	1,034	345
Magistrate shippers	1	0	—	—	—
All magistrates	85	37	58,214	1,573	685
Doleanten only	27	3	2,640	880	98
Doleanten professionals	3	3	1,008	336	336

TABLE 20—*Continued*

RENTEN PURCHASES BY AMSTERDAM LAY MEN, 1542–1565

MAGISTRATES, DOLEANTEN, AND NONPOLITICAL BUSINESSMEN

	Members of group	Number of renten buyers	Total bought	Average purchase per buyer	Average purchase per group member
				(In pounds)	
Doleanten brewers	0	—	—	—	—
Doleanten drapers	6	1	684	684	114
Doleanten grain dealers	11	2	2,398	1,199	218
Doleanten Baltic exporters	7	3	1,680	560	240
Doleanten merchants	14	2	2,700	1,350	193
Doleanten shippers	3	0	—	—	—
All Doleanten	71	14	11,110	794	156
Other professionals	10	5	3,776	755	378
Other brewers	8	2	1,956	978	244
Other drapers	21	2	360	180	17
Other grain dealers	57	16	17,850	1,116	313

TABLE 20—*Continued*

RENTEN PURCHASES BY AMSTERDAM LAY MEN, 1542–1565

MAGISTRATES, DOLEANTEN, AND NONPOLITICAL BUSINESSMEN

	Members of group	Number of renten buyers	Total bought	Average purchase per buyer	Average purchase per group member
				(In pounds)	
Other Baltic exporters	31	3	10,090	3,363	325
Other merchants	60	14	9,826	702	164
Other shippers	25	10	7,542	754	302
All others	211	52	51,400	988	244
All professionals	17	11	9,316	847	548
All brewers	17	7	8,796	1,257	517
All drapers	36	7	12,788	1,826	355
All grain dealers	79	22	25,910	1,178	328
All Baltic exporters	45	10	16,036	1,603	356
All merchants	85	20	16,662	833	196
All shippers	29	10	7,542	755	260
All businessmen and professionals	308	77	97,050	1,260	315

himself invested 1,800 in Holland renten; and Clement Volck-ertszoon Coornhert (684) was the brother-in-law of Hendrik Janszoon Crook, seven times schepen, who invested 1,236 in renten.[65] These young men doubtless joined in the grievance against the Dirkist government partly because the honor of public office had not come to them, as they might reasonably have expected it would. In any event the five of them account for nearly half (49.1%) of all the renten bought by Doleanten. As for the other sixty-six, their lack of interest in Holland renten provides a negative corroboration of the connection between office-holding and renten-buying. This conclusion needs qualification, however, since the Doleanten as a group were definitely younger than the magistrates,[66] and therefore less likely to feel the need of providing security for their families through the purchase of life annuities or other safe investments.

The other difference between the magistrates and their critics is more subtle. If one breaks Amsterdam's economic life down into the two broad areas mentioned earlier, information in table 20 suggests (as seems inherently likely) that business activities directly related to the Baltic trade were far more important than those which were not. Of the men listed in this table who were neither Dirkisten nor Doleanten, there were thirty-five brewers, drapers, and professional men, but about five times as many (172) grain dealers, Baltic exporters, merchants, and shippers. One would expect the city's ruling group to reflect in its composition this dominance of the Baltic

[65]The other large investors among the Doleanten were Claes Loen Cornelis-zoon, also known as Claes Boelens [Loen] inde Hamburg (1,164), whose father, uncle, and maternal grandfather had been leading figures in the ruling faction which preceded the Dirkists, and Lennart Janszoon Graeff (1,800), whose father (d. 1553) had been a member of the vroedschap. For all of these men, see Elias, *sub nomine.*

[66]Ages are known only for some of the Doleanten, as also for the magistrates, but twenty-two of the seventy can be recognized as sons of men who were prominent in the city's affairs about 1540, as magistrates, exporters (CC 23358–23366), or holders of commercial inventory valued in excess of 1,000 pounds (Meilink, "Gegevens aangaande Bedrijfskapitalen"): Brouwer-Ancher, 64–65, nos. 4, 8, 11, 12, 13, 16, 20, 24, 28, 29, 30, 31, 35, 36, 39, 43, 48, 49, 50, 55, 57, 59, and 60 (Elias has information on all these families).

trading interest. In fact, however, grain dealers, Baltic exporters, merchants, and shippers are somewhat less represented among the magistrates whose economic interests are identified here (twenty-nine of fifty-one, or 56.9%) than among the Doleanten (thirty-five of forty-four, or 79.5%). The richest and most prominent merchants often eschewed political activity; thus there were no officeholders among Amsterdam's six leading exporters during the period of the 100th penny tax,[67] and only two magistrates among the five men who together controlled about a third of the rye and wheat stocks inventoried in 1551.[68] To some extent, this apparent social division between a political and a commercial elite reflects the fact that the most active traders were often men who migrated to Amsterdam from elsewhere in Holland, from the northern Low Countries, or even from north Germany, like Arent Hudde, Jorriaen ter Meulen, Adriaan Reyerszoon Cromhout, and Adriaan Pauw. In a previous generation the fathers of Meester Hendrik Dirkszoon and Sijbrand Occo had been men of the same type, who might look forward to a political career not for themselves, but for their sons or sons-in-law.[69]

What is a bit more curious is that, although many magistrates lived along fashionable Warmoesstraat, few of them lived along the lower end of the street, which had inns catering to north German merchants and where the daily open-air grain exchange was held.[70] Moreover, of the eleven magis-

[67]Arent Hudde, Jaspar Craek, Karsten Roelofs, Meynaert Kuyl, Adriaan Reynaertszoon Cromhout, and Harman in 't Boot: Posthumus, *Uitvoer van Amsterdam*, 122–143, analyzes their exports.

[68]Aud. 1419:1: Gerrit Willekens (648 last), Gijsbert Janszoon van Berensteyn (131 last; chosen to the vroedschap in 1532), Pieter Pieterszoon van Neck (129 last), Jan Pieterszoon Kies (94 last), and Hendrik Corneliszoon in't Roomolen (70 last: chosen to the vroedschap in 1547), for a combined total of 1,072, of slightly over 3,000 last then found in the city. A last was a measure of volume equivalent to about eighty-five bushels.

[69]See Elias for Dirk Jan van Slooterdijk, Meester Hendrik's father, and Nübel, *Pompeius Occo,* for the father of Sijbrand Occo. Hudde was apparently from Kampen in Overijsel, Cromhout was from Medemblik, and Pauw's father had been a magistrate in Gouda (for these three, see Elias), while ter Meulen is called "from Bremen" in the 100th penny accounts (CC 23358).

[70]Tracy, "A Premature Counter-Reformation: The Dirkist Government of Amsterdam, 1538–1578," *Journal of Religious History*, XIII (1984): 150–167.

trates who were grain merchants, there are only three for whom large-volume transactions are suggested either in the 1551 grain census, or in famine-year sales recorded in the treasury accounts, and none of them was ever chosen for the key post of burgomaster.[71] Finally, it might be noted that the Dirkist party was peculiar among Holland's ruling oligarchies in that it had been brought to power by a single dramatic event some years previously. In 1535, a revolutionary faction among local Anabaptists whom the current governing party was shielding from persecution launched a sudden night attack on city hall. The original Dirkist leaders were men who had apparently felt all along that religious subversion should be dealt with more firmly. Years later, the stout Catholic loyalties of these same men and their descendants caused them to stand with the Spanish monarchy against the rebel towns of Holland, until they were ousted (1578) by a new, largely Protestant party led by former Doleanten.[72] Owing to these distinctive circumstances, the Dirkisten may have been an exception to the general rule that a town's dominant economic interest usually supplied much of its political leadership.[73]

[71]The three were Gijsbert Janszoon van Berensteyn (note 68), Jan Harmanszoon (note 56), and Hendrik Corneliszoon in 't Roomolen (note 68), who was first chosen burgomaster in 1567. Other magistrates known to have had an interest in the grain trade were the prominent burgomasters Gerrit Claeszoon Mattheus and Claes Doedeszoon (Appendix II*b*, no. 18), the latter's son Doedt Claes, together with Floris Floriszoon Kant in 't Sleutel, Jacob Janszoon van Keulen, Claes Jacobszoon Swieten van Leiden, Willem Corneliszoon Stickels, and Pieter Bicker Willemszoon, a miller.

[72]Ter Gouw, IV, 272–284; Albert F. Mellink, *Amsterdam en de Wederdopers in de 16e Eeuw* (Nijmegen: 1978); above, note 54.

[73]For example, Delft was thought to have suffered from misgovernment from its brewers: Neiborg to Mary of Hungary, 14 October 1551 (Aud. 1441:4); cf. Mary of Hungary to Sheriff Jan de Heuter, 21 August 1539 (Aud. 1528), and to Sheriff Dierick Pynss, 12 December 1541 (Aud. 1530), and the role of government regulations for brewers in the feud between Delft's magistrates and the regent's favorite, Dirk Duyst (Aud. 1441:4, nos. 3–5). Similarly, the sheriff and burgomasters of Gouda alleged they were unable to enforce a mandate from Brussels intended to protect small brewers against larger enterprises because "most of the vroedschap are brewers": to Mary of Hungary, 22 October 1549 (Aud. 1530). In the small city of Woerden (see below, note 89), a dependency of the Count of Egmont, Sheriff Gerrit van Renesse blamed resistance to his authority on his interference with illegal use of

The second level of comparison made possible by the information in table 20 concerns the renten-buying inclinations of men with different business interests. If one takes average purchase per group member as the best indication of interest in renten, professional men and brewers (who will be discussed separately) head the list, followed by grain dealers and shippers. That doctors and lawyers should regard state securities as safe and profitable investments that did not need watching is not surprising, and was perhaps especially common in administrative centers like Mechelen and The Hague, where investor confidence in such instruments was well established. Thus there were twelve advocates before the Grand Council in Mechelen who invested 18,764, and four physicians in The Hague who invested 11,126.[74] Among grain dealers, shippers, and merchants, much of the renten-buying was concentrated in the hands of a few prominent men, like Adriaan Pauw and Jan Pieterszoon Kies; they and six others bought 43.6 percent of all the renten listed in table 19 purchased by "nonpolitical" grain dealers, shippers, and merchants.[75] There are, however, some equally prominent names absent from the ten renten accounts examined here, such as Arent Hudde, Adriaan Cromhout, Jorriaen ter Meulen, and Jaspar Craek; Gerrit Willekens, who was (to judge from the 1551 grain census) Amsterdam's largest importer by far, is represented by a single purchase for 600 pounds, doubtless rather modest for him. In any case, whether one looks at grain dealers or professionals, the one thing that consistently stands out in table 20 is that magistrates were more likely to invest in renten than their economic and social peers.[76] As for

---

church land by "the burgomasters and their allies": for his long and lively refutation of the charges against him, Aud. 1656:2, no. 10.

[74]See also Appendix II*a*, nos. 18, 51, 71, and 93, and Appendix II*b*, nos. 11 and 42.

[75]See Appendix IIb, nos. 13, 14, 32, 43, and 49. Other large buyers were the grain dealers Simon Bauckeszoon (1,700), Simon Rijckert (1,368), and Hees Willemszoon (1,236).

[76]On Gerrit Willekens, above, note 68. If there were only twenty-one renten-buyers among the seventy-nine men who declared commercial inventory values in excess of 1,000 in 1543 (Meilink, "Gegevens aangaande Bedrijfskapitalen"), it was perhaps because many of these men were deceased

drainage boards. Since the early Middle Ages the county had been divided into drainage districts (*waterschappen*) separated from one another by lines of dikes. Maintenance of dikes and sluices, with limited powers of taxing landowners to support such costs, was entrusted to a drainage board, or *heemraadschap*, consisting of a *dijkgraaf* or *ambachtsheer* appointed by the count and a group chosen from among the chief landholders, or *ingelanden*.[88] Investment in the land may have been but one of many ways the burghers of Amsterdam acquired an assured income, but it was perhaps the only important form of investment for the notables of a small city like Woerden, where, according to an acerbic comment by the town's noble sheriff, burgomasters who saw fit to ride through the streets in a manure wagon were not much different from peasants.[89]

For purposes of comparison with table 20, one would ideally like to have some indication of how much capital wealthy Amsterdammers had tied up in land or others forms of relatively safe investment. Unfortunately, the materials for such a study, where they do exist, lie scattered in various places and cannot be assembled save by the kind of exhaustive survey of local archives which Thomas Brady has carried out for the patricians of Strasbourg during roughly the same period.[90] City treasury accounts and the records of occasional property taxes provide some information on excise tax–farmers and on holders of urban property. Though the Dirkist ruling party was accused by its adversaries of having a strong interest in real estate lying within the city walls,[91]

[88]De Vries, *The Dutch Rural Economy*, 28–29; S. J. Fockema Andreae, *Het Hoogheemraadschap van Rijnland* (Leiden: 1934), and "Embanking and Drainage Authorities in the Netherlands during the Middle Ages," *Speculum* 27 (1952): 158–167.

[89]Comment by Renesse (above, note 73), Aud. 1656:2, no. 10E.

[90]Thomas Brady, *Ruling Class, Regime, and Reformation at Strasbourg* (Leiden: 1979).

[91]Aud. 1441:3, no. 1, undated memo in French concerning charges against the Dirkist government by a group of property owners in the shipyard district, or *lastaige*, and the magistrates' response (see Ter Gouw, IV, 306–309, 416–431: the dispute began in 1542, when the burgomasters in time of war ordered buildings in this district razed instead of acceding to property-owner requests to extend the city walls so as to enclose the lastaige). The complaints

the 1553 hearth tax receipts do not indicate an unusual concentration of real estate in the hands of magistrates. The one thing that can be said is that, as usual, magistrate property owners were more likely than others to invest in Holland renten.[92] As for excise taxes, the treasury's most important receipts were the previously mentioned groote accijns (levied on beer, wine, and flour milling),[93] the weigh-house tax, paid by merchants who needed to have their goods weighed,[94] and the "pale money," or harbor fee, paid on goods ferried through the double pale of stakes which protected the harbor.[95] Contracts for collecting these taxes were awarded annually to the highest bidder.[96] For most of the period between 1542 and 1565, the "great excise" was collected by a syndicate formed among three magistrates, while the weigh-house was presided over by one prominent merchant.[97] For the "pale money" there was more competition, and the right to collect it often changed hands from year to year. As a group, the twenty-four men who held at least one of these contracts during the period in question were not conspicuous buyers of Holland renten, and those who did invest some of their

---

allege *inter alia* "que les gouverneurs de la ville veullent empescher ladite application [i.e., extension of the walls] pour leur singulier prouffit," while the magistrates give as one of their reasons for not extending the walls "que si ladite application se faisoit les deux pars de la ville anchienne yroient debut à perdicion et ne servoient les maisons iam ediffiez par les borgois."

[92]SH 551: taking a rental income of 100 pounds per year as a threshold, and excluding women (see above, note 40), there were 120 men who had a major investment in urban real estate. Among the 15 who were also magistrates, 8 bought renten, for an average per group member of 643 pounds; among the 105 others, 15 bought renten, for an average per group member of 158 pounds.

[93]Ter Gouw, III, 407–415.

[94]Ter Gouw, V, 32–34.

[95]Ter Gouw, IV, 115–116; V, 20–30.

[96]ASR 1543: owing to war-time conditions the weigh house was not farmed out for the year 1543–1544, but served by a man salaried by the city.

[97](Meester) Cornelis Garbrantszoon (Ruysch, brother-in-law of Dirk Hillebrandszoon Otter), Harman Otteszoon, and Floris Maartenszoon (van Alkmade) collected the groote accijns regularly from the late 1540s through 1565; Simon Gijsbertszoon Appelman contracted for the weigh house almost every year (on all four men see Elias, *sub nomine*).

capital in this way were mostly magistrates, including Dirk Hillebrandszoon Otter (Appendix II*b*, no. 7).[98]

For investment in land, however, the information to be found in city treasury records is fortuitous and indirect at best. For example, among the leaders of the ruling faction that preceded the Dirkists, Ruysch Jan Bethszoon was a *heemraad* (presumably of the drainage district of Amstelland), and Heyman Jacobszoon van Ouder Amstel was ambachtsheer of the nearby district of Amstelveen, a position to which the city had rights of nomination.[99] Among the Dirkisten, Joost Buyck is named as one of the ingelanden of the coastal district of Hontsbosch, near Alkmaar, while his elder brother Cornelis was dijkgraaf and ambachtsheer of Nieuwer Amstel, just south of Amsterdam.[100] The heemraden for Nieuwer Amstel during the same period (1550s) included Claes Gerritszoon Mattheus, frequently a burgomaster, and Simon Maarten Dirkszoon van den Ruwiel, frequently a schepen, who was also a draper and an urban property owner.[101] Further inferences can be drawn from the treasury records if one is willing to make an assumption. For discussions dealing with any particular trade, the magistrates customarily sent one of their number who had personal experience of the matter at hand. Meester Hendrik Dirkszoon was thus sent to Brussels to see about discontinuing an embargo on French wine, and Meester Cornelis Wouter Dobbens, a brewer, was dispatched to Leiden to consult with that city's brewers about a proposed new government ordinance.[102] Hence it seems reasonable to think

[98]Among the twenty-four, there were seven renten-buyers for a total of 9,852 (most of which is accounted for by Otter's 6,880), and an average per group member of 410 pounds.

[99]AJ 11 March 1523; ASR 1532, 1535. In his discussion of the waterschap of Amstelland and the subdistrict of Nieuwer Amstel, Ter Gouw, IV, 60–65, mentions that Heyman Jacobszoon was said to be able to travel from the walls of Amsterdam to the village of Ouderkerk without leaving his own land.

[100]ASR 1555, 1557.

[101]ASR 1542, 1554; the other heemraden (there were five, counting the dijkgraaf: Ter Gouw, IV, 60–65) were Jacob van Ems (on whom I have no information), and Jan Claeszoon inde Cat, an apothecary and later Doleant (see Elias).

[102]ASR 1549, 1550.

that those whom the city fathers sent to inspect dikes along the "ring" of Amstelland, or to deliberate on the affairs of the Hontsbosch drainage district (where representatives of Haarlem and Amsterdam were included *ex officio* in meetings of the heemraadschap), were men experienced in drainage and other rural issues. On this basis, a number of magistrates can be identified as having interests in the land, including leading figures like Meester Hendrik Dirkszoon and Dirk Hillebrandszoon Otter,[103] as well as Frans Janszoon Teyng, a brewer and occasionally a schepen, and Jan Claeszoon van Hoppen, town superintendent of public works and frequently a burgomaster during the 1560s.[104] Compared with other burghers who can be identified in the same way as investors in land, the magistrates were, once again, conspicuous as buyers of provincial renten (see table 22).

All in all, it is tempting to think that many of Amsterdam's magistrate buyers of renten were investors in land, especially since the highest renten purchases per buyer (see table 20) are found among those magistrates for whom no mercantile or manufacturing investments are known. But in the case of the brewers it was noted that men with similar economic interests did not necessarily show the same enthusiasm for Holland renten from one city to another, and evidence from Delft suggests the same may have been true for investors in land. In 1550 Delft's finances were in disarray, partly because of rebuilding expenses after the great fire of 1536. Necessary new taxes could only be authorized by the central government, which as a price for cooperation chose to exercise

[103]ASR 1564; connections with the land in Otter's case are also suggested by the fact that his father had been sent on similar missions (ASR 1533: Hillebrand Janszoon Otter), and that one of his daughters married Pieter Jacobszoon Schaep, owner of Croesbeek bij Heemstede, whose brother was also a landowner (Dirk Schaep Jacobszoon, lord of Batesteyn: on these families see Elias).

[104]ASR 1555, 1556, 1558, 1561, 1564. Simon Maarten Dirkszoon van den Ruwiel became ambachtsheer of Amstelveen in 1561. Other names mentioned in this connection are Jacob Gerritszoon Mattheus and Jacob Colijn. In addition, Elias notes the land-owning interests of Gerrit Willekens and his partner, Hendrik Pouwelszoon, as well as Pieter Gerrit Jacobszoon Koekebacker and Willem Pouwelszoon.

TABLE 22

Purchases of Holland Renten by Amsterdam Investors in Land, 1542–1565

	Members of group	Number of renten buyers	Total bought	Average purchase per buyer	Average purchase per group member
Magistrates	10	8	15,678	1,960	1,568
Other investors	11	4	3,496	874	318
All investors	21	12	19,174	1,598	913

its prerogative of dismissing all incumbent magistrates—burgomasters, schepenen, and the Council of Forty—in order to appoint others in their stead. The reason for this decision was that Delft's major brewers (like those of Gouda) had been battling efforts by Brussels to curb allegedly monopolistic practices in the industry, and the Council of State concluded that brewers had entirely too much influence in Delft's town hall.[105] Hence officials in The Hague drafted and sent to Brussels a list of magistrates identified according to their occupations, such as "brewers" or "renteniers." Marginal notes in the hand of Jacobus de la Torre, secretary of the Council of State, indicate some dissatisfaction with the result, so that an additional list was sent.[106] Probably to the further dissatisfaction of de la Torre, the final list, which is used for purposes of the following table, was almost entirely composed of men

[105] Above, note 73.

[106] Aud. 1441:4 no. 2 contains (1) a list of twelve names (the number needed for four burgomasters, seven schepenen, and a treasurer, with the controversial Dierick Duyst [above, note 73] added on as an alternate, provided he is wanted; this list is re-copied twice, with marginal comments by Jacobus de la Torre, on whom see Baelde, 318–319 (for a sample of de la Torre's hand, with signature, see his marginal comment on the Holland Procurator General's letter to Charles V, 1 March 1548, Aud. 1646:2, no. 8); (2) a similar list with Duyst as burgomaster; (3) another similar list that does not mention Duyst; (4) a much longer list of men who have previously served as burgomaster, schepen, or in other offices; (5) a still longer list of twenty-four former burgomasters and schepenen, plus the thirty-nine living members of the Council of Forty and two other former officials; and (6) a list of thirty-five names with no indication of previous offices, and with the notation that some are not qualified "for the service of the Emperor." Neiborch to Mary of Hungary, 14 October 1551 (Aud. 1441:4, no. 9) mentions sending on to Brussels a list of "several notables for the *loi* (= burgomasters plus schepenen) given him by Assendelft and Cornelis Suys of the Council of Holland (no. 3?), a list made up by Dierick Duyst (doubtless no. 2), a list by Neiborch himself, based on the others, which recommends Duyst for treasurer (no. 1), a list of previous officeholders drawn up by the town pensionary, Meester Huyck van den Eynde (probably no. 4), and a list by the lord of Andel, lieutenant of the Marquess of Veere, the current Stadtholder of Holland, and a burgher of Delft himself (a Jacob Gerritszoon Storm van den Andel, mentioned on several of the lists, is doubtless the same "lord of Andel"; his list can be identified with no. 6). De la Torre's comments, dated at one point 30 October 1551, are extremely difficult to read, but he suggests that someone from the Grand Council of Mechelen should investigate conditions there further; list no. 5 may have been one result.

who had already held one office or another. (The few who had not held office, or for whom no occupation is given, are eliminated here.) The uncertain line between a rentenier and a man engaged in commerce or industry is indicated by several entries that speak of a "rentenier, formerly a brewer" or a "rentenier, somewhat involved in commerce"; such men are called "renteniers/merchants" in table 23.

The group that stands out here is the brewer-magistrates, whose uncommonly large purchases were noted earlier in a different connection. At the other end of the scale, rentenier-magistrates showed little interest in Holland renten, whereas renteniers who still or within recent memory had other business interests were at least not remarkable in their purchases. Similarly, among members of the drainage board for the district around Leiden,[107] there were a few notable buyers of renten, but these men were also nobles who took part in meetings of the States of Holland—in other words, they had a political role, even if they would not be classed here as officeholders.

The point is that investors in land per se do not seem to have been unusually interested in Holland renten. Even if it be argued for other parts of Europe that those who invested in land did so mainly because they wished to live nobly, one should be very cautious about drawing similar conclusions for the Low Countries. Though the great age of reclamation

[107]Fockema Andreae, *Het Hoogheemraadschap van Rijnland*, 401, lists thirteen heemraden who held office between 1542 and 1565, of whom six invested a total of 5,292 in Holland renten, with the largest purchases by Willem van Lokhorst (2,300) and Jacob van der Does (1,404), noble deputies to the States of Holland who resided in Leiden.

[108]SH 1792, collection of 2 stuivers per morgen of arable land in connection with a bede for Prince Philip: land identified as "outside the dike" totals 1,262 morgen in the collection district of south Holland (Dordrecht), 624 in Delfland and Schieland (plus 2,800 for the four polders of Maasland, which all seem to have been new), and 112 for Arkel and Heusden, also in the southern part of the province. There are no such indications for the rest of Holland, save 270 morgen in the district of Friesland and Kenemergevolg (near Haarlem), very likely at Hontsbosch. Perhaps one reason for the concentration of such efforts in the Maas delta was the possibility of reclaiming land innundated in the great St. Elizabeth's day flood of 1421, which made Dordrecht an island (C. M. Davies, *The History of Holland and the Dutch Nation* [3 vols., London: 1861], I, 218).

TABLE 23

RENTEN PURCHASES (IN POUNDS) BY DELFT MAGISTRATES GROUPED BY OCCUPATION, 1542–1565

	Members of group	Number of Renten buyers	Total bought	Average per buyer	Average per group member
Renteniers	9	4	1,012	253	112
Rentenier/merchants	6	4	5,956	1,489	993
Brewers	18	10	36,210	3,621	2,012
Merchants & drapers	12	5	9,788	1,957	816
Totals	45	23	52,966	2,303	1,177

in Holland lay still in the future, this region already had a long history of improving the land, and in the middle decades of the sixteenth century there were projects for "inpoldering" new land along the Maas delta in southern Holland,[108] not far from Delft, which could attract capital from as far away as Brussels.[109] The Netherlander who invested heavily in land was likely as not a businessman interested in the most profitable use of his capital, and not particularly susceptible to the purely social appeal of living on a fixed income. If Amsterdammers who invested in the land were somewhat more interested in Holland renten then their Delft counterparts (though in both cases the evidence is admittedly slender), it may have been that northern Holland at this time offered fewer opportunities for putting capital into improving the land. Thus for the creators of a new, capitalistic form of agriculture, just as for those involved in a more traditional sector of the economy like brewing, there seems no general rule for linking particular economic interests with the purchase of Holland renten. The only general rule, as argued in this chapter, is that officeholders clearly lead the way in this form of investment in state debt.

V. In the larger view of Low Countries history, heavy investment in provincial renten seems to have been part of a social process by which magistrate families succeeded to positions of responsibility and influence formerly occupied by the provincial nobility. In an important new book on the

[109]Baudouin de Lannoy, lord of Molembaix and Knight of the Golden Fleece, vainly sought partial recompense from the States of Holland for his expenses in constructing a channel headland (*kolkerhooft*) at Oolkensplate: RSH 14 November 1548, 12 October, (?) November 1549; cf. Sandelijn, 14 November 1548, 2 October 1549, and, on a similar project in the same region funded by Maximiliaan van Bourgondie, Marquess of Veere and current Stadtholder of Holland, 9 October 1551. There were enough "foreigners" investing heavily in Holland agriculture to make it worthwhile for the States to attract renten capital from such persons by offering nonresidents who purchased in excess of 4,000 pounds in renten the privilege of exemption from the 10th penny tax on income from their Holland properties (SH 2341, refund of 40 pounds to Anthonis Sucquet, which means an annual income of 400 pounds, and, since all renten had by now been converted to the 1 : 16 rate, a capital of 6,400, or roughly what is indicated in Appendix IIa, no. 18).

nobility of Holland (1500–1650), Henk van Nierop shows that, roughly during the second quarter of the sixteenth century, nobles were abandoning their traditional prominent role in the officialdom of the county since many positions now demanded a more specialized knowledge of the law, or a greater time commitment than had formerly been expected. Owing to the pressures of Habsburg centralization, van Nierop argues, the business of office-holding was becoming more bureaucratic, and nobles chose to withdraw to their estates rather than to adapt to new circumstances.[110] It may be noted too that noble holdings were concentrated in the southern half of the province, not far from the Maas delta region where land reclamation projects were beginning to gain momentum, and perhaps made the idea of retiring to the land more attractive. Meanwhile, the vacuum left by the nobles was being filled by magistrate families, whose sons fashioned careers that moved back and forth between city hall and government bureaus in The Hague,[111] and married into other families (whether of noble or bourgeois origin) that had already been providing the Habsburgs with provincial officials for a generation or two.[112] In addition to a pattern of intermarriage,

[110]See chapter 6, note 23.

[111]For example, the Pijns family of Delft provided numerous officials for its native city as well as for The Hague (D. J. M. Wüstenhoff, "Genealogische aantekeningen betreffende het geslacht Pijns, Pijnssen," *De Wapenheraut* VII (1903): 430–436). Adriaan, or Aert, Sandelijn, perhaps the son of Arent Sandelijn, Councilor Ordinary of the Council of Holland (d. 1535; see Blécourt) was Councilor Extraordinary or without salary before becoming pensionary of Amsterdam and later a member of the vroedschap (Council of Holland to Mary of Hungary, 1 August 1547, Aud. 1646:1; Ter Gouw, VIII, 345.

[112]For example, two of Meester Hendrik Dirkszoon's sons were married to daughters of Meester Reynier Brunt, a native Amsterdammer and (see Blécourt) Procurator-General, or prosecuting attorney, on behalf of the emperor at the Hof van Holland, 1523–1536: Dirk Hendrikszoon Opmeer and Neel Reyniersdochter Brunt (Elias, I, 107), and SH 2280, purchase of a rente by Sijbrand Meester Hendrik Dirkszoonszoon and his wife, Lijsbeth Meester Reynier Bruntendochter. For the political and religious significance of this family connection, see Tracy, "A Premature Counter-Reformation: The Dirkist Government of Amsterdam." For another interesting connection—between Meester Vincent Corneliszoon van Mierop of the Council of Finance, and Meester Gerrit Hendrikszoon van Ravensberg, Holland's lead-

which is worthy of study in its own right, government officials and town magistrates also shared, as has been shown in this chapter, a habit of investing in State debt. In former days, it was doubtless expected of noble officials that they show loyalty to the prince by investing in renten secured by his domain income. Perhaps unconsciously, and without any trace of coercion, town regents and government officials of bourgeois origin were filling the same function by their large purchases of provincial renten.

Town magistrates might still like to think of themselves as simple merchants taking time out for public affairs,[113] but this idyllic self-image was increasingly remote from reality. As litigation became more complicated, often requiring some knowledge of Roman law, and as towns were called upon to defend their interests against the ever more ravenous demands of the Habsburg fisc, the business of local government (like the business of governing the whole county in Charles V's name) inevitably became more specialized,[114] and more time-consuming. How frequently the States of Holland convened during the fifteenth century is uncertain, but during the middle decades of the sixteenth century the States could meet on an average of once a month, for several days at a time.[115] To some degree, amateur politicians were being faced with a choice of whether or not they wished to make politics

---

ing purchaser of renten by far—see above, note 33. The fact that all of these important men are called "Meester," meaning (usually) the possession of a law degree, is certainly not incidental to an understanding of what they had in common; see above, note 64.

[113]Cf. the exchange between Stadtholder Hoogstraten and two leaders of the pre-Dirkist regime in Amsterdam, Allert Boelens and Cornelis Benninck, AJ 11 February 1530: "Hoogstraten seyde dat Allert Boelens ende Cornelis Benninck pensez vous deux seuls avoir le gouvernment de la ville . . . je scaurois bien trouver des aultres/ je vous coucheray si plat que ung chien/ daer op Allert Boelens seyde wy en begeerden 't Regieren vande stede nyet te hebben/ wy hebben genouch mit onse coopmanscape te doen."

[114]Above, note 64.

[115]For example, there were sixteen sessions for 1548, eleven for 1549, counting as sessions what RSH calls *dagvaarten*, but counting as one sessions held on consecutive days. The responsibility of burgomasters to represent their cities at such meetings was rotated, for example on a quarterly basis.

their profession, since it was difficult to combine public duties with a proper attention to one's private affairs. For example, the grain merchant Jan Harmanszoon in 't Goudenberg doubtless had to forgo an entire trading season in order to serve for 125 days running as Amsterdam's representative at the imperial Diet of Spires (1546).[116] Similarly, the man who served eight or nine times as burgomaster, or even five or six times as schepen, could hardly hope to keep pace with his erstwhile colleagues in a particular branch of commerce, and might naturally, even unbeknownst to himself, begin thinking of King Philip's officials in The Hague, or magistrates from other towns, as his true social peers. In these circumstances, investment in Holland renten or other instruments of State debt must have seemed a particularly sensible way of putting one's capital to good use.

From the standpoint of the central government in Brussels, it was surely a good omen for the future that magistrate families seemed willing to step into a social role being vacated by the nobility, pledging their capital as well as their talents to the service of the prince. From a strictly urban standpoint, however, the same social process boded ill for the ongoing struggle to preserve, against government encroachment, the network of special rights and privileges thought to be the foundation of each city's prosperity. Men who represented the interests of their city in dealings with the government could be brought to change sides, but in doing so they might earn the bitter enmity of erstwhile colleagues in city hall. The often-mentioned patrician feud in Amsterdam between Sheriff Baerdes and the Dirkist ruling party had its origin in just such a shift of allegiance, when the sheriff, who formerly served at the pleasure of the burgomasters, accepted reappointment at the hands of the regent, Mary of Hungary.[117] In a more subtle way, a city's particular interests might come to be perceived as endangered because the city fathers were too

[116]ASR 1544: Jan Harmanszoon in 't Goudenberg (above, note 56) and the pensionary, Meester Floris Hougaerden, represented Amsterdam at Spires, and had to be paid their travel and lodging expenses by the city, since the States of Holland refused to make their mission a provincial matter.

[117]J. J. Woltjer, "Het Conflikt tussen Willem Baerdes en Hendrik Dirkszoon."

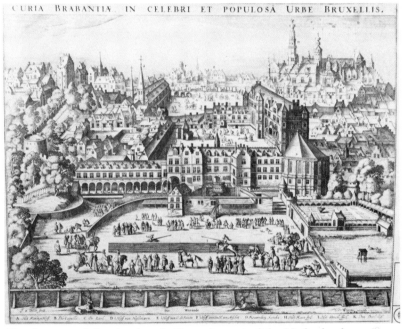

The former archducal palace in Brussels, seat of the Netherlands government under Mary of Hungary; engraving by B. de Momper. Reproduced by courtesy of the Koninklijk Huisarchief, The Hague.

Anonymous print of Mary of Hungary, Regent of the Netherlands,
1531–1555. Reproduced by courtesy of the Bibliotheque Royale/
Koninklijke Bibliotheek Albert I, Brussels.

Moreover, the line of reasoning suggested here remains con-jectural at best, since there has been no systematic study either of family and other connections between town magis-trates and government officials, or of the pattern of internal feuding which beset Holland's towns in the decades prior to the Revolt. But it is agreed on all sides that the Revolt was, among other things, an uprising in defense of provincial and urban privileges threatened by the centralizing policies of Philip II after 1566.[122] May it not, then, be pertinent to enquire whether this militant defense of local interests did not have a prehistory among groups of burghers who, like Amster-dam's Doleanten, came to believe that the traditional ruling elite of the town could no longer be relied on to protect them? As research into the background of the Revolt pursues its course, perhaps along the lines of questions indicated here, it may turn out that investment in renten was part of a long process by which magistrate families (or certain groups of them) cast their lot with the prince and his officials, only to lose forever their base of support at home.

[122]The best general treatment of the background of the Revolt is J. W. Smit, "The Netherlands Revolution," in *Preconditions of Revolution in Early Modern Europe*, Robert Forster, Jack P. Greene, eds. (Baltimore: 1970), 19–54; Smit also anticipates (33–34) the argument suggested here: "The town magistrates developed classic syndromes of role conflict. They were constantly reminded of their dependence upon the king and of their helplessness towards their own constituents."

close to the prince's officials in The Hague, or too little involved in the locally dominant branch of trade to understand its needs. Thus just as Amsterdam's Dirkist burgomasters saw Baerdes's ties to the regent as a threat to the city, townsmen who later joined in opposition to the burgomasters (the Doleanten) seem to have felt that the magistrates were somehow failing in their responsibility to protect the city's active trading interest.[118] Later still, former Doleanten and their allies would first oust from power the pro-Habsburg Dirkisten, thus bringing Amsterdam into the Revolt against Spain, and then reestablish the city's prosperity on traditional foundations (the Baltic trade), which the Dirkisten seem to have rather neglected.[119]

In Amsterdam, then, one may discern signs of a slow fusion of the city's ruling families with provincial officialdom to form a single ruling elite, characterized among other things by its penchant for investing in provincial renten. In turn, the alienation of the local governing party from its natural constituency—especially the Baltic merchants—seems to have contributed to the formation of an opposition group that persisted until the time of the Revolt, and indeed does much to explain Amsterdam's eventual adhesion to the rebel cause. To be sure, Amsterdam's internal history has no precise parallel elsewhere in Holland. Conflicts that pitted the sheriff (or some other representative of the regent's authority) against a locally dominant interest group were fairly common,[120] and a town's decision to join in the Revolt was often accompanied by the replacement or resignation of at least some members of the vroedschap. But Amsterdam is unique in the recognizable continuity of its factional conflicts both before and during the Revolt, and, unlike Amsterdam, most towns kept many of their former regents even after joining the Revolt.[121]

---

[118]Tracy, "A Premature Counter-Reformation: The Dirkist Government of Amsterdam."

[119]For the importance of the Baltic trade in the economy of the Dutch Republic, see chapter 6, note 4.

[120]Above, note 73.

[121]In the lists of officeholders for Dordrecht and Delft published respectively in Balen and Boitet, the few magistrates who resigned because they did not wish to be associated with the Revolt are noted as *glippers*.

"Subjugation of Ghent by Charles V" (1540: see p. 72), watercolor by J. C. Vermeyen. Reproduced by courtesy of the Bibliotheque Royale/Koninklijke Bibliotheek Albert I, Brussels.

J. M. Quinkhard, after M. van Heemskerk (?), portrait of Aert van
der Goes, Advocate of the States of Holland (1523–1545), author
of the first volume of RSH. Reproduced by courtesy of the Stichting
Iconographisch Bureau, The Hague.

Dirk Jacobszoon, portrait of Pompeius Occo (d. 1537), leading Amsterdam merchant, representative of the Fuggers, and father of the Dirkist magistrate Sijbrand Occo. Reproduced by courtesy of the Rijksmuseum, Amsterdam.

OBYT · 1588 ·   ÆTATIS · 82 ·

HÆC EST CANITIES BATAVI VENERANDA SOLONIS
  BVYCKIA QVO GAVDET GENS DECORATA VIRO
AMSTELDAMÆOS SACRI PARS MAGNA SENATVS
  REXIT CONSILIO, RELLIGIONE, FIDE
AT TANDEM EXPELLIT POPVLI MALE SVADA FVRENTIS
  SEDITIO, PATRIÆ QVI FVIT VSQVE PATER
SCILICET VT VIRTVS È CÆLO PRÆMIA SPERET
  INVIDA QVÆ MERITIS TERRA NEGARE SOLET

Anonymous, old-age portrait of Joost Buyck, a leading Dirkist
magistrate of Amsterdam. Reproduced by courtesy of the Museum
Amstelkring, Amsterdam.

Barend Dirkszoon, drawing of the 1535 execution of rebel Anabaptists in Amsterdam, showing the sixteenth-century city hall and the main square (the dam). Reproduced by courtesy of the Amsterdams Historisch Museum, Amsterdam.

A. van Wijngaerd, "View of Amsterdam," ca. 1550, showing the east or "Old Side" of the city, with Warmoesstraat running past the large church tower (the Oudekerk). Reproduced by courtesy of the Gemeentearchief, Amsterdam.

VI

Renten and Renteniers in
Seventeenth-Century Holland

Since Holland owes its place in European history to its achievements during the "Golden Century" following the break with Spain, it will be the purpose of this chapter
to show how lijfrenten and losrenten served as the backbone
of public borrowing in the seventeenth-century United Provinces, or Dutch Republic. Regrettably, there is no modern,
comprehensive survey of Netherlands state finance during
the republican era (1572–1795).[1] But Houtzager provides a

---

[1] F. N. Sickenga, *Bijdrage tot de Geschiedenis van de Belastingen in Nederland*
(The Hague: 1864). Both in the old *Algemene Geschiedenis der Nederlanden*, vols.
5–7, and in the new *Algemene Geschiedenis der Nederlanden* (15 vols. Haarlem:
1977–), vols. 6–8, there are only scattered references to public finance under
the Republic.

calendar of *Resolutions of the States of Holland* relevant to the renten,[2] permitting one to follow in outline the development of these annuities from 1572 to 1672, although the directives of the States raise a number of questions that could only be answered by a study of fiscal accounts,[3] which in turn would require a book far longer than this one. In what follows, it will first be helpful to indicate the sources of that uncommon prosperity which, in the first half of the seventeenth century, made the Dutch Republic the envy of Europe, and enabled it to create a public debt of unprecedented magnitude (I). It will then be possible to show that the Republic's techniques of public borrowing were, with some refinements, essentially those created by the Habsburg government of the sixteenth century (II). Finally, it will be appropriate to conclude with a brief comment on the renten-buying public of the seventeenth century (III).

I. As heartland of the seventeenth-century Republic, Holland was far different from the Habsburg province which, in the sixteenth century, struggled for a place in the sun alongside its then wealthier and more powerful neighbors to the south. Lineaments of an earlier era are nonetheless recognizable in each of the strands woven together to form a tapestry of prosperity in the Golden Age. First and foremost, it was traffic from the Baltic, Holland's traditional "mother trade," that continued to be the chief source of commercial wealth even as Amsterdam's wharves were lined with new and exotic wares from half way around the globe.[4] During the

---

[2]The citation form will be Houtzager RSH, that is, *Resolutiën van de Staten van Holland* (by date) as printed in Houtzager, *Hollands Lijf- en Losrenten voor 1672.*

[3]For example, when the States decreed a negotiatie (see p. 207), the proportion of lijfrenten, losrenten, and loans at interest or obligatiën is often not stated, and even if it is there is no telling if Holland's receivers were in fact able to place renten and loans in the stated proportions.

[4]The most recent summary treatment is Hans den Haan, *Moedernegotiatie en Grote Vaart* (Amsterdam: 1977); see also J. G. van Dillen, *Van Rijkdom en Regenten* (The Hague: 1970), 38–66. Charles R. Boxer, *The Dutch Seaborne Empire* (New York: 1968), 43, quotes an estimate from the 1660s that three-fourths of Amsterdam's commercial capital was still invested in the Baltic trade even at that date.

early years of the Revolt, and particularly after Amsterdam threw in with the rebels in 1578, Holland's merchants regained the lead in Baltic commerce, which had been slipping somewhat in recent decades.[5] They did so at a most fortunate moment in the history of Europe's grain trade. Beginning about 1590, long-term population trends opened up new markets in the Mediterranean, as (for example) Sicilian wheat dealers were no longer able to meet the demands of their traditional customers on the Italian mainland.[6] Baltic rye and wheat now became a reservoir for all Europe, and Holland's command of this precious resource was such that successive kings of Spain, much against their will, had to open the kingdom's northern ports to rebel shippers who carried not only grain but other bulk products grown scarce in southern Europe—even the timber used to build the Invincible Armada of 1588.[7]

Already in 1540, Hollanders boasted of a seagoing fleet of some four hundred vessels, greater in numbers (they said) than all the merchantmen of England, France, and Brittany combined.[8] About 1590, however, the ship-building district of northern Holland registed a leap forward with the development of the "flute" ship, tapered towards the deck as well as the keel, unusually seaworthy because of shallow draft, and so capable of being operated by a smaller crew, and thus more cheaply. The flute was ideally suited for the Baltic run, where ships sailed in convoys of a hundred vessels or more

[5]Christensen, *Dutch Trade to the Baltic around 1600*, 44–45, 90–102; Den Haan, *Moedernegotiatie en Grote Vaart*, 29–36, 44–46.

[6]Van Dillen, *Van Rijkdom en Regenten*, 65–70; den Haan, *Moedernegotiatie en Grote Vaart*, 55–59; and *Maritieme Geschiedenis der Nederlanden*, L. M. Akveld, S. Hart, W. J. van Hoboken, eds. (4 vols., Bussum: 1976–1980), II, 235–241.

[7]Den Haan, *Moedernegotiate en Grote Vaart*, 46–55.

[8]Meilink, *Rapporten en Betoogen nopens het Congiegeld op Granen*, 73, statement by the States of Holland in 1541 (Brittany was apparently still viewed by Hollanders as an independent seafaring nation), 400 "caravels"; see also 111, between thirty and forty "great hulks or caravel ships" were built in Holland each year. As to the number of herring busses, which were ocean-going vessels of a more modest kind, RSH, 15 July 1547, indicates that a war-time tax of 1 pound for each sixteenth "ship-part" for caravels and herring busses yielded 20,000 pounds, meaning a combined total of 1,250 caravels and busses.

to minimize the danger of attack, and where nautical speed and quickness of handling were not of great importance. It also symbolized the superior inventiveness of Holland's shipyards, whose low building costs and specially tailored products gave local merchants a competitive edge in several different branches of the carrying trade.[9]

Meanwhile, the great city of Antwerp had seen its seaborne commerce choked off by the vicissitudes of war. Briefly aligned with the Revolt, Antwerp fell to a long and brilliant seige by the Duke of Parma in 1585, and was subsequently cut off from the Maas estuary as rebel forces stubbornly held both banks of the Scheldt below the city.[10] Foreign merchants used to resorting to Antwerp now found that Amsterdam could serve just as well, especially since Jews from Iberia (where Portugal too was now ruled by the King of Spain) encountered fewer religious restrictions in the rebel provinces than in Spanish dominions.[11] The north was also enriched by waves of emigration from the southern Netherlands, as refugees sought either the freedom to practice their Protestant faith, or better economic opportunities, or a combination of both. For example, Leiden's moribund cloth industry was transformed into a dynamic export enterprise when Protestant weavers of light woolens from the Flemish town of Hondschoote migrated north in a body after Spanish troops occupied their native city.[12] In Amsterdam and elsewhere, emigrants from the south were instrumental in mounting a successful challenge to the Hispano-Portuguese monopoly of the Asian spice trade. For a time in the 1590s, the chimerical

---

[9]R. W. Unger, *Dutch Shipbuilding before 1800* (Amsterdam: 1978), 34–38; on new ship types, including the flute, *Maritieme Geschiedenis der Nederlanden*, II, 11–69; for the competitive advantages of Dutch shipbuilding, Violet Barbour, "Dutch and English Merchant Shipping in the 17th Century," *Economic History Review* II (1929/1930): 261–290.

[10]For the seige of Antwerp, L. van der Essen, *Alexandre Farnese* (5 vols., Brussels: 1933–1948), vols. 4 and 5.

[11]J. A. van Houtte, *An Economic History of the Low Countries* (New York: 1977), 187–189.

[12]W. Brulez, "De Diaspora der Antwerpse Kooplui op het Eind van de 16e Eeuw," *Bijdragen tot de Geschiedenis van de Nederlanden* 15 (1960): 297–306; J. Briels, *De Zuidnederlandse Emigratie, 1572–1630* (Haarlem: 1978). Posthumus, *Geschiedenis van der Leidsche Lakenindustrie*, vol. 2.

dream of sailing through unknown waters north of Russia in order to reach the riches of Asia found some support.[13] Far more important for the future was the first Dutch voyage (1595–1597) to the spice islands of the Moluccas chain, which brought investors a 500 percent profit, and launched several other ventures which, in 1603, merged to form the United East India Company, chartered by the States General, but governing its far-flung outposts as an autonomous corporation. Tiny Holland thus became the metropolis of a colonial empire.[14]

When the States General signed a Twelve Years' Truce with Spain in 1609, the profitable habit of preying on Hispano-Portuguese shipping in Asian and Atlantic waters was deprived of official sanction, but there were still other ways of creating new wealth. It was about this time that two Protestant kinsmen from the ecclesiastical principality of Liège, Elias Trip and Louis de Geer, relocated in Amsterdam and founded a trading company dealing in weaponry and metal wares, which soon was supplying capital and know-how for the development of rich copper lodes in Sweden.[15] The role which Amsterdam now played in Europe's copper trade is in some ways reminiscent of the past, since Sijbrand Occo (the Dirkist magistrate mentioned in chapter 5) and his father, as agents for the Fuggers, were responsible for bringing vast quantities of east European copper into Amsterdam by way of the Baltic, and then shipping it on to Antwerp along Holland's inland waterways.[16] The decisive difference was that, while not even the Trips or the de Geers ever attained anything like the

[13]Tracy, *True Ocean Found: Paludanus' Letters on Dutch Voyages to the Kara Sea, 1595–1596* (Minneapolis: 1979).

[14]On the United East India Company, the new *Algemene Geschiedenis der Nederlanden*, VII, 173–219; Boxer, *The Dutch Seaborne Empire*.

[15]F. Bredevelt van Veen, *Louis de Geer, 1587–1652* (Amsterdam: 1935); P. W. Klein, *De Trippen in de 17e Eeuw* (Leiden: 1965); Van Dillen, *Van Rijkdom en Regenten*, 314–317.

[16]See the references to trading in copper by the Fuggers and their Antwerp rival, Erasmus Schetz, in Tracy, "Shipments to Germany by Erasmus Schetz and other Antwerp Merchants during the Period of the 100th Penny Tax"; like Elias Trip in the seventeenth century, Schetz had a controlling interest in the Altenberg, or "Calamine Mountain," near Aachen, a major source of the mineral so vital in the copper-refining process.

wealth and power of the Fuggers, Amsterdam now housed within its walls the financial and commercial hegemony which in the previous century had been divided between Augsburg and Antwerp.

Amsterdam and its wealthy families were simply the most visible emblems of the great economic changes that occurred in Holland between roughly 1580 and 1620. The city's population swelled from a sixteenth-century high of about 35,000 in the 1550s to 105,000 in 1622, and continued growing thereafter until it reached nearly 200,000 in 1680.[17] In measuring the magnitude of growth in wealth one must of course discount for inflation, both because basic commodities like grain grew more costly, as measured in terms of units of silver, and because the silver content of the coinage was reduced (as in the sixteenth century, the money of account, now called the guilder, was reckoned at twenty silver stuivers, or *patards*). For present purposes, it will suffice to note that the silver *patard* had in 1660 about one-third of the purchasing power it had in 1580; in other words, inflation as measured in money of account (the guilder) was roughly 300 percent.[18] Even so,

[17]Pieter de la Court, *The True Interest and Political Maxims of the Republic of Holland* (London: 1746; Arno Press reprint, New York: 1972), 34, gives figures (based on a 1622 poll tax) of 115,022 for Amsterdam and 602,417 for all of Holland; on this friend of Johan de Witt and his treatise, see C. H. Wilson, *Profit and Power* (The Hague: 1978), 11–18. Jan De Vries, *The Dutch Rural Economy*, 90, sets the totals at 104,932 for Amsterdam in 1622, and 397,307 for all of Holland.

[18]This rough calculation is based on two statements in Van Houtte, *An Economic History of the Low Countries*, 212, 214, that the groat (2 groats = 1 stuiver, or patard) contained 0.4 grams of fine silver in 1568 and 0.25 in 1650, and that grain prices as expressed in silver rose 75 percent between 1580 and 1660. Over a span of eighty years, the ratio for the diminution of silver content of the coinage was thus 0.4 to 0.25, or 8 to 5, and the ratio for diminution in the purchasing power of constant units of silver was 175 to 100, or 7 to 4; to obtain a ratio for decline in the purchasing power of coinage, one multiplies the other ratios: 8/5 times 7/4 equals 56/20, or 14/5, roughly three to one. For a good general discussion of inflation during this period, see F. P. Braudel, F. Spooner, "Prices in Europe from 1450 to 1750," *Cambridge Economic History*, vol. 4, E. E. Rich and C. H. Wilson, eds. (London: 1967), 378–486. See also Jan De Vries, "An Inquiry into the Behavior of Wages in the Dutch Republic and the Southern Netherlands, 1500–1800," *Acta Historiae Neerlandicae* X (1978): 1–20.

the differences in wealth levels over the course of a generation or two are almost beyond belief. Claes Hendrikszoon Basgen (1468–1563), a wealthy Dirkist magistrate, left an estate of 55,850 pounds (guilders) of twenty patards, considered unusual at the time. Jacob Poppen (1576–1624), a member of the vroedschap and of the board of directors of the United East India Company, considered one of the richest men of his day, left an estate valued at 920,000 guilders of twenty patards— approximately six times greater than Basgen's, even if devalued by a factor of three, owing to inflation.[19] The wealth of the city as a whole can be charted through successive *capitale impositiën*, or percentage levies, on individual declarations of net worth in excess of a certain amount (as Van Dillen notes, declarations are sometimes found to indicate less than half the wealth which the declarer passed on to his heirs a few years later). For a *capitale impositie* of 1585, only seven Amsterdammers declared a net worth in excess of 70,000 guilders. For a 200th penny in 1631, there were 100 who declared in excess of 100,000 guilders, including 24 who reported more than 200,000. For another 200th penny in 1671, 200 declared in excess of 100,000, including 70 reporting more than 200,000; the sum total of wealth declared was 63,000,000 guilders in 1631, and 158,000,000 in 1671.[20]

Wealth of this magnitude offered a tempting target for a government hard pressed to meet its obligations, especially in time of war with Spain or later, England.[21] Theoretically, Holland was but one of seven provinces represented in the States General of the Netherlands, and was thus subject to a higher control. In practice, the States General convened at the *binnenhof* in The Hague, the old seat of the Council of Holland, just as the States of Holland did. Holland was assessed for 58.8 percent of the annual budgets drawn up by

[19]Elias, I, 247–248, 285–286.

[20]Van Dillen, *Van Rijkdom en Regenten,* 311–313; see also Peter Burke, *Venice and Amsterdam* (London: 1974), 55–61.

[21]On the Anglo-Dutch wars, see C. H. Wilson, *Profit and Power;* K. H. D. Haley, "De Republiek in de Tijd van het eerste Stadhouderloze Tijdperk," new *Algemene Geschiedenis der Nederlanden,* VIII, 266–281; and *Maritieme Geschiedenis der Nederlanden,* II, 346–354.

the States General, and actually paid for the Republic's wars and its normal governing functions in a somewhat higher proportion, since other provinces complained their quotas were too high, and were regularly in arrears.[22] Within Holland, though Amsterdam's preponderant influence was far greater than it had been in the sixteenth century, the formal structures of government and of political decision-making were more decentralized than had been the case in the Habsburg era. Although the nobility of Holland declined during the seventeenth century, both demographically and as a voice in the provincial States,[23] the towns enjoyed more autonomy than ever. The Court of Holland in The Hague no longer had the power to "evoke" cases from town courts at its own pleasure, and after 1572 there were eighteen cities represented in the States instead of six.[24] Moreover, unworkable though such a principle may seem, the rule of unanimity was now established, which meant that someone had to persuade recalcitrant towns to go along before anything could be formally decided by the States.[25] Persuasion of this kind and, in general, the task of providing an element of cohesion in a seemingly chaotic process of incessant consultation, fell to the Advocate of the States of Holland, who was now called the Councilor Pensionary or, to use the title customary in English, the Grand Pensionary. In the hands of men like Johan van Oldenbarnevelt (1586–1618), or Johan de Witt (1653–1672), this office, though provincial in nature, served as a kind of prime-ministership for the United Provinces.[26] Defenders of a more centralized conception of government were not lacking, especially among partisans of the successive

[22]Van Dillen, *Van Rijkdom en Regenten,* 270–272.

[23]Professor Henk van Nierop of the University of Amsterdam has completed a dissertation on *De Hollandse Adel, 1500–1650,* to be published this year (1984), of which he was kind enough to send me a copy of the concluding chapter.

[24]K. H. D. Haley, *The Dutch in the 17th Century* (London: 1972), 64–74.

[25]For example, the reduction of the interest rate for losrenten from 6.25 to 5 percent was delayed for two months until the other cities agreed to grant at least part of Delft's demand for special assistance in its renten debt (Houtzager RSH, 29 February–20 April, 1640).

[26]Jan den Tex, *Oldenbarnevelt* (2 vols., Cambridge: 1973); Herbert H. Rowan, *Johan de Witt* (Princeton: 1980).

Princes of Orange, who often chafed at the fragmentation of power in their country—for example, the five separate Admiralties, including three in Holland, each with its own jealously guarded territorial base.[27] But Their High and Noble Mightinesses, as deputies to the States of Holland now styled themselves, had good reason to be content with the status quo. Their forebears had not sustained a long and brutal war of independence merely in order to create a new centralizing authority of one kind or another, whether in the States General or in the person of the Prince of Orange.[28] However the wealth of Amsterdam and other cities was tapped for the needs of state, it would most emphatically have to be by the consent of Holland's urban oligarchies.

In keeping with the old principle that those who stood to gain from a service provided by the state should pay for it, the various Admiralties, charged with defense of the Dutch merchant fleet, were chiefly supported by taxes on shipping in and out of the country. Merchants trading with the Spanish Netherlands had to purchase licenses for the privilege of doing so, while those dealing with neutral or hostile nations had to pay a convoy fee.[29] For the general public in Holland, taxes were of three kinds. First, the old schiltal had given way to an annual *verponding*, or flat-rate tax, on the estimated value of land and buildings throughout the province; in time of need this could be collected at multiples of the usual rate.[30] Second, the States could decree a capitale impositie (as mentioned above in the case of Amsterdam) on a person's declared net worth in personal as well as real property; it could be a 100th penny, a 200th penny, or a 1,000th penny, any one of which might be levied more than once during the same

[27]*Maritieme Geschiedenis der Nederlanden*, II, 316–320: the five Admiralties were Amsterdam, Rotterdam (or the Maas), Enkhuizen (or West Friesland, part of Holland), Zeeland, and Friesland.

[28]For the running conflict between the House of Orange and the regenten of Holland's towns, especially just before and at the end of the "Stadtholderless period" from 1650 to 1672, see Pieter Geyl, *Orange and Stuart* (London: 1969), and *The Netherlands in the 17th Century, 1648–1715* (New York: 1964).

[29]H. Klompmaker, "Handel, Geld- en Bankwezen in de Noordelijke Nederlanden, 1580–1650," new *Algemene Geschiedenis der Nederlanden*, VII, 104–106.

[30]Van Dillen, *Van Rijkdom en Regenten*, 272.

year.[31] Finally, those whose net worth fell below the threshold for the capitale impositie, along with everyone else, contributed through multiple excise taxes, payable by the seller but at least in part passed on to the consumer. In the early years of the Revolt, the States inaugurated annual excise taxes on wine, beer, and other items of common use, much as was done during the 1550s to fund a new series of renten. In time, more and more items were added to the list—horned beasts, sheep, pigs, nursery trees, butter, cheese, honey, wax, flour, wool, silk, oil, refined sugar, paper, fish, and especially meat—until Holland was collecting forty-three separate excises, and the States were offering rewards to persons who could think of some new item that might be taxed.[32]

Even so, certain limits were respected, particularly as regards goods passing through the Netherlands to other destinations. Thus when the States of Zeeland called for a levy on imported grain, de Witt rejected their proposal, saying that the movement of grain must be kept free of burdens so that the Republic would continue to the "the granary of Europe." When his friend and confidant, the Leiden cloth-manufacturer Pieter de la Court, suggested a tax on English woolens finished in Holland and then re-exported, de Witt replied that imports ought not be taxed even if they directly competed with Holland products. In such matters, de Witt's biographer concludes, the Grand Pensionary "usually accepted the position of Amsterdam, the citadel of the trading interest."[33] Though Amsterdam was but one of eighteen cities voting in

[31]Houtzager RSH, 7 December 1634: since the renewal of war with Spain in 1621, there had been two 1,000th pennies, three 500th pennies, and four 200th pennies; van Dillen, *Van Rijkdom en Regenten,* 277, by 1692 it was common to collect a 100th penny twice yearly. P. W. Klein, "De heffing van de 100e en 200e penning van het vermogen te Gouda, 1599–1722," *Economisch-Historisch Jaarboek* XXXI (1967): 41–62, notes that although mercantile inventories and goods of all kinds were officially included in the definition of property to be taxed, the declarations on which collection was based were in practice limited to real property and "vermogenspapieren," that is, renten, obligatiën, and shares in trading companies. Beginning in 1680, valuation was formally restricted to real property and property rights that would be taxed in the verponding, plus paper wealth of the kind just indicated.

[32]Van Dillen, *Van Rijkdom en Regenten,* 272–276.

[33]Rowan, *Johan de Witt,* 187–189; on Pieter de la Court, see above, note 17.

the States, it contained about a sixth of Holland's population and roughly half its wealth,[34] and was thus able in most cases to block the adoption of measures it opposed.[35] Back in the Habsburg era, Amsterdam and its allies in the provincial States had constantly sought to convince a Brussels-based government that freedom of the transit trade was vital to Holland's middleman role; sometimes they were successful[36] and sometimes not. In the seventeenth century, this position, traditionally associated with Amsterdam, became a fixed principle of statecraft.

Since Holland was so much wealthier than it had been a hundred years earlier, and considerably more ingenious in taxing its people, the revenues of a (virtually) sovereign province were vastly superior to those once accorded to a sovereign prince. During the sixteenth century, Holland's ability to raise money in time of war—through collection of taxes like the schiltal as well as through the sale of renten—reached a high point in the 1550s, with a peak in one year of roughly 550,000 pounds of twenty patards.[37] Already by 1588 the now independent province was raising some 3,400,000, and by the mid-1630s the annual total for a wartime year was in excess of 10,000,000 guilders of twenty patards; for 1664, de Witt's friend Pieter de la Court estimates a revenue of 11,000,000 guilders for taxes levied by the States of Holland,

[34]See above, note 17, on Amsterdam's population. Van Dillen, *Van Rijkdom en Regenten*, 311–312, mentions that Amsterdam's share of a 200th penny tax was 63,000,000 guilders in 1631, and 158,000,000 in 1671 ("guilder" is a variant of the word *gulden*, as in the *Karolus gulden* of twenty stuivers dating from Charles V's reign). Figures for the whole province for 200th pennies of approximately the same dates are given in Houtzager RSH, 28 April 1640 (the 200th penny is expected to yield 800,000 guilders, meaning the capital of 160,000,000), and Pieter de la Court, *The True Interest and Political Maxims of Holland*, 20, the 200th penny of 1664 yielded 2,400,000, meaning a capital of 480,000,000.

[35]There were exceptions, as when the resistance of Amsterdam, Delft, and Rotterdam to withholding taxes on renten interest was worn down by the persistence of the measure's proponents: Houtzager RSH, 29 August–22 September, 1600, 22 February 1604, 21 November 1606–6 March, 1607.

[36]Notably in resisting the *congie,* or export duty, on Baltic grains (Meilink, "Rapporten en Betoogen nopens het Congiegeld op Granen").

[37]Tracy, "The Taxation System of the County of Holland under Charles V and Philip II," table 1.

including the three kinds of taxes mentioned above, but not the license and convoy fees which merchant shippers paid directly to the Admiralties.[38] Assuming an inflation rate between the 1550s and 1660s somewhat in excess of 300 percent, provincial revenue in the latter period was still at least five times greater than the highest total previously reached, and could moreover be sustained through decades of intermittent war with Europe's great powers, not merely for a few years. The cost of waging war nonetheless continued to outstrip the revenue-raising ability even of the wealthiest and best-governed states. In 1625 the Delegated Councilors, a permanent committee of the States of Holland, reported a running deficit for the province of 3,177,000 guilders from the time hostilities with Spain had been renewed after expiration of the Twelve Years' Truce in 1621. In 1641 the councilors reported a shortfall of 5,794,450.[39] Long-term financing was thus a continuing necessity, not merely to meet shortages of the kind just indicated, but even to meet Holland's quota of the Republic's annual budget in war-time years. Repudiation of the renten debt tracing back to the Habsburg-Valois wars was apparently never even considered by rulers of the fledgling Republic. Rather, their concern was to pay off the old debt in such a way as to improve the credit of the province, and make it possible to borrow on a much larger scale.

II. Development of the lijfrenten and losrenten during the first century of Dutch independence can conveniently be divided into four periods. From 1572 to 1596, new issues were few, and the chief problem faced by the States was how to make up arrears on renten sold prior to 1572. From about 1596 until the signing of the Twelve Years' Truce with Spain in 1609, Holland's credit improved to the point where rates could be progressively lowered, and many new renten were issued to cover debts to the English crown as well as the costs of continuing war with Spain. From 1621 to about 1643, the

---

[38]Houtzager, 51, 59; de la Court, *The True Interest and Political Maxims of Holland*, 20: to the figure of 11,000,000 for taxes levied by the States, de la Court adds 2,672,898 for fees paid to Holland's three Admiralties.

[39]Houtzager RSH, 9 December 1625, 5 December 1641.

last phase of what the Dutch call the Eighty Years' War (with Spain) was financed in good part by long-term securities, even as provincial credit kept improving, so that outstanding debt could be reduced to the unprecedented low rate of 5 percent, or 1 : 20. Finally, from 1652 to 1672, if the Republic survived a new series of wars with England and (at the end) France, it was in no small measure because long-term financing was controlled by the deft and sure hand of Johan de Witt.

"Renten of the five or six cities" (that is, issued before 1572) were a source of concern to the States during the early years of the Revolt. In 1575, noting that interest had not been paid for the past three years, the States decreed a temporary suspension of payments. Two years later it was decided to add unpaid interest to the principal balance while at the same time confiscating a portion of the capital for renteniers living in cities or provinces still loyal to the king of Spain. Meanwhile, new renten were still being issued, but at the high rates that had prevailed during the military and fiscal crisis of the 1550s, 1 : 12 for losrenten, and 1 : 6 for lijfrenten for one life.[40] Issues by the States were apparently infrequent; rather, most new renten were issued by individual cities, according to a quota system based on estimates of the wealth of each city and its surrounding rural district, and backed by "letters of indemnity" from the States.[41] The old domain revenues, which in the absence of a ruling count fell now to the States, continued, as before, to serve as security for renten issued by the receivers of domain income for each of the traditional collection districts.[42]

Before long, signs of improvement were noticeable. In 1586 the States authorized Holland's Receiver-General to pay all arrears on renten interest through 1583 and, in 1588, he was

[40]Houtzager, 45–52.

[41]Houtzager RSH, 10 January 1587, 19 September–7 October, 1589, 26 January 1591, 7–12 September 1597.

[42]Houtzager RSH, 5 March 1665, the *rentevoordeel*, or 1 percent savings on interest payments after the 1655 reduction to 4 percent, was 43,739 for the nine collection bureaus for domain revenue, meaning an outstanding capital of 4,373,900, or about 3 percent of the total indicated in de Witt's 1668 "Summing Up."

empowered to pay all arrears—to the extent that was possible. (As if to emphasize continuity with the past, the Receiver-General was Cornelis van Cuyck van Mierop, probably of the same family as Meester Vincent Corneliszoon, and related also to Meester Gerrit Hendrikszoon van Ravensberg, Holland's largest purchaser of renten during the 1550s.) In 1587 the States assumed direct responsibility for all losrenten which individual cities had sold for the needs of the province, and in 1591 cities were authorized to transfer lijfrenten sold for the needs of the province to the account of the States, if they so desired. After 1598, according to Houtzager, the *Resolutions of the States of Holland* contain no further references to arrears.[43]

The *Resolutions* as excerpted by Houtzager list ten new issues between 1597 and 1607 for a total capital of 2,250,000 guilders, plus several other issues for which no total is given. Apart from the customary los- and lijfrenten, long-term funds were also found through the sale of obligatiën. In the early sixteenth century, an obligatie was simply the personal bond of a great nobleman, or of an official entitled to collect some portion of the emperor's revenue. By about 1550, the term had been extended to include bonds issued in the corporate name of bodies like the States of Brabant or the States of Holland, promising the emperor's creditors in Antwerp that certain future revenues would be employed to satisfy their claims. Now, in the seventeenth century, an obligatie was a promissory note issued by the States, sold on the open market rather like the renten, but with some important differences. First, whereas a rentebrief was always inscribed in the buyer's name, an obligatie was made out to the bearer (or *toonder*, "one who shows").[44] Second, while renten were initially purchased from agents of one or another public body, obligatiën were initially marketed through investor syndicates, which collected for their services a brokerage fee amounting to an annual percentage of the capital, and fixed in 1607 at 0.05 percent.[45] Whenever the States required long-term funds,

---

[43]Houtzager, 45–52; on van Mierop, see chapter 2, note 122.
[44]Houtzager RSH, 15 May, 2 August 1657.
[45]Houtzager RSH, 27 February 1604, 27 July 1607.

they approved a "deal" (*negotiatie*) for a certain amount, authorizing the Delegated Councilors to raise the money through the sale of losrenten, lijfrenten, and obligatiën, with the proportions for each kind of sale sometimes fixed by the States, and sometimes left to the discretion of the Delegated Councilors. During the first decade of the seventeenth century, officials acting in behalf of the States were able to reduce the losrenten rate from 1 : 12 to 1 : 14 and eventually to 1 : 16 or 6.25 percent, the traditional rate that had prevailed through much of the sixteenth century; rates for lijfrenten and obligatiën declined proportionally.[46] The return on obligatiën was sometimes fractionally lower than for losrenten but, owing to the brokerage fee, they were nonetheless more costly to the government.[47] Because of this difference, the States preferred losrenten to obligatiën, and also took various measures to convert the latter into the former. For their part, however, some investors had a preference for obligatiën, perhaps because they were more easily convertible into cash through redemption, and certainly because they were not subject to the 40th penny sales tax that applied to losrenten traded on the secondary market.[48] The amount of renten debt outstanding during this period is not given in Houtzager's *Resolutions,* but it seems that annual interest charges for the total debt of the province were about 1,400,000 guilders in 1603; assuming for the sake of simplicity a debt consisting entirely of losrenten and obligatiën at the current rate of 1 : 12, this would mean a capital of at least 16,800,000. In 1609, when the Twelve

[46]Houtzager RSH, 25 July 1594, 7–12 August 1597, 28 August–15 September, 1601, 19–22 November 1603, 12 October, 30 November, 1605, 28 June–8 July, 1606, 28 June 1608, 23 February–5 May, 1611.

[47]Houtzager RSH, May 1607, obligatiën to be sold at 7 percent plus the half percent brokerage fee, while the rate for losrenten was 1 : 14, or 7.14 percent; 23 February, 12 October, 1604, obligatiën to be sold at 8 percent plus 1 percent for brokerage, while the rate for losrenten was 1 : 12, or 8.33 percent. By 1630 (Houtzager 141–142) both obligatiën and losrenten sold at 6.25 percent, or 1 : 16, except that the 0.05 percent brokerage fee still applied for the former.

[48]Above, note 44; Houtzager RSH, 24 February 1604, 7 June 1605, 9–26 September, 2 October, 1609; 28 April 1640, when the losrenten rate was lowered from 1 : 16 to 1 : 20, holders of losrenten were allowed to reclaim their original capital after one month's notice, but holders of obligatiën had to give six months' notice.

Years' Truce had brought nearly forty years of war with Spain to a temporary halt, the amount outstanding "at interest" (that is, in obligatiën alone) was 4,356,101.[49]

For the last phase of the Netherlands' war of independence (1620–1643), Houtzager's *Resolutions* list twenty-one issues of renten for a total capital of 13,800,000 guilders, plus a few others for which no amount is indicated. Despite the fact that Holland's annual tax revenues reached 10,000,000 guilders during this period, there were still deficits, as noted earlier, of more than 3,000,000 in 1625, and nearly 6,000,000 by 1641. Meanwhile, the debt for obligatiën alone was calculated at 10,531,071 in 1630.[50] During this period some refinements were made in the process of selling renten, and others were proposed. For example, in 1625 a 200th penny tax was levied in the form of a forced purchase of renten, but with options, so that wealthy Hollanders could choose whether to have their contributions credited as losrenten or lijrenten. In 1637 creditors of the provincial government were given the option of accepting payment in the form of los- or lijfrenten, a measure which only makes sense on the presumption of a strong demand for these annuities.[51] Three years earlier, in 1634, the States settled a long-standing argument about the merits of a withholding tax on renten income. During the early years of the century, the States had occasionally voted such taxes despite strong initial objections (from Amsterdam, Delft, and Rotterdam) that measures of this kind "harmed the credit of the province." By 1634, the proponents of a withholding tax were not only outvoted but instructed never to bring the proposal to the floor again.[52] During the same year, the deputies also considered a proposal for what one is tempted to call zero-coupon lijfrenten, according to which investors would receive five times their original capital after eighteen years had elapsed, but nothing in between. Renten of this kind might have some appeal, it was suggested, as a dowry for one's daughters (rather like the bank of dowries in Medi-

---

[49]Houtzager RSH, 19–23 November 1603, 11 November–23 December, 1609.
[50]Houtzager, 141–142.
[51]Houtzager RSH, 6–15 April 1625, 17 January 1637.
[52]Above, note 35; Houtzager RSH, 4–20 May 1634.
[53]Rowan, *Johan de Witt*, 180–181.

cean Florence). But Hollanders were by now very choosy
about investment opportunities, and a five-for-one return
after eighteen years was considerably less than what could
be gotten for the same period by reinvesting the annual interest income from ordinary losrenten (as de Witt remarked
some years later, most Holland renteniers apparently rein-
vested their interest income instead of consuming it).[53] Hence
when the plan was brought back for discussion some months
later, it was dismissed as "not being to the taste of anyone
who understands even a little about investing money."[54]

There was in fact little need for gimmicks or special incen-
tives to bolster the strong demand for States of Holland renten. As early as 1634, the Delegated Councilors thought it
would be possible to convert outstanding debt from the 1 : 16
rate to an unprecedented 1 : 20, or 5 percent, and in 1640 this
plan was put into effect, both for losrenten and obligatiën,
with the stipulation (as in the sixteenth century) that investors
who did not wish to accept the lower rate could choose to
have their capital returned. Money for redemptions was to
be found not by a new issue of renten (as in the 1550s), but
by levying a 200th penny to create a sinking fund.[55] It says
much for the popularity of Holland renten that, although the
total losrenten and obligatiën debt, extrapolating from earlier
and later figures, may conservatively be estimated at
40,000,000 or 50,000,000 guilders,[56] a sinking fund of only

[54]Houtzager RSH, 13 December 1634 (point 11 of proposal to the States by
the Delegated Councilors), 30 June 1635 (final dismissal of the idea, with
quote). Simple interest on a 100-pound lijfrente for one life at the current
rate of 1 : 11 would total 198 pounds after eighteen years (plus 100 pounds
for the original capital), but compound interest (achievable by reinvesting
the income each year at the same rate) would be 554 pounds after eighteen
years, plus 100 for the original capital; what the Delegated Councilors proposed would have yielded only 500 pounds all told after eighteen years, or
154 pounds less.

[55]Houtzager RSH, 29 February through 28 April, 1640; instead of using a
200th penny, as the Delegated Councilors originally proposed, 800,000 for
the sinking fund was found by a negotiatie at the new rate of 5 percent.

[56]For a figure that suggests a minimum debt of 16,800,000 in 1603, see
above, note 49; Houtzager, 78–85: de la Court in 1655 estimated the renten
debt at 140,000,000, and de Witt's careful "Summing Up" in 1668 gives a
figure of nearly 132,000,000 for 1667. At such a rate of growth, 40,000,000 or
50,000,000 would seem a conservative guess for 1640.

800,000 was considered sufficient to meet any demands for redemption. Holland's role in the overall finances of the United Provinces is indicated by the fact that when the States General undertook some years later (1649) a similar reduction of its debt from 6.25 to 5 percent, the sinking fund established for this purpose was only about 125,000.[57] In other words, assuming the same ratio between the size of the sinking fund and the total amount outstanding, the province carried a debt roughly six times that of the "Generality" to which it was theoretically subordinate.

Though hostilities between Spain and the Netherlands were not formally concluded until the Treaty of Westphalia in 1648, there had been little fighting in the Low Countries since 1643, and hence little need for massive public spending. Meanwhile, however, tensions had been mounting between the Republic and its erstwhile ally, England, as disputes over fisheries, cloth manufacturing, and control of the Asian spice trade proved insoluble. The first Anglo-Dutch war broke out in 1652, nearly coinciding with the accession of a young man of only twenty-seven years to the venerable office of Grand Pensionary of Holland. Johan de Witt's father, a magistrate of Dordrecht, had been one of the "Lovensteiners," a group of Delegated Councilors whom Stadtholder William II, Prince of Orange, had imprisoned in Lovenstein castle in an effort to subjugate the States to his will. Following William's sudden death in 1650, the Lovensteiners were released in triumph, and the States allowed the title of stadtholder to lapse, not to be revived again until the French invasion of 1672 provoked a great political crisis, which cost de Witt his life, and thrust into the limelight his great foe, William III, Prince of Orange and later king of England. From 1650 to 1672, then, the political dominance of Holland's town oligarchies was unfettered by any Orangist claims in behalf of executive power, while the Republic faced a fiscal test of strength even more severe than during the long war with Spain. It was de Witt who

---

[57]Houtzager RSH, 5 May 1649, Holland's contribution to the sinking fund for States General renten was 74,000; assuming Holland paid its usual quota of 58.8 percent the total sinking fund would be 125,850.

managed, with supreme skill, both the foreign policy and the finances of the United Provinces.[58]

For a time, the States had ceased offering lijfrenten for sale,[59] apparently in the belief that losrenten were less of a charge on the public fisc, even though they were not extinguished by the death of the beneficiary. But in 1653 a special committee on finances, of which de Witt was a member, persuaded the States to adopt an annual 1,000th penny tax, proceeds of which were to fund lijfrenten at the rate of 1 : 11 for one life. Each city issued an amount of lijfrenten equal to eleven times the 1,000th penny assessment for the town itself and the surrounding rural district; as beneficiaries died the resulting savings were to be employed to retire principal. This plan continued in effect for eight years, but at the end of 1661 the States dropped the 1,000th penny tax and assumed responsibility for the outstanding lijfrenten.[60]

Meanwhile, losrenten continued to enjoy great popularity, so much so that they traded on the secondary market at a premium of 5 to 7 percent over par value. Accordingly, in 1655 de Witt proposed a reduction of the interest rate from 5 to 4 percent, and the States agreed.[61] Two years later the advantages hitherto enjoyed by holders of obligatiën were nullified when these bonds were ordered converted to losrenten; each bond had to be brought to the office of one of the fiscal agents of the States, to have the word *toonder* (bearer) crossed out and replaced with the owner's name. The intent of this change was that obligatiën now became subject to the 40th penny transfer tax.[62] To reduce the renten debt, the States decreed that the "interest advantage" (*rentevoordeel*) derived from the 1 percent reduction in annual interest pay-

[58]Rowan, *Johan de Witt*, is by far the most thorough account of the Grand Pensionary's career, but see also the new *Algemene Geschiedenis der Nederlanden*, VIII, 265–281; Wilson, *Profit and Power;* and the studies of Pieter Geyl, cited above, note 28.

[59]Houtzager RSH, 8 December 1642, a question was raised as to whether the States should start selling lijfrenten again, but at 1 : 11 or even 1 : 13 for one life instead of the former rate of 1 : 9. There is no further reference to lijfrenten in Houtzager RSH until the 1,000th penny proposal of 1653.

[60]Houtzager RSH, 13 August 1653, 18, 27 September, 1–2 December, 1661.

[61]Houtzager RSH, 10 March, 30 April, 7 August, 1655.

[62]Houtzager RSH, 2 August 1657.

ments should be used to make redemptions and not for any other purpose; with some exceptions, notably during the second Anglo-Dutch war, this principle was adhered to.[63] But even as rates were brought to a new low and plans for retiring old debt were put into place, the Republic's need for long-term financing was greater than ever. By de Witt's estimate, Holland borrowed some 70,000,000 guilders between 1655 and 1670. A few years earlier (1668), he presented the States with a "Summing Up" for outstanding renten debt through the end of 1667:

Losrenten	119,405,278	(@ 4%)
Lijfrenten	12,568,438	(@ 9.11% or less)
Total	131,973,716	

In 1652, prior to the conversion to 4 percent in 1655, annual interest charges had been 6,991,474, but as of 1668 they were down to 5,823,580, a reduction of some 17 percent, despite the prodigious public borrowing of the intervening years. For the third Anglo-Dutch war, beginning in 1668, de Witt had provided Holland with, in Rowan's words, "a reserve fund of 7,000,000 guilders, not to speak of its enormous resources in credit."[64]

One of de Witt's particular convictions was that lijfrenten were under-utilized as a means of public finance. Lodewijk Huyghens, mathematician-brother of the famous scientist, suggested that a differential rate structure based on age would make lijfrenten more attractive to investors, and de Witt

---

[63]Houtzager RSH, 28 February 1657, since this use of the rentevoordeel was not reducing the debt quickly enough, the States voted to set aside an extra 1,000,000 guilders each year for the same purpose. For decisions to use the rentevoordeel for needs of war against England, Houtzager, RSH 1 November 1664, 15 December 1664, 5 February 1665, 5 March 1667; see also 23 March 1669, the rentevoordeel for one year is estimated at 1,250,000, meaning a total debt of 125,000,000 which gives added confirmation to the figure presented in de Witt's "Summing Up" of 1668.

[64]Houtzager, 85–86, misquoted by Rowan, *Johan de Witt*, 180, when he says that, under de Witt, Holland's debt was reduced from some 7,000,000 guilders in annual interest payments to 1,168,000; the confusion comes from the fact that, in the figures as given by Houtzager and here in the text, annual payments were reduced *by* 1,168,000 under de Witt's stewardship.

quickly adopted the idea as his own. In 1669 he devised a questionnaire for receivers of local tax districts, asking them to list birth and (as appropriate) death dates for beneficiaries of all the lijfrenten they had sold beginning in 1655. Getting the information needed for specially hired bookkeepers to construct a mortality table took a bit of time and prodding, but by 1671 de Witt was able to present to the States a celebrated treatise on *De Waerdye van Lijfrenten Vergelyken met Losrenten*, or *The Worth of Life Annuities as Compared with Heritable Annuities*, of the same face value. Some of the more complicated aspects of de Witt's proposals were not acceptable to the States, but they did agree to begin issuing lijfrenten at the now customary rate of 1 : 14 for one life, with the novel proviso that rates would be proportionally higher for older beneficiaries and lower for younger ones.[65] Meanwhile, investors in various parts of the Dutch Republic were beginning to form private societies along the same lines, providing a form of income security that took into account the life-expectancies of beneficiaries.[66] This is of course the point at which it becomes possible to speak of a transition from public lijfrenten to the private insurance industry.

One of the small ironies of history is that it was de Witt's great political enemy in the Netherlands, Prince William III of Orange, who later presided over the successful transfer to England of the Dutch system of public borrowing which de Witt himself had done so much to perfect. Behind this irony lies another. The use of los- and lijfrenten described in this book was devised by Habsburg officials in the reign of Charles V and, in the case of Holland, imposed on an unwilling province. But in the long period of civil war in the Low Countries which followed, it was not the Habsburg monarchy that derived the most benefit from this ingenious method for attracting funds from wealthy folk, but rather its enemies in

[65]Houtzager, 92–100, cites a modern edition of de Witt's *Waerdye* in a Dutch life-insurance journal: J. P. van Rooijen, "De Witt's *Waerdye van Lijfrenten naer Proportie van Losrenten*," *De Levensverzekering* 11 (1934): 117–142.

[66]J. C. Riley, "That Your Widows May Be Rich: Providing for Widowhood in Old Regime Europe," *Economisch- en Sociaal-Historisch Jaarboek* 45 (1982): 58–76.

the northern provinces, especially the burghers who ruled Holland. Clio smiles, it seems, not on those who invent something, but on those who use it well.

III. The *Resolutions of the States of Holland* offer only the most occasional information about investors in the provincial debt. For example, when the interest rate was reduced from 5 percent to 4 percent in 1655, the University of Leiden complained to the States that it thereby suffered an annual income loss of 6,431 guilders, which means a capital investment of 643,100.[67] Moreover, perhaps because los- and lijfrenten accounts for this period have never received any scholarly attention, students of Holland's urban elites have not had a great deal to say about their investments in government debt. The focus of discussion has been on the transition of town *regenten* from a group of merchants to a group of rentiers in the broad sense of investing chiefly in land and adopting a noble manner of living. The question has been not so much whether such a transition occurred (for that it did occur seems admitted by all), but when and how. By about 1700, if not somewhat earlier, the ruling oligarchy of towns in Holland and Zeeland, including (somewhat later than the rest) Amsterdam, no longer consisted of men with an active interest in trade. The regenten of this era were more closely related to one another than in the past, less willing to admit newcomers to their ranks, and given to parceling out offices by means of "contracts" drawn up in advance. For Amsterdam in particular, Roorda and van Dijk have found convincing growth, from 1650 to 1750, in two important indices of rentier status, that is, owning a villa and not listing any occupation on tax declarations. Burke's examination of probate records for Amsterdam suggests an equally strong growth in the tendency to invest in government annuities. Thus Jacob Poppen, who was mentioned earlier as leaving an estate valued at 920,000 guilders in 1624, had roughly a third of his wealth tied up in Holland renten, but by the early eighteenth century the comparable figures for other large estates sometimes ran as high as 76 percent, 80 percent, or even 95 percent.[68]

[67]Houtzager RSH, 6 October 1656.

But impressionistic statements of this kind perhaps raise more questions than they answer. One would wish to know whether active merchants invested as much in renten as landowners did, or perhaps began doing so as commercial opportunities became less attractive.[69] In light of the discussion in chapter 5, one would also like to know if officeholders in the Republic continued to lead the way in investing in state debt, and if institutions (like the University of Leiden) increased their buying as these investments appeared to become more and more secure. For the present, however, two concluding remarks may suffice. First, it is at least not self-evident that the purchase of renten correlates more with one kind of wealth than another. Indeed, the very notion of a distinction between merchants and rentiers need not have the same significance for the Dutch Republic (prior to about 1675 or 1700) that it seems to have had for other parts of Europe. For the history of seventeenth-century France, for example, there is at least one school of thought that argues for a clear-cut distinction between the *noblesse de la robe*, or (to use Lublinskaya's term) the "feudal bourgeoisie," and the *bourgeoisie commercante*, both in the perceptions of contemporaries, and in terms of a genuine conflict between the trading interest and the economic priorities of the rentier.[70] But Holland in the sixteenth century had town regents who invested heavily in state debt,

[68]D. J. Roorda, "The Ruling Class in Holland in the 17th Century," *Britain and the Netherlands* II (1964): 109–132; H. van Dijk and D. J. Roorda, "Social Mobility under the Regents of the Republic," *Acta Historiae Neerlandicae* IX (1976): 76–102; and Peter Burke, "From Entrepreneur to Rentier," in *Venice and Amsterdam*, 101–114.

[69]Burke, *Venice and Amsterdam*, 111, suggests a connection between declining commercial opportunities and investment in state debt when he says that a fall in grain prices was followed ca. 1650–1670 by "a period of decline in Amsterdam trade as a whole," while "At this point Jan de Witt was making investment in the public debt an attractive proposition." But it is hard to see what de Witt did (e.g., in lowering the interest rates) to make renten "more attractive" than they were prior to 1650, and there is no a priori reason to think Amsterdam's merchants refrained from buying renten until the city's trade began to decline.

[70]Pierre Deyon, *Amiens, Capitale Provinciale*, 114–119; A. Lublinskaya, *French Absolutism, the Critical Phase* (Cambridge: 1968), chapters 1, 3; for a critique of the Marxist concept of class as applied to seventeenth-century history, Roland Mousnier, *La Venalité des Offices* (Paris: 1964).

while still representing the province's commercial interests quite vigorously in their dealings with the central government, and there is no reason to think the same combination of interests was not common in the seventeenth century. To return once more to the solitary case of Jacob Poppen, he was a member of the United East India Company's board of directors as well as an important buyer of Holland renten, and he also had considerable wealth tied up in the kind of agricultural investment that might properly be called capitalistic.[71] Indeed, it seems that the very word *capitalist* was of seventeenth-century Dutch origin: after about 1650, when the 200th penny began to be levied on a graduated scale, those in the top wealth category were known as *capitalisten*, and those in the next category down were called "half capitalists." At a time when the hereditary nobility of the province was dwindling in numbers and influence, and when the mercantile elite had for the most part not yet adopted noble manners, historians ought to be wary of making sharp distinctions between one kind of capitalisten and another.[72]

Second, it is at least possible that the one thing most closely associated with large investments in state debt was not holding a certain kind of wealth but, as in the sixteenth century, exercising a public charge. When de Witt proposed the renten interest reduction of 1655, he expected some opposition from the States because, he said, the renteniers whose income would be diminished by such a measure were the very men who had to vote its approval in the States.[73] That public policy should be controlled by the holders of public debt would surely have been viewed as a nightmare by princely governments of the early modern era. In a sense, the whole practice

[71]Elias, I, 286: Poppen was "one of the first *hoofdingelanden* and entrepreneurs" for drainage of the Beemster, a large lake a few miles inshore from Hoorn and Edam in northern Holland.

[72]Van Dillen, *Van Rijkdom en Regenten*, 275; Burke, *Venice and Amsterdam*, 104–105, cites a complaint which the historian Aitzema records (1652) of the Amsterdam regents, that they were no longer merchants, but now derived their incomes from "houses, lands, and renten," but only to note that Aitzema himself does not endorse this view, and that eighteen of thirty-seven town council members in 1652 were merchants or manufacturers.

[73]Rowan, *Johan de Witt*, 180–181.

of having the provincial States of the Habsburg Netherlands issue renten had developed as a means of freeing the government from the clutches of the Fuggers and other great firms, so that Charles V would be owing money to great numbers of his subjects instead of to a small number of bankers. In the process of making this shift, however, control of tax revenue had to be relinquished into the hands of the very same urban oligarchs, sitting in the States, whose successful avoidance of burdens had so often offended the government's sense of equity. But what is just and what works best are not necessarily the same. Equitable or not, control of fiscal policy by men who themselves had heavy investments in state debt was the real genius of the Netherlands system of public borrowing, both in its Habsburg beginnings and in its seventeenth-century grandeur.

Conclusion

The financial revolution described in this book took place over a span of about fifty years, and represents one stage of a much longer historical development. It is surely one of the hallmarks of the modern state that it not only enjoys an assured revenue, but can project this revenue some distance into the future, by carrying a long-term debt that may exceed its annual income by some considerable amount. Neither the empires of antiquity nor the princely states of the Middle Ages had the capacity to mobilize future resources for present needs in this way. But within the smaller and more manageable arena defined by town walls, the practice of issuing annuities to fund major expenditures was not unknown among ancient cities,[1] and, after a long hiatus, was reborn again among European cities of the twelfth and thirteenth centuries. While Genoa raised capital by creating special taxes

---

[1]Houtzager, 12–17, citing a marble table from Miletus 205 B.C.

for the benefit of lender syndicates, Venice and the Tuscan cities preferred using interest-bearing forced loans, possibly because the inherent fairness of the forced loan was more suitable to their steadfastly republican institutions. When cities in northern France and the Low Countries began creating a funded debt in the latter half of the thirteenth century, they chose the method of selling rentes on the open market, possibly because these towns, themselves subject to a prince, lacked the power of coercing their own citizens as effectively as Venice or Florence could. Just as the cities (especially in Italy) provided, within their territorial limits, an early model of effective government, these various fiscal expedients marked off a new level of achievement in the complicated business of managing state debt.

From the vantage point of the thirteenth or fourteenth century, it was not self-evident that this same achievement could be repeated at higher levels of political integration, that is, by utilizing as the foundation for long-term debt the revenues of an entire kingdom, or even just an entire province. By this time kings were already borrowing on a short-term basis against particularly lucrative domain revenues (like the export duty on wool in England),[2] and rentes or juros secured by similar revenues are known from at least the later fourteenth century in France, and somewhat earlier in Castile.[3] But though this method of creating a funded debt worked quite well in some instances, notably in sixteenth-century Castile, it also had built-in limitations, especially in an age when theorists were beginning to proclaim the doctrine of absolute monarchy. Symbolic of the problem is the oft-noted inconsistency between Bodin's contention that the king of France is subject to no human authority, and his insistence that the king is bound by natural law to keep faith with his creditor-subjects.[4] For if the king were truly absolute, why need he have scruples about assigning to another purpose revenues

---

[2]Richard Kaeuper, *Bankers to the Crown: the Riccardi of Lucca and Edward I* (Princeton: 1973), 27–46.

[3]Chapter 1, notes 28, 41.

[4]Ernst Hinrichs, "Das Fürstenbild Bodins und die Krise der französische Renaissancemonarchie," in *Jean Bodin*, Horst Denzer, ed. (Munich: 1973), 281–302, especially 287–294; Perry Anderson, *Lineages of the Absolutist State* (London: 1979), 50.

pledged for debt service—as was so often done anyway, without benefit of absolutist theory? If subjects balked at entrusting their money to the promises of such a king, well and good, let them be coerced. In this sense the evolution of monarchical institutions in western Europe made it more rather than less difficult to create a long-term debt that rested on the full faith and credit of the king.

Apart from the prince himself, parliamentary bodies were the only institutions that could pledge the resources of the realm in such wise as to provide satisfactory assurance to potential creditors. In the sixteenth century, many realms had functioning representative bodies whose writ was coterminous with the king's (e.g., England, Castile, Poland), but for various reasons none of these bodies became involved in the management of long-term debt. Instead, the task of creating a wider field for the kind of public debt pioneered by city-states was left to provincial parliaments whose territories were intermediate between the medieval city-states and the emerging nation states both in size and in the difficulties of political integration. In Germany, the estates of many secular principalities assumed new responsibilities for debt, but in a limited way, since it appears they merely shouldered existing debts of the prince, and did not issue any new instruments of indebtedness. Rather, the Low Countries were the land of promise for fiscal innovation at the provincial level. Here, in proportion as the central government was historically weak, the provincial states were uncommonly experienced in the management of their own affairs, and seem to have enjoyed an unusual degree of moral authority. One doubts there were provincial bodies anywhere else in Europe which could presume to coerce inhabitants of their territories to buy renten, as the States of Holland routinely did, albeit with the permission of the regent. Moreover, since the Low Countries combined a burgeoning commercial economy with an inveterate tradition of provincial liberties, the burghers who sat in its provincial parliaments probably had more political leverage than in any other princely state in Europe. Here, if anywhere, a government that wished to create a long-term debt would be compelled to do so in ways that satisfied the wishes of potential investors.

If the funded debt that developed in the Habsburg Netherlands was in many ways a product of this general background, its shape and character were determined more con-
cretely by three specific events. First, agents of the central
government were able to persuade the States, as early as
1515, to adopt the novel principle of collective responsibility
for the issuance of renten; this in itself was no mean achievement, given the fact that noble-burgher conflicts and intra-
urban jealousies were at least as common in these provinces
as they were elsewhere in Europe. The one problem with
these renten, from the standpoint of the government, was
that the ordinaris bede could only bear so much of an interest
rate burden. But in 1542—this was the second step—Mary of
Hungary and her advisers induced the States to accept the
"novel expedients," which included new provincewide excise
and land taxes, as well as a new series of renten that came
to be funded by these taxes. Finally, in 1553 the regent and
the States agreed to abandon the custom (prevalent hitherto
in Holland, at least) of forced buying; it was this decision,
encouraged no doubt by currently high levels of interest rates,
which as it were opened the tap and allowed urban capital
to flow freely into the refinancing of state debt. The end
product of these decisions deserves to be recognized as a
financial revolution, not so much because by these means the
government could raise unprecedented sums during the great
war of the 1550s, but rather because it marks the first time in
European history that the future revenues of whole provinces
could be mobilized for present needs through the mechanism
of credit. The later fiscal accomplishments of the Dutch Republic would certainly differ in magnitude from what had
been achieved under the Habsburgs, but not in kind. For if
Holland's funded debt under de Witt was (allowing for inflation) fully thirty or forty times larger than what it had been
in the 1550s, it was in both cases roughly twelve times greater
than the annual provincial revenues by which it was funded.[5]

[5]Tables 7, 8, pp. 94, 96: during the 1550s, the States of Holland issued
roughly 1,250,000 in renten, against annual excise and land tax revenues of
approximately 100,000 per annum; chapter 6, notes 38, 64: Holland in the
1660s had annual revenues of 11,000,000, as against a debt of 131,000,000.

Dickson's book, quoted in the opening pages of this study, describes the third and final stage in the slow evolution of modern long-term debt, that is, the transfer of Dutch techniques of public borrowing to a more fully integrated nation state; only in England was there, at this time, a parliament that could pledge the full faith and credit of an entire kingdom (in contrast, the States General of the Netherlands borrowed money on a much less ambitious scale than did the single province of Holland).[6] Between the Venetian ligatio pecuniae of 1262[7] and Dickson's "financial revolution in England" lie nearly 500 years of European political development, during which a whole network of clearly medieval institutions gives way to others that are recognizably modern. The fiscal strand of "modernity" is perhaps less studied and less well understood than some others, especially as regards the question of funded or long-term debt, but it is not for that reason least in importance. Venturing into territory that is not well explored, this study perhaps raises more questions than it answers. But it has nonetheless brought to light a phenomenon whose importance will doubtless continue to be recognized even as further research is done—that is, the Netherlands financial revolution that marks one of the watersheds of European fiscal development.

[6]Chapter 6, note 57.
[7]Chapter 1, note 7.

Appendixes

Abbreviations for Appendixes
(see also Abbreviations, p. vii)

Comm. ADB

Communication from M. W. van Boven, gemeente archivaris, Archiefdienst, Breda.

Comm. ARAB

Communication from Carlos Wyffels, algemene rijksarchivaris, Algemeen Rijksarchief, Brussels.

Comm. CP

Communication from Professor Carla R. Philips, History Department, University of Minnesota, Minneapolis.

Engelbrecht

E. A. Engelbrecht, *De Vroedschap van Rotterdam* (see Bibliography)

Comm. GABZ

Communication from W. A. van Ham, adjunct archivaris, Gemeente Archief, Bergen-op-Zoom.

Comm. GAH	Communication from J. J. Temminck, archivaris, Gemeente Archief, Haarlem.
Comm. GAM	Communication from P. W. Sijnke, gemeente archivaris, Gemeente Archief, Middelburg.
Comm. GA'sG	Communication from H. Bordewijk, archivaris, Gemeente Archief, 's Gravenhage (The Hague).
Comm. GAV	Communication from C. H. J. Peters, gemeente archivaris, Gemeente Archief, Vlissingen (Flushing).
Comm. RAZ	Communication from R. C. Hol, head of external services, Rijkarchief in Zeeland, Middelburg.
Comm. SAA	Communication from G. De Gueldre, adjunct bibliothecaris, Stadsarchief, Antwerp.
Comm. SAH	Communication from Jan van der Heijden, Stadsarchief, 's Hertogenbosch.
Comm. SAL	Communication from Marcel Peters, Stadsarchief, Leuven.
Comm. SASD	Communication from H. Uil, adjunct streekarchivaris, Streekarchief van Schouwen-Duiveland en Sint-Philipsland, Zierikzee.
Vitale	Vito Vitale, *Breviario di Storia di Genoa* (2 vols. Genoa: 1955).

Prefatory Remarks

The figure of 2,000 Holland pounds as a threshold for large investment is arbitrarily chosen. Expressed in other terms, 2,000 pounds would buy a house along Amsterdam's Warmoesstraat or, depending on price fluctuations, between 3,000 and 4,000 bushels of rye on the Amsterdam exchange (see chapter 2, notes 40, 41).

For those who purchased renten more than once, as most of these buyers did, "total purchase" will almost always exceed the amount invested at any one time, since some of the capital from earlier purchases will have been redeemed. In most cases, the place of purchase is given after the name of the buyer. Where a buyer is listed as burgher or magistrate of a certain city, the purchase occurs there, unless otherwise noted. Under "Source" are given numbers of the accounts where relevant purchases are booked. For Appendixes I*a* and I*b* (renten sold between 1515 and 1534 and secured by the beden), these numbers refer to GRK; for Appendixes II*a* and II*b* (renten sold between 1542 and 1565, and secured by provincial excise and land taxes), the reference is to SH. Buyers are sometimes identified in the accounts as to occupation and place of residence. More often, it is necessary to check appropriate printed sources, or make inquiries at local archives. Under "Identification" are abbreviated titles of published works (see Abbreviations at the beginning of the book), or references to letters from local archivists (see previous page). For "Officials and kin," the key is as follows:

    * = Official of the central government

   ** = Magistrate or appointed official of a town

  *** = Official for enclave of noble jurisdiction

    + = Immediate kin of officials in any of above senses

APPENDIX 1a

BUYERS OUTSIDE HOLLAND, 1515–1534

	Total	Officials and kin	Source	Identification
1. Antoine de Lalaing, Count of Hoogstraten, Head of Council of Finance, Stadtholder of Holland	40,806	*	Ch. IV, n. 23	Baelde
2. Silvester Pardo, member of the *consulado* of Castilian wool merchants in Bruges	14,400		3435	Comm. CP
3. Dame Marie van Halmale, *Margravinne* of Aarschot, purchased for a convent in Leuven	13,008	+	3435	
4. Wilhelm, Count of Rennenberg, military commander in Holland at the time of purchase	10,000	*	3432	Ch. 4, n. 24
5. Jean Micault, Receiver-General for All Finances, Mechelen	8,000	*	Ch. 2, note 54	Baelde
6. Jacques de Marseilles, *voorsuyer* for his imperial majesty, Brussels	6,400	*	3435	
7. Sebastiaen van den Berge, Receiver for Sluys (Flanders), Sluys	4,700	*	3424, 3432 3435	

8. Prior of the Carthusian monastery, Cologne	4,160		3435
9. Pouwels Verspeye, burgher of Nieuwpoort (Flanders)	4,128		3424, 3432
10. Jan van Burkele, burgher of Bruges	3,600		3435
11. Lady Johanna Benedicta Pelerynsdochter, Bruges	2,880		3435
12. Pieter Gribonal, Councilor Ordinary of the Council of Flanders, Bruges	2,720	*	3424, 3432
13. Nicholas de Marchie, advocate before the Grand Council, Mechelen	2,640		3418, 3432 3435
14. Jan van der Straete, burgher of Bruges	2,592		3424
15. Franchois Banzam, Bruges	2,400		3432, 3435
16. Anthoina Voet, Bruges	2,304		3435
17. Lady Elizabeth 's Vrient, Bruges	2,160		3424, 3432
Totals	126,898	85,634	

APPENDIX I*b*

BUYERS WITHIN HOLLAND

	Total	Officials and kin	Source	Identification
1. Lord Gerrit, lord of Assendelft, First Councilor of the Council of Holland, The Hague	2,793	*	3424, 3432	Blécourt Holleman
2. Lady Gherrijt Claesdochter, widow of Meester Jacob Pijns, Fiscal Advocate of the Court of Holland, The Hague	2,628	+	3424, 3432 3435	Blécourt Chap. 5, n. 111
3. The prelate, Godshuys van der Lee	2,400		3424, 3432	
4. The prelate, Benedictine monastery of Egmond	2,300		3432	
5. Meester Eewout Lievenszoon van Hoogelande, burgomaster of Middelburg two times, advocate before the Court of Holland	2,016	**	3435	Comm. RAZ Comm. GAM Ch. 4, n. 40
Totals	12,137	7,437		

APPENDIX II*a*

BUYERS OUTSIDE HOLLAND, 1542–1565

	Total	Officials and kin	Source	Identification
1. Erich, Duke von Braunschweig-Kalenberg (Brussels)	64,000		2289	Ch. 3, n. 71
2. Lady Josyna van Daele, daughter of no. 7, wife of Gerard Sterck, Receiver-General for All Finances, Antwerp	18,000	+	2286	Comm. SAA
3. Lord Diederik van der Lippe, lord of Blyenbeek	18,000		RSH 5 Nov. 1564	
4. Jan Hendrikszoon Smit, burgomaster of Vlissingen in 1554 (Middelburg)	16,800	**	2281, 2347	Comm. GAV Houtzager
5. Meester Adriaan de Proost, Town Secretary of Middelburg	14,400	**	2278, 2280 2347–2348	
6. Lord Lodewijk van Vlaanderen, lord of Praet, member of Council of State, Stadtholder of Holland (Brussels)	12,000	*	2282	Baelde
7. Arent van Daele, merchant and magistrate of Antwerp, father of nos. 2, 9	12,000	**	RSH 10 Mar. 1558	Comm. SAA

APPENDIX II*a*—*Continued*

BUYERS OUTSIDE HOLLAND, 1542–1565

	Total	Officials and kin	Source	Identification
8. Quiryn Claes Ewoutszoon, member of the poor relief board, Zierikzee	11,520	**	2278–2280 2281–2282 2286–2287 2347	Comm. SASD
9. Meester Pieter van Daele, dean of Aalst, son of no. 7, Antwerp	10,000		2287	Comm. SAA
10. Lady Adriana van Nassau (from an illegitimate branch), widow of Dirk van Assendelft, Sheriff of Breda and brother of App. I*b*, no. 1, Breda	8,400	+	2282	Holleman
11. Hendrik Hujoel, merchant of Antwerp	8,100	*	2281	Comm. SAA
12. Meester Philips Lang van Wellenbach, Chancellor of Brabant, Brussels	7,800	*	2280–2281	
13. Lady Marie [Eewoutsdochter Lievens] van Hoogelande, [daughter of App. II*a*, no. 5], widow of Meester Jacob de Valladolid, four times burgomaster of Middelburg	7,016	+	2280, 2282 2286 2347–2348	Comm. GAM

14. Jan Anthoniszoon Pieters, draper and magistrate of Zierikzee	6,872	**	2280, 2282 2347–2348	Comm. SASD
15. Adriaan Jasparszoon Creyt of Vlissingen (Middelburg)	6,600		2281, 2286	
16. Joost Olivierszoon of Veere (Middelburg)	6,600		2281, 2286 2348	
17. Marcus de Florenis (5,400 in Mechelen, 1,200 in Middelburg)	6,600		2286, 2348	
18. Meester Anthonis Sucquet, advocate before the Grand Council, Mechelen	6,480		2277–2279 2281	
19. Cornelis Ocker Simonszoon, merchant and burgomaster of Zierikzee, lord in Kempenshofstede, father of no. 53	6,402	**	2277 2280–2282 2286 2347–2348	Comm. SASD
20. Meester Joost Ban, Keeper of the Great Seal, Brussels	6,400	*	2348	
21. Lord Hieronymus Sandelijn, lord of Herenthout, *Rentmeester van Beavesterschelde*, Collector of the Zeeland Toll, Middelburg	6,000	*	2286, 2348	
22. Giorgio Doria, son of the Marquess of Genoa [Andrea Doria], Antwerp	6,000		2280	Vitale I 224?

	Total	Officials and kin	Source	Identification
23. Jacob De Witte Jacobszoon, burgomaster of Zierikzee, with his brother Witte Jacobszoon De Witte	6,000	**	2286	Comm. SASD
24. Lady Margriet Jacobsdochter, widow of App. Ib, no. 5, Middelburg	5,500	+	2208, 2275 2277, 2280	
25. Jacob Hendrikszoon van Grypskerke, treasurer for the new sluice and the watermill, member of old noble family, Middelburg	5,178		2278 2281–2282 2286, 2347	Comms. GAM, RAZ
26. Adriaan Lievenszoon Yemants, magistrate of Zierikzee, nephew of no. 89	4,776	**	2280–2281 2286 2347–2348	Comm. SASD
27. Anna Vighe, widow of Albert Prouninck, merchant and magistrate of 's Hertogenbosch	4,596	+	2347	Comm. SAH
28. Michiel Romboutszoon Cools, magistrate of Zierikzee, son-in-law of no. 41	4,540	**	2281, 2286 2347–2348	Comm. SASD

29. Court Jacobszoon of Middelburg, grootschipper, with his wife Geertruyt Cornelisdochter (2,700 in Amsterdam, 1,776 in Middelburg)	4,476		2278, 2280 2347–2348	
30. Hendrik Wishagen, Mechelen	4,200		2277, 2280 2286, 2347	
31. Cornelis Bouwenszoon Diericx, magistrate of Zierikzee	4,168	**	2278, 2280 2287, 2348	Comm. SASD
32. Lady Anna van Passenroede, wife of Leonard van der Kecke, burgomaster of Brussels, with her brother Jan	4,044	+	2348	Comm. ARAB
33. Lord Arnoult van Zuylen, lord of Hoffelaken, Utrecht	4,008		2286, 2347	
34. Lady Alyt van Assendelft, widow of Andries Millink, lord of Waalwijk, niece of App. I*b*, no. 1, daughter of App. II*a*, no. 10, Breda	4,000	+	2348	Comm. ADB
35. Anthonis Succa et al., Leuven, as executors of an estate; mentioned in BN as a "secretary of Emperor Charles V"	4,000	*?	2347	Comm. SAL
36. Lord Gerrit van Veltwijk, member of the Council of State, Brussels	4,000	*	2280	Baelde

APPENDIX IIa—*Continued*

BUYERS OUTSIDE HOLLAND, 1542–1565

	Total	Officials and kin	Source	Identification
37. Viglius Zuichemius van Aytta, President of the Council of State, Brussels	4,000	*	2348	Baelde
38. Hendrik vander Perre, innkeeper in "Reyenburg," Mechelen	3,950		2275, 2278 2281, 2287 2347	
39. Meester Albert Bouwenszoon, Procurator of the Grand Council, Mechelen	3,904	*	2277, 2280 2347–2348	
40. Gabriel Moyal, merchant of Antwerp	3,900		2279, 2281 2347	
41. Wisse Barentszoon Pech, magistrate-merchant, Zierikzee, father-in-law of no. 28	3,900	**	2280–2281 2347	Comm. SASD
42. Jan Anthoniszoon Block of Veere (Middelburg)	3,760		2348	
43. Roelant Tournay, *Griffier* of Dinant, in the ecclesiastical principality of Liège (Brussels)	3,600	**	2280	

44. Franchois van der Cruyce, wealthy merchant of Antwerp	3,600		2347	Comm. SAA
45. Remy de Halut, Mechelen	3,600		2280	
46. Lady Jacqueline Pels, widow of Willem Pieterszoon, Mechelen	3,600		2278	GRM
47. Lord Lauweryns van der Lamen, lord of Blockeryn (Maastricht)	3,600		2282	
48. Lady Johanna Herlin, widow of Jacob van Hoogelande (relationship to no. 24, if any, unknown)	3,600		2277	Comm. GAM
49. Marinus Willem Jacobszoon van Duiveland, magistrate of Zierikzee, father-in-law of no. 64	3,264	**	2280–2281 2347	Comm. SASD
50. Gillis Byt, Mechelen	3,200		2277–2278 2286–2287 2348	
51. Meester Jan van Schutteput, advocate before the Council of Brabant, Brussels	3,200		2348	Comm. ARAB
52. Laurens Baickenszoon of Veere (Middelburg)	3,024		2282	

APPENDIX IIa—Continued
BUYERS OUTSIDE HOLLAND, 1542–1565

	Total	Officials and kin	Source	Identification
53. Ocker Cornelis Ockerszoon, *heemraad* of Schouwen, magistrate of Zierikzee, son of no. 19	3,000	**	2286, 2348	Comm. SASD
54. Meester Laurens Clercq, Chancellor of Brabant, Brussels	3,000	*	2278–2279 2347	
55. Augustijn van der Dijk Romboutszoon, Mechelen	3,000		2286	
56. Joost Verleyen with his wife Anna Staes, Mechelen	3,000		2286–2287 2347	
57. Jan Simonet, builder of a house on the dam (1547), Middelburg	2,880		2286, 2348	Comm. RAZ
58. Meester Jan Lent with his wife, Margriet ten Luttkenhuys, Utrecht	2,844		2279, 2280	
59. Meester Pieter Claeszoon, Middelburg	2,800		2280–2281 2347	

No.	Name	Amount		Reference	Source
60.	Meester Jan Vlierden, Secretary of the Council of State, brother of no. 61, Brussels	2,720	*	2347–2348 2279	Baelde
61.	Meester Daniel Vlierden, physician to Mary of Hungary, Brussels, brother of no. 60	2,710	*	2280–2281	
62.	Francois van Eeghere, Mechelen	2,640		2275, 2277 2348	
63.	Andries Jacobszoon de Jonge, Middelburg	2,600		2280–2282 2286 2347–2348	
64.	Cornelis Willem Simonszoon Stavenisse, *heemraad* of Schouwen, magistrate of Zierikzee, son-in-law of no. 49	2,560	**	2348	Comm. RAZ
65.	Lord Floris Gribonal, lord of Berking and Plessy, Member of the Grand Council, Mechelen	2,500	*	2286, 2348	
66.	Meester Aernt van Meerbecke with his wife, Margriete Snellincx, Mechelen	2,440		2287	
67.	Nicholas Boenart, barber of his imperial majesty, Brussels	2,400	*	2280, 2347	
68.	Maître Philibert de Bruxelles, member of the Council of State, Brussels	2,400	*	2281, 2286	Baelde

APPENDIX II*a*—Continued

BUYERS OUTSIDE HOLLAND, 1542–1565

	Total	Officials and kin	Source	Identification
69. Lord Eustachius de Croy, *Protonotarius vicarius*, Brussels, possibly = Eustache de Croy, lord of Rumenghen (d. 1585), or Eustache de Croy, lord of Creseque (d. 1610)	2,400		2280	Comm. ARAB
70. Philip Danchy Philipszoon, Bruges	2,400		2277	
71. Meester Christoffel Gout, advocate before the Grand Council, Mechelen	2,400		2286, 2347	
72. Jonker Arnoult van Groenevelt, lord of Noefville, Utrecht	2,400		2282, 2286	
73. Lady Margriete van der Noot Adolfsdochter, daughter of the late Chancellor of Brabant, Brussels	2,400	+	2348	Comm. ARAB
74. Lady Jacomine Potters, widow of Joost van Schutteput, Brussels	2,400		2281	
75. Meester Joachim Roelants, M.D., with his wife, Lady Cornelia Pels, Mechelen	2,400		2280, 2286	

No.	Name	Amount		References	Comm.
76.	Hubrecht Robertszoon, Antwerp	2,400		2347	
77.	Anna Verleyen, widow of Joost Snellincx, Mechelen	2,400		2277–2278	
78.	Lieven de Wael Corneliszoon, magistrate of Zierikzee, with his wife, Lady Geneveva Aernt Claesdochter	2,400	**	2282, 2286	Comm. SASD
79.	Jan Harmanszoon Hubert, magistrate of Zierikzee, brother of no. 87	2,386	**	2282, 2286 2347	Comm. SASD
80.	Willem Simon Maartszoon, wealthy merchant, lord of Stavenisse and Cromstrijen, magistrate of Zierikzee	2,320	**	2278, 2280 2282	Comm. SASD
81.	Adriaan Soetman, Zierikzee	2,304		2286–2287 2347–2348	
82.	Adriaan van Campen, Middelburg	2,288		2281, 2348	
83.	Franchois van Baersvelt with his wife, Anna 'Sberen, Mechelen	2,280		2286–2287 2347–2348	
84.	Cornelis Franchois Tas, burgomaster of Middelburg, 1567, 1570	2,208	**	2282, 2348	Comm. RAZ
85.	Nicholas Stenbor, Bergen-op-Zoom, majordomo of Anna van Bergen, Dame of Arenberg, sister of the Marquess of Veere (Mechelen)	2,200	***	2282, 2347	Comm. GABZ

APPENDIX IIa—Continued
BUYERS OUTSIDE HOLLAND, 1542–1565

	Total	Officials and kin	Source	Identification
86. Gerard Schape with his wife, Anna van der Wiel, Brussels	2,200		2347–2348	
87. Anthonis Harmanszoon Hubert, Zierikzee, brother of no. 79	2,172		2280–2281 2347	
88. Jan vander Perre, merchant of Middelburg	2,160		2286	Comm. RAZ
89. Yemant Claeszoon Yemants van der Lisse, prominent magistrate of Zierikzee, Auditor of Accounts for Zeeland, uncle of no. 26	2,160	** (*)	2286	Comm. SASD
90. Anthonis Moens with his wife, Joanna Daniels, Mechelen	2,160		2278–2279 2287 2347–2348	
91. Cornelis Sebastiaen Otteszoon, Zierikzee	2,116		2280–2281 2347	

		Comm. SAA
92. Ollaert Gilliszoon, on behalf of the orphans of Jaspar Eewoutszoon van Hooogelande [son of App. I*a*, no. 5?], Middelburg	2,106	2281, 2347
93. Meester Joris de Tromper, advocate before the Grand Council, Mechelen	2,100	2277–2278
94. Cornelis Pieterszoon of Veere, Middelburg	2,016	2282, 2348
95. Collaert Gilliszoon Tsoggaert, as administrator for an estate, Middelburg	2,016	2281, 2347
96. Wolfaert Herten, burgher of Cologne, factor for the Strasbourg merchant Balthasar Coninck, Antwerp	2,000	2348
Totals	482,828 231,266	

APPENDIX IIb
BUYERS IN HOLLAND, 1542–1565

	Total	Officials and kin	Source	Identification
1. Meester Gerrit Hendrikszoon van Ravensberg, frequently burgomaster of Haarlem after 1557, son-in-law of Meester Vincent Corneliszoon van Mierop, member of the Council of Finance	22,568	**	2279–2280 2347–2348 2289	Comm. GAH
2. Jan Jan Aper Melis van Melisdijk, magistrate of Delft, son of burgomaster Jan Aper Melis van Melisdijk	14,400	**	2282, 2287 2347	Boitet
3. Pieter van Halmale, property owner and member of the orphans' board, The Hague	11,920		2280, 2347	Comm. GA'sG
4. Clara van Zandvoort Willemsdochter, Haarlem	8,400		2348	
5. Jan Janszoon Sasbout, magistrate and brewer of Delft	8,000	**	2287, 2348	Boitet de la Torre
6. Sijbrand Occo, magistrate, draper, and factor for the Fuggers, Amsterdam	7,840	**	2279, 2282 2285, 2287 2347	Elias Nübel

	Amount		Pages	Source
7. Dirk Hillebrandszoon Otter, burgomaster, tax farmer, possibly investor in land, Amsterdam	6,880	**	2275, 2280 2285, 2289 2347–2348	Elias ASR
8. Frans Dirk Gouvertszoon Meerman, magistrate and brewer, Delft	6,864	**	2279–2280 2349	Boitet de la Torre
9. Dr. Hippolytus Persijn, member of the Council of Holland, later President of the Council of Utrecht	6,748	*	2275, 2279 2347–2348	Blécourt
10. Splinter van Harghen, lord of Oosterwijk, with his wife, Lady Magtild van Wijngaerden, The Hague	6,600		2275, 2282 2347	Comm. GA'sG
11. Meester Cornelis Schuyten, M.D., The Hague	5,834		2347–2348	Comm. GA'sG
12. Jan Barendszoon in 't Romenijboot, wine merchant, and his wife, Jaepgen Jansdocther Lepeltack, Amsterdam	5,640		2279–2280 2289 2347–2348	Elias
13. Jan Jacobszoon Dommer, rope-walk owner, Amsterdam	4,794		2279 2281–2282 2347	Elias
14. Pieter Foppeszoon, Norway merchant and soap-boiler, Amsterdam	4,420		2279, 2282 2347	Elias

APPENDIX II*b*—*Continued*

BUYERS IN HOLLAND, 1542–1565

	Total	Officials and kin	Source	Identification
15. Meester Cornelis Aertszoon van der Dussen, town secretary and magistrate of Delft, rentenier, formerly a tailor	4,260	**	2277–2278 2280–2281	Boitet de la Torre
16. Heyman Adriaanszoon van Blyenburch, Sheriff of Dordrecht	4,128	*	2279–2281 2347	Balen
17. Hendrik Janszoon Persijn van Haarlem, magistrate and linen merchant, Delft	4,080	**	2275, 2277	Boitet de la Torre
18. Claes Doedeszoon, magistrate and grain dealer, Amsterdam	4,060	**	2275 2278–2279 2281 2347–2348	Elias
19. Gerrit Hendrikszoon Stuver, magistrate of Haarlem	4,000	**	2347–2348	Comm. GAH
20. Gerburch Claesdochter, widow of Pompeius Occo, mother of no. 6	4,000	+	2278–2279 2281	Elias

	Amount		Pages	Source
21. Meester Quiryn Weytsen, Councilor Ordinary, Council of Holland, The Hague	4,000	*	2287, 2348	Blécourt
22. Aert Corneliszoon van der Myle, magistrate of Dordrecht	3,876	**	2275, 2278 2279	Balen
23. *Gasthuismeesteren* and *Gasthuismoeders*, St. Pieter's Gasthuis (hospital), Amsterdam	3,848		2282 2347–2348	Ter Gouw
24. Meester Aernt Sasbout, Councilor Ordinary, Council of Holland, The Hague	3,640	*	2279–2282 2289	Blécourt
25. Jacob Splinter, Auditor in the Chamber of Accounts, The Hague	3,448	*	2208, 2280 2282, 2348	
26. Cornelis Hoogeveen Melis, magistrate of Rotterdam	3,432	**	2348	Engelbrecht
27. Gerrit Peng Eggertszoon, son of Egge Garbrantszoon Paf, magistrate of Amsterdam	3,406	+	2279–2280 2287, 2289 2347	Elias
28. Meester Quiryn Aertszoon van der Hoog, magistrate and brewer of Delft	3,280	**	2277 2279–2280 2347	de la Torre Boitet

APPENDIX II*b*—*Continued*
BUYERS IN HOLLAND, 1542–1565

	Total	Officials and kin	Source	Identification
29. Meester Aert Sandelijn, town pensionary and member of the vroedschap, Amsterdam	3,200	**	2278–2280 2284, 2287 2347	Elias
30. Maarten Jacobszoon van Alkmaar, wine merchant, Amsterdam	3,200		2279–2280 2284, 2347	Elias
31. Joost Sijbrandszoon Buyck, leading magistrate and draper, Amsterdam	3,200	**	2208, 2275 2279, 2282 2347	Elias
32. Jan Pieterszoon Kies, lumber merchant and grain dealer, Amsterdam	3,200		2289, 2347	Elias
33. Meester Philips Coebel, native of The Hague, member of the Privy Council in Brussels (The Hague)	3,200	*	2289	Baelde
34. Pieter Corneliszoon of Monnikendam, ship captain, (Amsterdam)	3,172		2282 2347–2348	

21. Meester Quiryn Weytsen, Councilor Ordinary, Council of Holland, The Hague	4,000	*	2287, 2348	Blécourt
22. Aert Corneliszoon van der Myle, magistrate of Dordrecht	3,876	**	2275, 2278 2279	Balen
23. *Gasthuismeesteren* and *Gasthuismoeders*, St. Pieter's Gasthuis (hospital), Amsterdam	3,848		2282 2347–2348	Ter Gouw
24. Meester Aernt Sasbout, Councilor Ordinary, Council of Holland, The Hague	3,640	*	2279–2282 2289	Blécourt
25. Jacob Splinter, Auditor in the Chamber of Accounts, The Hague	3,448	*	2208, 2280 2282, 2348	
26. Cornelis Hoogeveen Melis, magistrate of Rotterdam	3,432	**	2348	Engelbrecht
27. Gerrit Peng Eggertszoon, son of Egge Garbrantszoon Paf, magistrate of Amsterdam	3,406	+	2279–2280 2287, 2289 2347	Elias
28. Meester Quiryn Aertszoon van der Hoog, magistrate and brewer of Delft	3,280	**	2277 2279–2280 2347	de la Torre Boitet

APPENDIX IIb—*Continued*
BUYERS IN HOLLAND, 1542–1565

	Total	Officials and kin	Source	Identification
29. Meester Aert Sandelijn, town pensionary and member of the vroedschap, Amsterdam	3,200	**	2278–2280 2284, 2287 2347	Elias
30. Maarten Jacobszoon van Alkmaar, wine merchant, Amsterdam	3,200		2279–2280 2284, 2347	Elias
31. Joost Sijbrandszoon Buyck, leading magistrate and draper, Amsterdam	3,200	**	2208, 2275 2279, 2282 2347	Elias
32. Jan Pieterszoon Kies, lumber merchant and grain dealer, Amsterdam	3,200		2289, 2347	Elias
33. Meester Philips Coebel, native of The Hague, member of the Privy Council in Brussels (The Hague)	3,200	*	2289	Baelde
34. Pieter Corneliszoon of Monnikendam, ship captain, (Amsterdam)	3,172		2282 2347–2348	

No.	Name		Amount	References	Source
35.	Gerrit Adriaanszoon Cool, Rotterdam		3,138	2275, 2282 2348	Engelbrecht
36.	Meester Dominicus Boot, Councilor Ordinary, Council of Holland, The Hague	*	3,088	2279–2280 2347–2348	Blécourt
37.	Lord Jacob van Duvenvoorde, lord of Opdam, frequently a noble deputy to the States of Holland		3,060	2279, 2347	RSH
38.	Pieter Boel Allertszoon, grain merchant, *Doleant*, son of a leading pre-Dirkist magistrate, Amsterdam	+	3,054	2279, 2347	Elias
39.	Meester Cornelis De Jonge, lord of Baardwijk, *heemraad* of Delfland, member of the Chamber of Accounts, and *rentemeester* for the lord of Wassenaer, The Hague	* ***	3,044	2275 2280–2281 2347–2348	Comm. GA'sG
40.	Beatris Korssendochter, widow of Willem Jacobszoon in "Cologne," magistrate of Delft	+	3,000	2348	Boitet
41.	Pieter Jan Aper Melis van Melisdijk, magistrate of Delft, brother of no. 2	**	3,000	2347	Boitet
42.	Meester Cornelis De Huyten, M.D., The Hague		3,000	2280	
43.	Adriaan Reynertszoon Pauw, merchant of Amsterdam		3,000	2279–2280 2285	Elias

APPENDIX IIb—*Continued*
BUYERS IN HOLLAND, 1542–1565

	Total	Officials and kin	Source	Identification
44. Jan Pijns, *baljuw* of Egmond and of Wassenaer, The Hague	2,976	***	2275, 2279 2280–2281	Comm. GA'sG
45. Pieter Kantert Willemszoon, leading magistrate of Amsterdam	2,912	**	2279, 2281 2289, 2348	Elias
46. Huissittenmeesteren (poor relief board), St. Nicholas parish, Amsterdam	2,904		2279, 2281 2347	Ter Gouw
47. Grietken Reyer Lepeltacksdochter, Amsterdam	2,800		2348	
48. Meynaert van Heussen, Sheriff of Haarlem	2,724	*	2278, 2280 2282	RSH
49. Hendrik Janszoon Haek, merchant of Amsterdam	2,700		2279, 2282 2284, 2347	Elias
50. Mariken Bartoutsdochter, widow of Meester Cornelis Willemszoon, Rotterdam	2,696		2281, 2348	

	Amount		References	Source
51. Jonge Jan Duvenszoon, magistrate and stockfish dealer, Amsterdam	2,652	**	2279–2280 2347	Elias
52. Melis Adriaanszoon, Rotterdam	2,592		2280, 2282	
53. Meester Albert Kantert, magistrate of Amsterdam, son of no. 45	2,568	**	2278–2279 2281, 2285 2348	Brouwer-Ancher
54. —— for the orphans of Pieter Jan Aper Melis van Melisdijk (no. 41), Delft	2,400		2287	
55. Meester Hendrik Dirkszoon, leading magistrate and wine merchant, Amsterdam (600 in The Hague)	2,400	**	2279, 2282 2286, 2347	Elias
56. Heylige Geestmeesteren (poor relief board), Haarlem	2,400		2279, 2348	
57. Aelken Jan Willemsdochter, widow of Harman Ellartszoon van Diemen, magistrate of Amsterdam	2,400	+	2347	Elias
58. Jan Ewoutszoon van der Stocke, magistrate and brewer, Rotterdam	2,384	**	2208, 2277 2348	Engelbrecht
59. Jan Pieterszoon Korver, merchant of Amsterdam (1,504 in Gouda)	2,380		2348	Elias

APPENDIX II*b*—*Continued*

BUYERS IN HOLLAND, 1542–1565

	Total	Officials and kin	Source	Identification
60. Dirk Corneliszoon, grain dealer, Delft	2,364		2282, 2347	
61. Luduwe Arisdochter Boelens, daughter of a leading pre-Dirkist magistrate, sister of no. 38, widow of Anthonis van Houff (their son was also a magistrate), Amsterdam	2,340	+	2279 2347–2348	Elias
62. Lord Willem van Lokhorst, frequently a noble deputy to the States of Holland, Leiden	2,300		2287, 2348	RSH
63. Elizabeth Dirksdochter, widow of Hendrik Janszoon Persijn (no. 17), magistrate of Delft	2,240	+	2282 2347–2348	Boitet
64. Cornelis Huygenszoon, Rotterdam	2,180		2208, 2282 2289, 2348	
65. Dirk Corneliszoon Van Oudewater, magistrate of Gouda	2,168		2348	Walvis
66. Frans Janszoon Teyng, magistrate and brewer, Amsterdam	2,160	**	2280, 2285	Elias

67. Joris Corneliszoon Stierman, Rotterdam	2,144		2348	
68. Lucas Meynaertszoon van Alkesteyn, magistrate of Amsterdam	2,096	**	2279, 2284 2348	Elias
69. Gasthuismeesteren, Our Lady Hospital, Amsterdam	2,025		2279, 2285 2347–2348	Ter Gouw
70. Lady Alyt van Anzael, The Hague	2,016		2278, 2282	
71. Dirk Corneliszoon van Reynegom, tollmaster of the Gouda toll, Gouda	2,016	*	2278, 2280 2347–2348	
Totals	288,859 179,564			

Select Bibliography

Manuscripts and Manuscript Collections

Amsterdam, Gemeentearchief
    Andries Jacobszoon, "Prothocolle van alle die reysen . . . bij mij Andries Jacops gedaen . . ." (2 vols., 1523–1538) = AJ
    "Stadsrekeningen," 1531–1566 = ASR
    Adriaan Sandelijn, "Memoriaelboek" (4 vols., 1548–1571) = Sandelijn
Brussels, Algemeen Rijksarchief
    "Chambre des Comptes" = CC
    "Papiers de l'Etat et de l'Audience" = Aud.
    "Comptes des Receveurs Generaux de toutes les finances" (film copy of "Chambre des Comptes," Series B, Archives du Departement du Nord, Lille) = Lille B
Dordrecht, Stadsarchief
    "Tresoriers Rekeningen" = DTR
Gouda, Stadsarchief
    "Stadsrekeningen" = GSR

Haarlem, Gemeentearchief
"Tresoriers Rekeningen" = HTR
The Hague, Rijksarchief van Zuid-Holland
"Grafelijkheids Rekenkamer" = GRK
"Staten van Holland voor 1572" = SH
Leiden, Stadsarchief
"Tresoriers Rekeningen" = LTR

Published Sources

Michel Baelde, "Onuitgegeven Dokumenten betreffende de 16e Eeuwse Collaterale Raden," *Bulletin de la Commission Royale d'Histoire*, CXXXI (Brussels: 1965), 129–229.

————. *De Domeingoederen van de Vorst omstreeks het Midden van de XVIe Eeuw (1551–1559)* (Brussels: 1971).

M. Balen, *Beschryving van der Stadt Dordrecht* (Dordrecht: 1677).

A. S. de Blécourt, E. M. Meijers, *Memorialen van het Hof van Holland, Zeeland and West-Friesland van de Secretaris Jan Roosa* (3 vols., Haarlem: 1929) = Blécourt.

R. Boitet, *Beschrijving der Stad Delft* (Delft: 1729) = Boitet.

Bouwstoffen voor de Geschiedenis van de Levensverzekeringen en Lijfrenten in Nederland, directors of the Algemene Maatschappij voor Levensverzekering en Lijfrenten, eds. (Amsterdam: 1897).

A. J. M. Brouwer-Ancher, "De Doleantie van een deel der burgerij van Amsterdam in 1564 en 1565," *Bijdragen en Mededelingen van het Historisch Genootschap te Utrecht* XXIV (1903): 59–200 = Brouwer-Ancher.

E. C. G. Brünner, "De Adviezen van de 'Conseil et Chambre des Comptes de Hollande' en van den Conseil Privé in zake der voorgenomen Nieuwe Verponding," *Bijdragen en Mededelingen van het Historisch Genootschap te Utrecht* XLIII (1922): 129–160.

Pieter de la Court, *The True Interest and Political Maxims of the Republic of Holland* (London: 1746; Arno Press reprint New York: 1971).

Albertus Cuperinus, *Chronicke*, in C. R. Hermans, *Verzameling van Kronyken, Charters en Oorkonden betreffende de Stad en Meijerij 's Hertogenbosch* (3 vols., 's Hertogenbosch: 1847–1848).

Institutio Principis Christiani, Otto Herding, ed., in *D. Erasmi Opera Omnia*, Vol. IV:1 (Amsterdam: 1974).

Erasmus, the Correspondence of, R. A. M. Mynors, D. F. S. Thomson, translators; notes by Wallace Ferguson (note on coinage by John Munro) = *Erasmus, Collected Works of*, vol. 1 (Toronto: 1974).

R. Fruin, ed., *Informatie op het Staet van Holland in 1514* (Leiden: 1866).

Rudolf Häpke, ed., *Niederländische Akten und Urkunden zur Geschichte der Hanse* (2 vols., Leipzig: 1913).

J. H. Kernkamp, *Vijftiende-Eeuwse Rentebrieven van Noord-Nederlandse Steden* (Groningen: 1961).

P. A. Meilink, "Gegevens aangaande Bedrijfskapitalen in den Hollandschen en Zeeuwschen Handel in 1543," *Economisch-Historisch Jaarboek* VIII (1922): 263–277.

———. "Rapporten en Betoogen nopens het Congiegeld op Granen, 1530–1541," *Bijdragen en Mededelingen van het Historisch Genootschap te Utrecht* XLIV (1923): 1–124.

Resolutiën van de Staten van Holland (289 vols., Amsterdam: 1789–1814) = RSH

J. Th. de Smidt, E. I. Strubbe, J. van Rompaey, H. de Schepper eds., *Chronologische Lijsten van de Geëxtendeerde Sententiën en Procesbundels berustende in het Archief van de Grote Raad te Mechelen* (4 vols., Brussels: 1966–1983) = GRM.

J. Walvis, *Beschryving der Stad Gouda* (Gouda: 1714) = WALVIS.

Secondary Works

Algemene Geschiedenis der Nederlanden, J. A. van Houtte, ed. (12 vols., Amsterdam: 1949–1958).

(Nieuwe) Algemene Geschiedenis der Nederlanden, D. P. Blok, ed. (15 vols., Haarlem: 1977–).

Miguel Artola, *La Hacienda Real del Antiguo Regimen* (Madrid: 1982).

Michel Baelde, *De Collaterale Raden onder Karel V en Filips II, 1531–1578* = *Verhandelingen van de Koninklijke Vlaamse Akademie van Wetenschappen, Letteren en Schone Kunsten van België, Klasse der Letteren* XXVII (Brussels: 1965) = Baelde.

———. "Financiële Politiek en Domaniale Evolutie in de Nederlanden onder Karel V en Filips II, 1530–1560," *Tijdschrift voor Geschiedenis* LXXVI (1963): 14–33.

Jeremy D. Bangs, "Holland's Civic *Lijfrente* Loans (XVth Century): Some Recurrent Problems," *Publication du Centre Européen d'Etudes Burgundo-Medianes* 23 (1982): 75–82.

Violet Barbour, "Dutch and English Merchant Shipping in the 17th Century," *English Historical Review* II (1929/1930): 261–290.

A. Beaujon, *Overzicht der Geschiedenis der Nederlandsche Zeevisscherijen* (Leiden: 1885).

Bartolomé Bennassar, *Valladolid au Siècle d'Or* (Paris: 1967).

Peter Blickle, *Landschaften im Alten Reich* (Munich: 1973).

P. J. Blok, "De Financiën van het Graafschap Holland," *Bijdragen en Mededelingen voor Vaderlandsche Geschiedenis* 3e Series, III (1886): 36–130.

———. *Geschiedenis eener Hollandsche Stad* (4 vols., The Hague: 1910–1918).

William Bowsky, *The Finances of the Commune of Siena* (Oxford: 1970).

C. R. Boxer, *The Dutch Seaborne Empire* (New York: 1968).

P. Brachin, L. J. Rogier, *Histoire du Catholicisme Hollandais depuis le XVIIe Siècle* (Paris: 1974).

Thomas Brady, *Ruling Class, Regime, and Reformation at Strasbourg* (Leiden: 1979).

Karl Brandi, *Emperor Charles V* (London: 1939).

Fernand Braudel, "Les Emprunts de Charles V sur le Place d'Anvers," in *Charles-Quint et son Temps* (Paris: 1959), 190–201.

Fernand Braudel, F. Spooner, "Prices in Europe, 1450–1750," *Cambridge Economic History of Europe*, vol. 4, E. E. Rich, C. H. Wilson, eds. (London: 1967), 378–486.

P. Brouwers, *Les Aides et Subsides dans le conté de Namur au XVIe Siècle* (Namur: 1934).

E. C. G. Brünner, *De Orden op de Buitennering van 1531* (Utrecht: 1918).

W. Brulez, "De Diaspora der Antwerpse Kooplui op het Eind van de XVIe Eeuw," *Bijdragen tot de Geschiedenis der Nederlanden* XV (1960): 297–316.

Peter Burke, *Venice and Amsterdam* (London: 1974).

Ramon Carande, *Carlos V y sus Banqueros* (3 vols., Madrid: 1943–1957).

F. L. Carsten, *Princes and Parliaments in Germany* (Oxford: 1959).

Alvaro Castillo Pintado, "Dette Flottante et Dette Consolidée en Espagne de 1557 à 1600," *Annales* XVIII (1963): 745–759.

———. "Los Juros de Castilla: Apogeo y Fin de un Instrumento de Credito," *Hispania* (Madrid) XXIII (1963): 43–70.

———. "*Decretos y Medios Generales* dans le system financière de Castille: le crise de 1596," *Melanges en honneur de Fernand Braudel* (2 vols., Toulouse: 1973), I, 137–144.

Federico Chabod, *Lo Stato e la Vita Religiosa a Milano nell' Epoca di Carlo V* (Turin: 1971).

Pierre Chaunu, "L'Etat de Finance," in *Histoire Economique et Sociale de France*, Fernand Braudel, ed., vol. 1 (Paris: 1977), 129–148.

Aksel E. Christensen, *Dutch Trade to the Baltic about 1600* (Copenhagen: 1941).

J. Craeybeckx, *Un Grand Commerce d'Importation: les Vins de France aux Pays Bas au XVIe Siècle* (Paris: 1958).

J. S. van Dalen, *Geschiedenis van Dordrecht* (2 vols., Dordrecht: 1931–1936).

C. M. Davies, *The History of Holland and the Dutch Nation* (3 vols., London: 1861).

H. De Buck, *Bibliographie der Geschiedenis van Nederland* (Leiden: 1968).

Rogier De Gryse, "De Gemeenschappelijke Groote Visscherij van de Nederlanden in de XVIe Eeuw," *Bijdragen tot de Geschiedenis der Nederlanden* VII (1952): 32–54.

————. "De Konvooieering van de Vlaamse Vissersvloot in de 15e en 16e Eeuwen," *Bijdragen tot de Geschiedenis der Nederlanden* II (1948): 1–24.

Jean Delumeau, *Vie Economique et Sociale de Rome dans le Seconde Moitié du XVIe Siècle* (2 vols., Paris: 1957–1959).

H. De Man, *Jacques Coeur, königlicher Kaufmann* (Bern: 1950).

Julian Dent, *Crisis in Finance: Crown, Financiers, and Society in 17th Century France* (Newton Abbot: 1973).

H. De Ridder-Symoens, "De Universitaire Vorming van de Brabantse Stadsmagistraten en Funktionarissen: Leuven en Antwerpen, 1430–1580," *Verslagboek van de Vijfde Colloquium "De Brabantse Stad"* ('s Hertogenbosch: 1978), 21–125.

Jan De Vries, *The Dutch Rural Economy in the Golden Age* (New Haven: 1974).

Pierre Deyon, *Amiens, Capitale Provinciale* (Paris: 1967).

P. J. Dickson, *The Financial Revolution in England: A Study in the Development of Public Credit, 1688–1756* (London: 1967).

H. van Dijk, J. Roorda, "Social Mobility under the Regents of the Republic," *Acta Historiae Neerlandicae* IX (1976): 76–102.

J. G. van Dillen, *Van Rijkdom en Regenten* (The Hague: 1970).

J. C. van der Does, *Maarten van Rossum* (Utrecht: 1943).

Heinz Dollinger, *Studien zur Finanzreform Maximilians I von Bayern in den Jahren 1598–1618* (Göttingen: 1968).

Antonio Dominguez Ortiz, *Politica y Hacienda de Felipe II* (Madrid: 1960).

Richard Ehrenberg, *Capital and Finance in the Age of the Renaissance* (New York: 1928).

Johan E. Elias, *De Vroedschap van Amsterdam* (2 vols., Amsterdam: reprinted 1963) = Elias.

E. A. Englebrecht, *De Vroedschap van Rotterdam, 1572–1795* = Vol. V, *Bronnen Voor de Geschiedenis van Rotterdam* (Rotterdam: 1973).

H. A. Enno van Gelder, Marcel Hoc, *Les Monnayes des Pays Bas Bourguignons et Espagnols, 1434–1713* (Amsterdam: 1960).

G. Espinas, *Les Finances de la Commune de Douai des Origines au XVIe*

Siècle (Paris: 1902).

L. van der Essen, *Alexandre Farnese* (5 vols., Brussels: 1933–1948).

S. J. Fockema Andreae, *Het Hoogheemraadschap van Rijnland* (Leiden: 1934).

———. "Embanking and Drainage Authorities in the Netherlands during the Middle Ages," *Speculum* XXVII (1952): 158–167.

Van Gelder, see under Enno.

Robert Genestal, *Les Monastères comme Etablissements du Credit en Normandie aux XIIe et XIIIe Siècles* (Paris: 1901).

Pieter Geyl, *Orange and Stuart* (London: 1969).

———. "The National State and the Writers of Netherlands History," in his *Debates with Historians* (The Hague: 1955), 179–197.

———. *The Netherlands in the 17th Century, 1648–1715* (New York: 1964).

J. A. Goris, *Etude sur les Colonies Marchandes Meriodionales à Anvers de 1478 à 1567* (Leuven: 1925).

P. Gorissen, "De Prelaten van Brabant onder Karel V: hun Confederatie, 1534–1544," *Standen en Landen—Anciens Pays et Assemblées d'Etat* VI (1953): 1–127.

Nelly Gottschalk, *Fischereigewerbe und Fischhandel der niederländischen Gebieten im Mittelalter* (Bad Worishofen: 1927).

Pierre Goubert, *Beauvais et le Beauvaisis, 1600–1730* (Paris: 1960).

Ferdinand H. M. Grapperhaus, *Alva en de Tiende Penning* (Zutphen: 1982).

J. C. Grayson, "The Civic Militia in Amsterdam," *Bijdragen en Mededelingen tot de Geschiedenis der Nederlanden* XCV (1980): 35–63.

Gordon Griffiths, *William of Hornes, Lord of Hèze, and the Revolt of the Netherlands* (Berkeley: 1954).

Hans den Haan, *Moedernegotiate en Grote Vaart* (Amsterdam: 1977).

Rudolf Häpke, *Die Regierung Karls V und der europäische Norden* (Lübeck: 1914).

K. H. D. Haley, *The Dutch in the 17th Century* (London: 1972).

Henri Hauser, "La Crise de 1557–1559 et le Boulversement des Fortunes," *Melanges Offerts à A. Lefranc* (Paris: 1936), 307–319.

Jacques Heers, *Gênes au XVe Siècle* (Paris: 1961).

Otto von Heinemann, *Geschichte von Braunschweig und Hannover* (3 vols., Gotha: 1882).

Herbert Helgig, *Gesellschaft und Wirtschaft der Markgrafschaft Brandenburg im Mittelalter* (Berlin: 1973).

Alexandre Henne, *Histoire au Règne de Charles V en Belgique* (10 vols., Brussels: 1858–1860).

———. *Histoire de Belgique sous le Règne de Charles V* (2 vols., Brussels: 1865).

F. A. Holleman, *Dirk van Assendelft, Schout van Breda, en de zijnen* (Zutfen: 1953) = Holleman.

J. A. van Houtte, *An Economic History of the Low Countries* (New York: 1977).

Dirk Houtzager, *Hollands Lijf- en Losrenten voor 1672* (Schiedam: 1950) = Houtzager.

Jane de Iongh, *Margaretha van Oostenrijk* (Amsterdam: 1947).

————. *De Koningin: Maria van Hongarije, Landvoogdes der Nederlanden, 1505–1558* (Amsterdam: 1966).

H. P. H. Jansen, "Holland's Advance," *Acta Historiae Neerlandicae X* (1978): 1–20.

G. Janssens, "Een Onderzoek naar het Bronnenmateriaal voor het Bestuderen van de Politieke Aktiviteiten van de Staten van Brabant, 1567–1577," *Standen en Landen—Anciens Pays et Assemblées d'Etat* LXX (1977): 339–353.

I. J. G. Kam, *Waar Was dat Huis in de Warmoesstraat* (Amsterdam: 1968).

Julius Kirshner, "The Moral Problem of Discounting Genoese *Paghe, 1450–1550,*" *Archivum Fratrum Praedicatorum* (1977): 109–167.

P. W. Klein, "De Heffing van de 100e en 200e Penning van het Vermogen te Gouda, 1599–1722," *Economisch-Historisch Jaarboek* XXXI (1967): 41–62.

————. *De Trippen in de XVIIe Eeuw* (Leiden: 1965).

Bruno Kuske, *Das Schuldenwesen der deutschen Städten im Mittelalter* (Tübingen: 1904) = *Zeitschrift für die gesamte Staatswissenschaft,* Ergänzungsheft XII.

Frederick C. Lane, "Public Debt and Private Wealth, particularly in 16th Century Venice," *Melanges en Honneur de Fernand Braudel* (2 vols., Toulouse: 1973), I: 317–325.

F. H. J. Lemmink, *Het Ontstaan van de Staten van Zeeland en hun Geschiedenis tot 1555* (Rozendaal: 1951).

H. Lemonnier, *Histoire de la France,* E. Lavisse, ed., vol. 5:2 (Paris: 1911).

J. C. van Loenen, *De Haarlemse Brouwindustrie voor 1600* (Amsterdam: 1950).

A. Lublinskaya, *French Absolutism, the Critical Phase* (Cambridge: 1968).

Gino Luzzato, *Il Debito Pubblico della Repubblica di Venezia, 1200–1500* (Milan: 1963).

N. Maddens, *De Beden in het Graafschap Vlaanderen tijdens de Regering van Karel V (1515–1550), Standen en Landen = Anciens Pays et Assemblées d'Etat,* vol. 72 (Heule: 1978) = Maddens.

————. "De Invoering van de 'Nieuwe Middelen' in het Graafschap

Vlaanderen tijdens de Regering van Keizer Karel," *Belgische Tijdschrift voor Filologie en Geschiedenis* = *Revue Belge de Philologie et d'Histoire* LVII (1979): 342–363, 861–898.

———. "De Opstandige Houding van Gent tijdens de Regering van Keizer Karel, 1515–1540," *Appeltjes uit het Meetjesland* XXVIII (1977): 203–239.

Maritieme Geschiedenis der Nederlanden, L. M. Akveld et al., eds. (4 vols., Bussum: 1976–1980).

Martin, see under Ruiz.

Ernest McDonnell, *Beguines and Beghards in Medieval Culture, with Special Reference to the Belgian Scene* (New Brunswick, N. J.: 1954).

Christine Meek, "Il Debito Pubblico nella Storia Finanziaria di Lucca," *Actum Luce* III (1974): 7–46.

P. A. Meilink, *Archieven van de Staten van Holland voor 1572* (The Hague: 1929) = Meilink.

A. F. Mellink, *Amsterdam en de Wederdopers in de XVIe Eeuw* (Nijmegen: 1978).

Richard Moderhack, *Braunschweigische Geschichte im Überblick* (Braunschweig: 1977).

Anthony Molho, *Florentine Public Finance in the Early Renaissance* (Cambridge, Mass.: 1971).

Michel Mollat, "Récherches sur les Finances des Ducs Valois de Bourgogne," *Revue Historique* CCLXIX (1958): 285–321.

Roland Mousnier, *La Venalité des Offices* (Paris: 1964).

B. Munier, "Kardinaal Willem van Enckevoirt, 1464–1534, en de Overdracht van de Temporaliteiten van het Bisdom Utrecht," *Mededelingen van het Nederlands Historisch Instituut te Rome*, 3e Series, VII (1953): 122–168.

Henk van Nierop, *De Hollandse Adel, 1500–1650* (Amsterdam: 1984).

M. L. J. C. Noordam-Croes, "Antoon van Lalaing, Graaf van Hoogstraten," *Jaarboek Koninklijke Hoogstratens Oudheidkundig Kring* XXXVI (1968): 1–174.

Otto Nübel, *Pompeius Occo* (Tübingen: 1978).

Geoffrey Parker, *The Spanish Road and the Army of the Netherlands* (Cambridge: 1972).

———. *The Dutch Revolt* (Ithaca: 1977).

———. "The Development of European Finance," in *Fontana Economic History of Europe*, vol. 2 (New York: 1977).

Leo Peters, *Wilhelm von Rennenberg, ein rheinischer Edelherr zwischen den konfessionellen Fronten* (Kempen: 1979).

Carla R. Philips, *Ciudad Real, 1500–1700* (Cambridge, Mass.: 1979).

Pintado, see under Castillo.

Henri Pirenne, *Histoire de Belgique* (7 vols., Brussels: 1902–1932).

——. *Early Democracies in the Low Countries* (New York: 1914).

Götz Freiherr von Pölnitz, *Anton Fugger* (3 vols., Tübingen: 1958–1967).

N. W. Posthumus, *Geschiedenis van de Leidsche Lakenindustrie* (3 vols., The Hague: 1908–1933).

——. *De Uitvoer van Amsterdam* (Leiden: 1971).

Volker Press, *Calvinismus und Territorialstaat: Regierung und Zentralbehörden der Kurpfalz, 1559–1619* (Stuttgart: 1968).

I. Prins, *Het Faillissement der Hollandsche Steden: Amsterdam, Dordrecht, Leiden en Haarlem in het jaar 1494* (Amsterdam: 1922).

Brian Pullan, "The Occupations and Investments of the Venetian Nobility in the middle and late 16th Century," in *Renaissance Venice*, J. R. Hale, ed. (Totowa, N.J.: 1973), 527–594.

F. Rachfahl, *Margaretha von Parma, Staathalterin der Niederlanden* (Munich: 1898).

Récherches sur les Finances Publiques en Belgique—Acta Historica Bruxellensia, III (2 vols., Brussels: 1967–1970).

Maurice Rey, *Le Domaine du Roy et les Finances Extraordinaires sous Charles VI* (2 vols., Paris: 1965).

Jelle Riemersma, *Religious Factors in Early Dutch Capitalism* (The Hague: 1967).

B. van Rijswijk, *Geschiedenis van het Dordtsche Stapelrecht* (The Hague: 1900).

J. C. Riley, "Life-Annuity Based Loans in the Amsterdam Capital Market towards the End of the 17th Century," *Economisch-Historisch Jaarboek* XXXVI (1973): 102–130.

——. "That Your Widows May be Rich: Providing for Widowhood in Old-Regime Europe," *Economisch- en Sociaal-Historisch Jaarboek* XLV (1982): 58–76.

L. J. Rogier, *Geschiedenis van het Katholicisme in de Noordelijke Nederlanden in de 16e Eeuw* (2 vols., Amsterdam: 1947).

J. M. Romein, "Spieghel Historiael: De geschiedsschrijving van de Tachtigjarige Oorlog," *Tijdschrift voor Geschiedenis* LVI (1941): 225–257.

J. P. van Rooten, "De Witts *Waerdye van Lijfrenten naer Proportie van Losrenten*," *De Levensverzekering* XI (1934): 117–142.

D. J. Roorda, "The Ruling Class in Holland in the 17th Century," *Britain and the Netherlands* II (1964): 109–132.

Paul Rosenfeld, "The Provincial Governors from the Minority of Charles V to the Revolt," *Standen en Landen—Anciens Pays et Assemblées d'Etat*, XVII (Leuven: 1959), 1–63.

Herbert H. Rowan, *Johan de Witt* (Princeton: 1980).

Felipe Ruiz Martin, "Un Expediente Financiero entre 1560 y 1575,"

Moneda y Credito 92 (1965): 1–58.

Alfred Schmidtmayer, "Zur Geschichte der bremischen Akzise," *Bremisches Jahrbuch* 37 (1937): 64–69.

B. Schnapper, *Les Rentes au XVIe Siècle* (Paris: 1957).

Johannes Schulter, *Die Markgrafschaft Brandenburg* (5 vols., Berlin: 1961–1969).

A. J. Slavin, ed., *The New Monarchies* (New York: 1959).

J. W. Smit, "The Netherlands Revolution," in *Preconditions of Revolution in Early Modern Europe*, Robert Forster, Jack P. Greene, eds. (Baltimore: 1970).

H. Soly, "The 'Treason of the Bourgeoisie': A Myth? Some Considerations on the Behavior Pattern of Antwerp Merchants," *Acta Historiae Neerlandicae* VIII (1975): 31–49.

O. Sperling, "Herzog Albrecht der Beherzte als Gubernator von Friesland," *Abhandlungen zu den Jahresberichten des königlichen Gymnasium zu Leipzig*, 1891–1892.

Peter Spufford, "Coinage, Taxation, and the Estates General of the Burgundian Netherlands," *Standen en Landen—Anciens Pays et Assemblées d'Etat* XL (1966): 61–88.

J. E. A. L. Struik, *Gelre en Habsburg, 1492–1528* (Arnhem: 1960).

G. Taal, "Het Graafschap Zeeland en zijn Verhouding tot Holland in de Landsheerlijke Tijd," *Archief van de Zeeuwsch Genootschap* V (1965): 51–96.

H. Terdenge, "Zur Geschichte der holländischen Steuern," *Vierteljahrschrift für Wirtschafts- und Sozialgeschichte* XVIII (1925): 95–167.

Jan den Tex, *Oldenbarnevelt* (2 vols., Cambridge: 1973).

J. M. J. Thurlings, *De Wankele Zuil* (Nijmegen: 1971).

E. M. A. Timmer, "Grepen uit de Geschiedenis der Delftsche Brouwnering," *De Economist* LXX (1920): 358–373.

James D. Tracy, "Heresy Law and Centralization in the Habsburg Netherlands: Conflicts between the Council of Holland and the Central Government over Enforcement of the Placards," *Archiv für Reformationsgeschichte* 73 (1982): 284–307.

————. *The Politics of Erasmus: A Pacifist Intellectual and His Political Milieu* (Toronto: 1978).

————. "Habsburg Grain Policy and Amsterdam Politics: The Career of Sheriff Willem Dirkszoon Baerdes, 1542–1566," *Sixteenth Century Journal* XVIII (1983): 293–319.

————. "Shipments to Germany by Erasmus Schetz and Other Antwerp Merchants during the Period of the 100th Penny Tax, 1543–1545," forthcoming in *Journal of European Economic History*.

————. "The System of Taxation in the County of Holland under Charles V and Philip II," forthcoming in *Economisch- en Sociaal = Historisch Jaarboek*.

———. "A Premature Counter-Reformation: The Dirkist Government of Amsterdam, 1538–1578," *Journal of Religious History* XIII (1984): 150–167.

———. *True Ocean Found: Paludanus' Letters on Dutch Voyages to the Kara Sea, 1595–1596* (Minneapolis: 1979).

Richard Trexler, "Florence by Grace of the Lord Pope . . ." *Studies in Medieval and Renaissance History* IX (1972): 115–212.

Winfried Trusen, "Zum Rentenkauf im Späten Mittelalter," *Festschrift für Hermann Heimpel* (3 vols., Göttingen: 1972), II, 140–158.

Modesto Ulloa, *La Hacienda Real de Castilla en el Reinado de Felipe II* (Madrid: 1977).

R. W. Unger, *Dutch Ship-Building before 1800* (Amsterdam: 1978).

R. van Uytven, "Plutokratie in de 'Oude Demokratiën' der Nederlanden," *Handelingen van de Koninklijke Zuid-Nederlandse Maatschappij voor Taal- en Letterkunde en Geschiedenis* XVI (1962): 373–409.

Richard Vaughan, *Duke Charles the Bold* (London: 1973).

Fabiano Veraja, *Le Origini della Controversia Teologica sul Contratto di Censo nel XIII Secolo* (Rome: 1960).

Karel Jan Willem Verhofstad, S.J., *De Regering van de Nederlanden in de Jaren 1555–1559* (Nijmegen: 1937) = Verhofstad.

Cinzio Violante, "Imposte Dirette e Debito Pubblico a Pisa nel Medioevo," in *L'Impôt dans le Cadre de la Ville et d'Etat* (Brussels: 1966), 45–94.

A. C. J. de Vrankrijker, *Geschiedenis van de Belastingen* (Bussum: 1969).

H. van der Wee, *The Growth of the Antwerp Market* (3 vols., Antwerp: 1963).

H. van Werveke, *De Gentsche Stadsfinanciën in de Middeleeuwen*, Academie Royale de Belgique, Classe des Lettres, Sciences Morales et Politiques, Memoires in 8o, 2e Serie, XXXIV (Brussels: 1934).

C. H. Wilson, *Profit and Power* (The Hague: 1978).

Martin Wolfe, *The Fiscal System of Renaissance France* (New Haven: 1972).

J. J. Woltjer, "Het Conflikt tussen Willem Baerdes en Hendrik Dirkszoon," *Bijdragen en Mededelingen betreffende de Geschiedenis van de Nederlanden* LXXXVI (1971): 178–199.

A. M. van der Woude, *Het Noorderkwartier* (3 vols., Wageningen: 1972).

Sherrin Wyntjes, "Survivors and Status: Widowhood and Family in the Early Modern Netherlands," *Journal of Family History* (1982): 396–405.

Index

Note: The word *renten,* without further qualification, refers here only to renten issued by the States of Holland; other annuities of the same type are listed under the city or provincial states issuing them, and so specified, e.g., "renten of Delft," or "renten of Flanders."

—Dirkisten, Hendrik, ruling faction, 163, 166, 173, 190; Catholic and Habsburg loyalties, 173, 191; economic interests, 171–173, 179; party leaders, 160; as renten-buyers, 167, 168–170
—Doleanten, 163, 164, 166, 190–191; economic interests, 171–172; as renten-buyers, 167, 168–170; and Protestantism, 173
—Doleantie, 160, 163, 165, 166
—drapers, 168–170, 176, 177
—foundations, charitable and religious, 135, 146
—government, 47, 124
—grain dealers, 164, 165, 166; in relation to magistrates, 172, 173; as renten-buyers, 168–170, 174, 175
—gratiën, 53, 54, 55
—groote accijns, 15, 17, 56 n. 96, 180, tax-farmers, 180
—hearth tax, 155–156 n. 40, 180
—investors in land, 181–183, 187
—magistrate renten-buyers, 157, 162, 168–171, 174; magistrate-brewers, 175–176; investors in land, 182; tax-farmers, 180
—magistrates, 149, 151, 180
—market for renten, 1515–1534, 131, 132, 137; 1542–1565, 137, 143, 145; size of purchases, 152, 154
—merchants, 165, 166; as renten-buyers, 168–170, 172
—patriciate, 148, 163, 214
—population, 48, 49, 198
—professionals, 165, 168–170, 171, 174
—prominent magistrates, 160–161. See also Hendrik Dirkisten
—property owners, 116, 155, 179
—renten: sales of, 15, 17, 133; sold apart from other great cities, 34, 57–58, 59–60, 78–79; sold on

city's bede quota, 45. See also magistrates as renten-buyers; market for renten
—renten of Amsterdam, 15, 17, 133
—schiltal quota, 48 n. 66, 51
—shippers, 165, 166, 168–170, 172
—and States of Holland, 52 n. 84; in the Dutch Republic, 200, 202–203, 208
—treasury surplus, 49
—Warmoesstraat, 40 n. 40, 172
—wealth of, 137, 161, 199, 201
—woolen industry, 49, 165, 167
Anglo-Dutch Wars, 210, 212
Annuities, 1, 3–5, 26, 141; life annuities, 13
Antwerp (the city): Baltic trade, 49, 118; decline of, 196; government, 36, 47; loans to central government, 42, 44, 67; as market for renten, 118–119, 144, 154; renten sold on its bede quota, 45; toll, 31
Antwerp exchange: bankers, 42, 57, 105; interest rates for government loans, 40, 44, 64, 91; loans to central government, 39 n. 26, 43, 65, 79; resorted to unwillingly by government, 40, 41; security demanded, 42, 43, 84; used by receivers for the beden, 42, 64
Artois, County of, 34; beden of, 34; and grain trade, 111; renten of, 46 n. 56, 78; States of, 45–46 n. 56, 76, 77, 99
Assendelft, Gerrit van, First Councilor of the Council of Holland, 3, 48 n. 65, 51, 147; as buyer of renten, 126, 152, 228; on fiscal issues, 56, 126

Baltic trade, 81, 111, 165–167; after 1572, 191, 194, 195, 197; Amster-

Designer: UC Press Staff
Compositor: Prestige Typography
Printer: Braun-Brumfield
Binder: Braun-Brumfield
Text: 10/12 Palatino
Display: Palatino

Designer: UC Press Staff
Compositor: Prestige Typography
Printer: Braun-Brumfield
Binder: Braun-Brumfield
Text: 10/12 Palatino
Display: Palatino

merchants and grain dealers at large, though a few of them did invest sizable amounts in renten, it does not appear that as a group they were diverting capital away from productive investment towards the refinancing of state debt. The case of the brewers calls for special comment, owing to their apparently high level of interest in renten in both Amsterdam (table 20) and, as noted earlier, in Delft. Production in Holland's brewing towns seems to have declined during the first half of the sixteenth century, as brewers complained that government regulations aimed at preventing monopoly were preventing them from competing effectively in their usual export markets.[77] Amsterdam did not produce for export, and its breweries were not very numerous.[78] One gets a glimpse of a very different industry in Gouda, geared to export, from a list of brewers drawn up in connection with a dispute between large- and small-scale operators in 1546. Ninety-eight active brewers are mentioned, who between them produced 4,716 "brews" the previous year, for an average of 48 each. Among these men and women, there were fifteen men (of whom nine were also magistrates) who invested in Holland renten. The renten-buying brewers were apparently towards the larger end of the production scale, since their average for the year had been 65 brews. There is no such list available for the brewers of Delft, whom the central government in its regulation efforts found generally as troublesome as their counterparts in Gouda, but there is a document (shortly to be discussed more fully) which identifies current and prospective magistrates by occupation, in-

---

by the 1550s, when the real market for Holland renten began. Among this group too, however, magistrates were far more likely to invest than their nonpolitical colleagues: among nineteen magistrates there were nine buyers with an average purchase per group member of 489 pounds; among sixty others there were twelve buyers and an average purchase per group member of 180 pounds.

[77]Van Loenen, *De Haarlemse Brouwindustrie voor 1600*, 47–56, 139–143; above, note 73.

[78]Ter Gouw, V, 49–51: since brewing water had to be imported in special waterships, the Amstel being foul, breweries are marked on Anthonis' 1544 sketch of the city by long pipes called "well gallows" (*putgalgen*), of which Ter Gouw counts ten; other sources indicate nine breweries in 1509, and ten in 1546. See also above, note 61.

cluding brewers.[79] These two sources permit a comparison with Amsterdam, albeit one which is confined to brewers who happened also to be magistrates (see table 21).

TABLE 21

PURCHASES OF RENTEN BY MAGISTRATE-BREWERS, 1542–1565

	(number of buyers) / average purchase per buyer	
	Magistrate brewers	*Other magistrates*
Amsterdam	(5) 1,368	(32) 1,602
Delft	(10) 3,621	(21) 1,544
Gouda	(9) 698	(20) 370

The salient point of this comparison in table 21 is that magistrate brewers outspent their political peers in buying renten in the two cities where brewing was an export industry, but not in Amsterdam, where output was for local consumption, and was probably not as much affected by difficulties in Holland's export markets. In Delft and Gouda, if not in Amsterdam, it does appear that difficulties in this particular industry led to a disinvestment in favor of (perhaps among other things) state securities like the Holland renten.

Drapers occupy the lowest end of the scale among renten-buyers grouped by economic interest. Amsterdam's overland connection with south German markets for its woolen cloth was severely disrupted by the first Schmalkaldic War (1546–1547) and seems not to have been rebuilt, since production figures were never again as high as they were during the early 1540s. Moreover, like other heavy woolens produced elsewhere, the bolts of green cloth produced in Holland (notably Leiden) suffered in competition with lighter fabrics like

[79]The list is attached to a petition from Gouda dated 9 August 1546 (Aud. 1656:1). Van Loenen, *De Haarlemse Brouwindustrie voor 1600*: in a given week, the typical brewer usually produced one "brew," a quantity which, depending on the type of beer involved, could mean anything from fourteen to forty barrels. For the source of the information on Delft brewers in table 21, see below, note 106.

English kerseys and says from various towns in the southern Netherlands.[80] Of the total amount that "all drapers" invested in renten, over half was accounted for by Sijbrand Occo and Joost Buyck, two leading magistrates who had other and perhaps more important sources of income.[81] Finally, it might be noted that two subcategories of the "Baltic exporters" group, herring-packers and soap-boilers, bought almost no renten, while the trade in French wines, or *romenij*, was apparently prosperous enough to permit some quite large purchases, notably by Jan Barendszoon in 't Romenijboot.[82]

Along the spectrum of mercantile interests, then, interest in Holland renten seems to have been high among export brewers, whose industry was in decline, and low (at least in Amsterdam) among woolen cloth manufacturers, whose economic problems were perhaps even more severe. Among other groups (like grain merchants and shippers) there is no noticeable pattern of renten-buying and, from the evidence presented here, no indication that a large amount of capital was being diverted from still-profitable sectors of the local economy into the refinancing of State debt. One is left with the conclusion that office-holding was far and away the one thing most likely to influence a wealthy person's decision to invest in the annuities issued by the States of Holland. It remains now to test this conclusion against one more set of possibilities, relating to the economic interests of those whom sixteenth-century Dutch-speakers called "renteniers."

IV. Like the French term from which it is derived, the word *rentenier* denoted someone living on a fixed income. Originally, like the institution of the rente itself, the term had primary reference to landed property, and it seems to have retained this connotation in the sixteenth century, even though there were by now several other types of fixed income available to wealthy investors. In addition to providing credit to land-owning peasants, often in the form of private rentes,

[80]Posthumus, *Geschiedenis van de Leidsche Lakenindustrie*, vol. 1, and the article cited above, note 63.
[81]See above, note 46, and below, note 100.
[82]Appendix II*b*, nos. 12, 30, and 55.

one could lend to urban property-holders on the same basis, or purchase ecclesiastical tithes, or bid for tax-farming contracts, usually for the collection of city or provincial excise taxes. One could also bid for the contract to manage one or more of the prince's domain revenues, or, finally, purchase renten of the kind issued by cities and provincial States.[83]

Scholars like De Vries and van der Woude have made it clear that an innovative specialized agriculture was an important ingredient in the economic dynamism of the Low Countries,[84] but the role of urban investors remains to be clarified, at least for the Habsburg period. The draining of inland lakes which altered the face of the northern Netherlands did not begin until the latter decades of the sixteenth century, and was thus roughly coterminous with the creation of the Dutch Republic.[85] Long before this time, however, burghers were providing capital in return for the constitution of renten on peasant land,[86] and were also acquiring title to rural properties. Thus when the province of Utrecht, newly added to the Habsburg dominions, adopted a tax on land in 1530, three towns across the frontier in Holland—mighty Amsterdam and little Oudewater and Schoonhoven—protested that their burghers would thereby become subject to taxation in two provinces.[87] During the early sixteenth century it was common enough for town-dwellers to sit on Holland's traditional

[83]That the terms *rentier* and (in Dutch) *rentenier* were not used primarily for financiers or investors in public rentes is suggested by a circumlocution employed in a communication from the States of Flanders (dated 1558, Aud. 650:171–174), speaking of "ceulx non estans marchans ayans leur deniers courrans à fret et finance."

[84]De Vries, *The Dutch Rural Economy;* A. M. van der Woude, *Het Noorderkwartier* (3 vols., Wageningen: 1972), III, 521–526, notes that in part of Holland's "northern quarter" where the soil was more productive, opportunities for investment by burghers, nobles, and cloisters were great, and percentages of land owned by the peasants were accordingly diminished.

[85]De Vries, *The Dutch Rural Economy,* 192–196.

[86]Property inventories, as recorded by the orphan bureau (*weeskamer*) of Amsterdam in cases where one or more parents died while one or more of their children were still minors, are indicative of such investments early in the sixteenth century (e.g., "Inbrengstregisters van het Weeskamerarchief," Gemeentearchief of Amsterdam, III, 83v, 249v).

[87]AJ 12 May, 2 October 1530, 6 January 1531; RSH 28 November 1530, 8 January 1531.